HENRY DAVID THOREAU

AN AMERICAN LANDSCAPE

HENRY DAVID THOREAU
by
SAMUEL WORCESTER ROWSE
Concord Free Public Library

Henry David Thoreau

An American Landscape

Edited and Illustrated by

Robert L. Rothwell

With an Introduction by
Robert Finch

PARAGON HOUSE
New York

First edition, 1991
Published in the United States by
Paragon House Publishers
90 Fifth Avenue, New York, NY 10011
Copyright © 1991 by Robert L. Rothwell
All rights reserved.
No part of this book may be reproduced, in any form,
without written permission from the publishers,
unless by a reviewer who wishes to quote brief passages.

Library of Congress Cataloging-in-Publication Data
Thoreau, Henry David, 1817–1862.
[Journal. Selections]
American lanscape / Henry David Thoreau ; compiled and
illustrated by Robert L. Rothwell.—1st ed.
p.   cm.
Consists of selections from the author's Journals.
ISBN 1-55778-491-4 : $22.95
1. Thoreau, Henry David, 1817–1862—Diaries.   2. Authors,
American—19th century—Diaries.   3. Landscape—United States.
I. Rothwell, Robert L.   II. Title.
PS3053.A2   1991
818'.303—dc20   91-12824
                                                                              CIP

Manufactured in the United States of America

Designed by Robert Reed

ACKNOWLEDGMENTS

For help and suggestions offered, I am particularly indebted to Walter Harding, presently Secretary of The
Thoreau Society, and to Anne R. McGrath, The Thoreau
Lyceum, in Concord, Mass., and Mrs. Marcia Moss of The
Concord Free Public Library, Concord, Mass. I wish to
also give my appreciation to those people of Concord
whom I have briefly encountered and who have contributed to this book unknowingly by their hospitality.

Many thanks also goes to my family for their perseverance, proof reading, and much other helpful assistance.

CONTENTS

CHAPTER VI YEAR 1854, AGE 36–37

CHAPTER VII YEAR 1855, AGE 37–38

CONTENTS

CHAPTER XI YEAR 1859, AGE 41–42

CHAPTER XII YEAR 1860 AND 1861, AGE 42–44

MAP OF
CONCORD, MASS.
Showing Localities mentioned by
Thoreau in his Journals

Compiled by Herbert W Gleason
1906
SCALE OF MILES

FOR INDEX TO MAP SEE OVER

NOTE TO MAP OF CONCORD

The material used in this Map of Concord has been derived from a variety of sources. The town bounds, streets, and residences have been taken from a township map of Middlesex County made by H. F. Walling in 1856, reference also being had to a local map of Concord by the same engineer, dated 1852, on which credit for the surveys of White Pond and Walden Pond is given to "H. D. Thoreau, Civ. Engr." The course of the Concord River is drawn from an elaborate manuscript plan of Thoreau's, based on earlier surveys, showing the river from East Sudbury to Billerica Dam. This plan, on which Thoreau has entered the results of his investigation of the river in the summer of 1859, is now in the Concord Public Library. The outlines of Walden and White Ponds have also been taken from Thoreau's original surveys, now in the Concord Library. Loring's and Bateman's Ponds are according to surveys by Mr. Albert E. Wood of Concord, and Flint's Pond is from a survey for the Concord Water Works by Mr. William Wheeler, also of Concord.

All names of places are those used by Thoreau, no attention being given to other names perhaps more current either in his own time or at present. Only such names of residents are given as are mentioned in the Journal.

A few old wood roads, pasture lanes, etc. (Thoreau's preferred highways), are indicated, as to their general direction, by dotted lines.

The irregularity of the northeastern boundary of Concord arose from the fact that when Carlisle was set off from Concord in 1780, the farmers living on the border were given the option of remaining within the bounds of Concord or of being included in the new town. In 1903 the Massachusetts Legislature abolished this old division and continued the straight line forming the western half of the boundary directly to the river.

The identification of localities which were named by Thoreau apparently for his personal use alone has been accomplished, so far as it has proceeded, by a careful study of all the Journal references to each locality, an examination of a large number of Thoreau's manuscript surveys, and an extended personal investigation on the ground. Many of these localities are given more than one name in the Journal, and in a few cases the same name is given to different localities. Where doubt exists as to any particular location, the name is omitted from the map.

Hon. F. B. Sanborn, Judge John S. Keyes, Dr. Edward W. Emerson, the Misses Hosmer, and others among the older residents of Concord have been consulted in the preparation of the map, and have kindly supplied helpful information from their personal acquaintance with Thoreau.

December, 1906. H. W. GLEASON.

EDITOR'S PREFACE

Why this book of journal selections? The sheer bulk of the *Journal of Henry David Thoreau* (two million words) is intimidating to all but the most devoted Thoreau enthusiast. And since I believe that the entries on the landscape have no equal in all of American literature, I have spent several years gathering them together for this collection.

One of Thoreau's original ideas for keeping the journal was to use it as a source for future books and essays. There is such a wealth of entries on the landscape that one could speculate Thoreau himself might have had a book of landscape writings in mind.

Thoreau's family lived in Concord, Massachusetts, where his father, John Thoreau, had a pencil manufacturing business. The father was an ordinary man who tended to his business and family and was very much at home with life in the small town. Thoreau's mother was a dynamic woman with a strong personality who dominated the household and her four children. One of the sons' death, John's, at age twenty-seven, was a severe blow to Henry as the two were very close. John was open and gregarious while his brother was quiet and introspective. Henry thought he was not particularly worth meeting in person but that the best of him was to be found in his writings.

Thoreau could not make a living by writing; *Walden* and *A Week on the Concord and Merrimack Rivers* were his only books to be published during his lifetime. A Harvard graduate, he worked as a pencil maker, carpenter, day laborer, lecturer, and surveyor.

Thoreau was a contemporary and close friend of Ralph Waldo Emerson and Ellery Channing, both renowned literary figures of his day and neighbors in the village. Channing was Thoreau's most frequent companion on his walks whenever he did not go alone and is referred to as C. in the Journal. Emerson played an important role in Thoreau's literary and personal life and was considered for a long time to be Thoreau's mentor until *Walden* and some other writings became well accepted.

Thoreau lived most of his life in and around Concord. A dedicated walker and saunterer, he routinely spent hours each afternoon recording what he saw on his walks. I do not believe it is well understood why a thorough knowledge of his native landscape was so important to Thoreau's writings. A traveler sees what there is to see at only one point in time. Thoreau, by constantly observing his favorite places in Concord, was able to record how these places changed during all the seasons throughout his life. An example is the accumulated journal entries pertaining to the Concord River scenery. These observations present a complete picture of the river that no writer could ever achieve in a few visits. It was from this dedication to recording his native landscape in his journal on nearly a daily basis that such poignant writing evolved.

As these selections show, Thoreau always prized the touch of man in nature for the ideal landscape. A pioneer conservationist, he criticized some of the local farmers for their insensitive uses of the land, though he praised the beauty of the rocky farm pastures sloping down to the river, or an ideal white farmhouse perched on the hillside. Thoreau was one of the first to speak out for the preservation of the environment.

The first entries in the journal were made in 1837 and the last in 1861. The selections used here are in chronological order and all are dated and titled. Many of my illustrations represent actual places in present day Concord, Massachusetts, and the surrounding area. None of the illustrations try to depict an exact location described in the accompanying selection and only a similarity or suggestion pertaining to the selection is intended.

I sincerely hope these writings will be enjoyable reading for all, be they familiar with Thoreau or not.

—ROBERT ROTHWELL, 1991

INTRODUCTION

THOREAU'S JOURNAL HAS OFTEN been referred to as the "quarry" from which he mined much of his published writings. True as this is, the journal was for Thoreau himself not so much a quarry as a laboratory of the mind. Kept for nearly a quarter of a century, its more than two million words show us better than any biography his development as a writer, a reader, a moral philosopher, a naturalist, and an observer of the human condition, including his own.

Thoreau claimed that he never tired of a familiar landscape, or of the "great poem" of the seasons, because he himself was constantly changing and that he was always viewing his surroundings with the eyes of "this ever new self." That Thoreau never stagnated as a thinker or an observer, never fell into the trap of comfortably repeating old truths or reflex descriptions, is shown nowhere more clearly than in his journal entries on landscape.

Thoreau's best landscapes are always those with which he finds some way to identify personally. At Walden he made spiritual identification with the pond he immortalized, seeing in its depths and clarity the kind of serenity and purity of existence that he sought there. The narrator of *Walden* is a magnificently constructed literary persona, closed and apparently self-contained, like the waters in which he saw his aspirations reflected. In his travel writings, particularly *Cape Cod* and *The Maine Woods,* many of the best moments come from Thoreau's attempts, not always successful, to identify with new and wilder landscapes and to comprehend them with ideas and perspectives developed in the relatively domesticated fields and woods of his native Concord.

What we get in the journal, however, particularly after he left Walden in 1847, is a more personal, candid, complex, speculative and open-ended Thoreau, one whose quest for a comprehensive understanding of man's relationship with nature remains strong and determined, but whose answers grow less certain—not only as the Transcendental principles of his youth seem less adequate to the complexity of his experience, but as his intellectual view of nature-at-large is widened by new readings in aesthetics and natural history.

The earliest landscape descriptions exhibit the typical Romantic impulse to see nature as a reflection and measure of the observer's spiritual life. Landscape served, Thoreau said, as a source of "tropes and symbols to describe my inner moods." This approach, applied with a genial, charming lightness in *A Week on the Concord and Merrimack Rivers* and transmuted into dense, complex symbolism in *Walden,* changes markedly in the journals of the 1850s.

One important influence on Thoreau at this time was the writings of the eighteenth-century English painter William Gilpin. Following his encounter with Gilpin's work in 1852, Thoreau adopted a more "painterly" approach to his landscapes. That is, his descriptions become more visually analytic; he seeks not merely to render the effects of landscape, but to understand their components and causes: how, for instance, sunlight is filtered by the structure of white pine leaves, or how the perception of light on snow is affected by temperature.

Even more important was Thoreau's encounter with Charles Darwin's descriptions of South American landscapes in *The Voyage of the Beagle.* Darwin's provocative observations on natural adaptation and selection led Thoreau to a new sense of landscape as something more than a static and pleasing view, or a source of Transcendental metaphors. Nature, it seemed, had an energetic will of its own, more powerful than Thoreau had guessed and less subject to his poetic control. In *Walden* he had intuitively celebrated the forces of eternal creation and renewal. Now Thoreau began to see those forces made newly manifest in the familiar woods and fields around him.

Increasingly, through the 1850s, the Journals are filled with detailed notes on such subjects as seed dispersal, the role of squirrels in the distribution of oaks, and the patterns of forest succession. Rather than simply asserting the transforming power of nature through brilliant images Thoreau was now recording it as well through scientific analysis and observation.

This change in the emphasis of the journal entries has led some critics to complain that, especially in his last years, Thoreau the poet and philosopher was increasingly displaced by Thoreau the natural historian and, too often, the mere recorder of facts. Certainly the later journal volumes contain more factual natural history. But as these selections amply show, Thoreau never abandoned the search for that "higher truth" which those facts might reveal, not just about the workings of nature but of humanity's relationship to it. Many of the most provocative passages of the later journals are arguments for the need to combine personal response and connection with scientific understanding.

If anything, the relationship between self and nature becomes more intimate and personal in the later journals. In fact, one of the more interesting changes in his approach to landscape is the way in which Thoreau becomes more absorbed in its literal effects on him. Increasingly Thoreau uses himself as a measure of nature, describing it in terms of how it reacts on his own body: He stands up in his boat on the river to gauge the strength of the wind on his frame. He observes the effect of shade on his own eyes. He drenches himself in storms to measure their force, and slogs about in swamps "to bathe (my) eyes in greenness." He climbs a large blueberry bush and finds "a comfortable seat" as a means of assessing its size. He analyzes the texture of ice by seeing how far he can slide on it in rubbers and records the progress of spring by noting the day on which he sheds his outside coat, or can sit at evening with the window open. (There is, of course, a poignant irony here in that such willful exposure to the elements in the face of the progressive deterioration of an always frail constitution may have hastened Thoreau's death. One biographer has even suggested that it was his ground-level examination of pine stumps in November 1860 that brought on his last and fatal bout with tuberculosis.)

From a reader's point of view, the most attractive quality in these selections may be Thoreau's growing affectionate identification with his native landscape. From the start, perhaps in part to justify a temperamental propensity for home-sticking, Thoreau asserted the importance of knowing one's local landscape well, coining his famous boast that he had "travelled a good deal in Concord" and preaching the futility of seeking one's contentment or interest in life in foreign landscapes. Whatever his motives, he practiced what he preached, not only studying the fauna and the flora of his native township in careful and loving detail, but visiting and revisiting familiar haunts—Walden Pond, the Cliffs, Fair Haven Bay, Baker Farm, Lee's Hill, the Bedford Levels, Deep Cut, Sunset Reach, Conantum, Hubbard's Bridge, Orchis Swamp, the Sudbury Meadows, and above all his beloved Concord River—so that there is in his later descriptions of these places a rich patina of experience, a depth of accumulated self-history—what Barry Lopez calls "the sense of memory moving across landscape."

This recognition of Thoreau's long attachment to his native landscape culminates in the entry for November 1, 1858, surely one of the most remarkable passages in the entire journal, and as moving a tribute to one's home town as can be found in literature. In its unusually personal tone, its deep humanity, its strong sense of his own mortality, its candid acknowledgment of hopes and achievements, failures and disappointments, coupled with the indomitability of a spirit "that does not know when it is beaten," it is as close as we ever come to seeing Henry wear his heart on his sleeve. It takes a lifetime of devotion to place to produce a passage as good as this.

When Thoreau died in 1862, the bulk of the journal's manuscript was left unprepared for publication. Nonetheless its achievements, as represented in the following pages, are impressive by any measure. One finds here incomparable renderings of the countryside in Concord, Maine, Mount Monadnock, and other New England scenes; passages that form the basis of such superb late essays as "Walking" and "Wild Apples"; vivid, fully-realized portraits of a number of local trees; ground-breaking appreciations of the aesthetic and environmental value of wetlands in an age which still regarded swamps and marshes as "wasteland" to be "reclaimed" for agriculture and commerce; brilliant insights on the art of seeing and the role of the imagination in nature writing; and seminal statements on local landscape preservation that have been incorporated into modern landscape architecture and have provided rallying cries for local conservation movements across the country.

Moreover, in his recognition of the holistic character of landscape—that is, the ecological and psychological importance of place—Thoreau laid the groundwork for the modern tradition of nature writing, whose primary intent has been the reintegration of human sensibilities in its relation to nature. Like the "strong and beautiful bug" entombed for sixty years in the apple-wood table in *Walden,* the seed he planted in his voluminous journals lay dormant for many decades, but has flowered in our own century in the work of those great conservationist and nature writers from John Muir to Barry Lopez who brought to their own disciplines and landscapes Thoreau's powerful sense of nature as the shaper of man.

—Robert Finch
Brewster, Massachusetts
April 1991

Chapter I

Year

1837 to 1847

Age

20–30

837

Nov. 21.   The World from Nawshawtuct

ONE MUST NEEDS CLIMB a hill to know what a world he inhabits. In the midst of this Indian summer I am perched on the topmost rock of Nawshawtuct, a velvet wind blowing from the southwest. I seem to feel the atoms as they strike my cheek. Hills, mountains, steeples stand out in bold relief in the horizon, while I am resting on the rounded boss of an enormous shield, the river like a vein of silver encircling its edge, and thence the shield gradually rises to its rim, the horizon. Not a cloud is to be seen, but villages, villas, forests, mountains, one above another, till they are swallowed up in the heavens. The atmosphere is such that, as I look abroad upon the length and breadth of the land, it recedes from my eye, and I seem to be looking for the threads of the velvet.

Thus I admire the grandeur of my emerald carriage, with its border of blue, in which I am rolling through space.

1838

Jan. 21. Sparkling Ice

EVERY LEAF AND TWIG was this morning covered with a sparkling ice armor; even the grasses in exposed fields were hung with innumerable diamond pendants, which jingled merrily when brushed by the foot of the traveller. It was literally the wreck of jewels and the crash of gems. It was as though some superincumbent stratum of the earth had been removed in the night, exposing to light a bed of untarnished crystals. The scene changed at every step, or as the head was inclined to the right or the left. There were the opal and sapphire and emerald and jasper and beryl and topaz and ruby.

Such is beauty ever,—neither here nor there, now nor then,—neither in Rome nor in Athens, but wherever there is a soul to admire. If I seek her elsewhere because I do not find her at home, my search will prove a fruitless one.

Sept. 5. The Wonder of a River

FOR THE FIRST TIME it occurred to me this afternoon what a piece of wonder a river is,—a huge volume of matter ceaselessly rolling through the fields and meadows of this substantial earth, making haste from the high places, by stable dwellings of men and Egyptian Pyramids, to its restless reservoir. One would think that, by a very natural impulse, the dwellers upon the headwaters of the Mississippi and Amazon would follow in the trail of their waters to see the end of the matter.

1839

April 4. In the Morning

THE ATMOSPHERE OF MORNING gives a healthy hue to our prospects. Disease is a sluggard that overtakes, never encounters, us. We have the start each day, and may fairly distance him before the dew is off; but if we recline in the bowers of noon, he will come up with us after all. The morning dew breeds no cold.

Twilight on the river.

We enjoy a diurnal reprieve in the beginning of each day's creation. In the morning we do not believe in expediency; we will start afresh, and have no patching, no temporary fixtures. The afternoon man has an interest in the past; his eye is divided, and he sees indifferently well either way.

April 30. Illuminated Pictures

OF SOME ILLUMINATED PICTURES which I saw last evening, one representing the plain of Babylon, with only a heap of brick-dust in the centre, and an uninterrupted horizon bounding the desert, struck me most. I would see painted a boundless expanse of desert, prairie, or sea, without other object than the horizon. The heavens and the earth,—the first and last painting,—where is the artist who shall undertake it?

840

March 8. The Brooks

IN THE BROOKS THE slight grating sound of small cakes of ice, floating with various speed, is full of content and promise, and where the water gurgles under a natural bridge, you may hear these hasty rafts hold conversation in an undertone. Every rill is a channel for the juices of the meadow. Last year's grasses and flowerstalks have been steeped in rain and snow, and now the brooks flow with meadow tea,—thoroughwort, mint, flagroot, and pennyroyal, all at one draught.

March 21. Here Is Not All the World

THANK FORTUNE, WE ARE not rooted to the soil, and here is not all the world. The buckeye does not grow in New England; the mockingbird is rarely heard here. Why not keep pace with the day, and not allow of a sunset nor fall behind the summer and the migration of birds? Shall we not compete with the buffalo, who keeps pace with the seasons, cropping the pastures of the Colorado till a greener and sweeter grass awaits him by the Yellowstone? The wild goose is more a cosmopolite than we; he breaks his fast in Canada, takes a luncheon in the Susquehanna, and plumes himself for the night in a Louisiana bayou. The pigeon carries an acorn in his crop from the King of Holland's to Mason and Dixon's line. Yet we think if rail fences are pulled down and stone walls set up on our farms, bounds are henceforth set to our lives and our fates decided. If you are chosen town clerk, forsooth, you can't go to Tierra del Fuego this summer.

March 30. My Undisputed Territory

PRAY, WHAT THINGS INTEREST me at present? A long, soaking rain, the drops trickling down the stubble, while I lay drenched on a last year's bed of wild oats, by the side of some bare hill, ruminating. These things are of moment. To watch this crystal globe just sent from heaven to associate with me. While these clouds and this sombre drizzling weather shut all in, we two draw nearer and know one another. The gathering in of the clouds with the last rush and dying breath of the wind, and then the regular dripping of twigs and leaves the country o'er, the impression of inward comfort and sociableness, the drenched stubble and trees that drop beads on you as you pass, their dim outline seen through the rain on all sides drooping in sympathy with yourself. These are my undisputed territory. This is Nature's English comfort. The birds draw closer and are more familiar under the thick foliage, composing new strains on their roosts against the sunshine.

1841

Jan. 30. Snowflakes Settle

THE SNOW FALLS ON no two trees alike, but the forms it assumes are as various as those of the twigs and leaves which receive it. They are, as it were, predetermined by the genius of the tree. So one divine spirit descends alike on all, but bears a peculiar fruit in each. The divinity subsides on all men, as the snowflakes settle on the fields and ledges and takes the form of the various clefts and surfaces on which it lodges.

Feb. 8. My Journal Is That of Me

MY JOURNAL IS THAT of me which would else spill over and run to waste, gleanings from the field which in action I reap. I must not live for it, but in it for the gods. They are my correspondent, to whom daily I send off this sheet postpaid. I am clerk in their counting-room, and at evening transfer the account from day-book to ledger. It is as a leaf which hangs over my head in the path. I bend the twig and write my prayers on it; then letting it go, the bough springs up and shows the scrawl to heaven. As if it were not kept shut in my desk, but were as public a leaf as any in nature. It is papyrus by the riverside; it is vellum in the pastures; it is parchment on the hills. I find it everywhere as free as the leaves which troop along the lanes in autumn. The crow, the goose, the eagle carry my quill, and the wind blows the leaves as far as I go. Or, if my imagination does not soar, but gropes in slime and mud, then I write with a reed.

Feb. 28. The Author's Character

NOTHING GOES BY LUCK in composition. It allows of no tricks. The best you can write will be the best you are. Every sentence is the result of a long probation. The author's character is read from title-page to end. Of this he never corrects the proofs. We read it as the essential character of a handwriting without regard to the flourishes.

March 7–10. Harmony with Nature

THE APRIL SHOWER SHOULD be as reviving to our life as to the garden and the grove, and the scenery in which we live reflect our own beauty, as the dewdrop the flower. It is the actual man, not the actual Nature, that hurts the romance of the landscape. "He poisons the ground." The haymakers must be lost in the grass of the meadow. They may be Faustus and Amyntas here, but near at hand they are Reuben and Jonas. The woodcutter must not be better than the wood, lest he be *worse.* Neither will bear to be considered as a distinct feature. Man's works must lie in the bosom of Nature, cottages be buried in trees, or under vines and moss, like rocks, that they may not outrage the landscape. The hunter must be dressed in Lincoln green, with a plume of eagle's feathers, to imbosom him in Nature. So the skillful painter secures the distinctness of the whole by the indistinctness of the parts. We can endure best to consider our repose and silence. Only when the city, the hamlet, or the cottage is viewed from a distance does man's life seem in harmony with the universe; but seen closely his actions have no eagle's feathers or Lincoln green to redeem them. The sunlight on cities at a distance is a deceptive beauty, but foretells the final harmony of man with Nature.

April 10. What We See

WE ARE AS MUCH as we see. Faith is sight and knowledge. The hands only serve the eyes. The farthest blue streak in the horizon I can see, I may reach before many sunsets. What I saw alters not; in my night, when I wander, it is still steadfast as the star which the sailor steers by.

April 15. The Gods and Man

THURSDAY. THE GODS ARE of no sect; they side with no man. When I imagine that Nature inclined rather to some few earnest and faithful souls, and specially existed for them, I go to see an obscure individual who lives under the hill, letting both gods and men alone, and find that strawberries and tomatoes grow for him too in his garden there, and the sun lodges kindly under his hillside, and am compelled to acknowledge the unbribable charity of the gods.

April 26. The Indian

THE CHARM OF THE Indian to me is that he stands free and unconstrained in Nature, is her inhabitant and not her guest, and wears her easily and gracefully.

Aug. 9. Reading History

I READ HISTORY AS little critically as I consider the landscape, and am more interested in the atmospheric tints and various lights and shades which the intervening spaces create than in its groundwork and composition. It is the morning now turned evening and seen in the west,—the same sun, but a new light and atmosphere. Its beauty is like the sunset; not a fresco painting on a wall, flat and bounded, but atmospheric and roving, or free. But, in reality, history fluctuates as the face of the landscape from morning to evening. What is of moment in it is its hue and color. Time hides no treasures; we want not its *then,* but its *now.* We do not complain that the mountains in the horizon are blue and indistinct; they are the more like the heavens.

Aug. 12. Beholding a Mountain

WE TAKE PLEASURE IN beholding the form of a mountain in the horizon, as if by retiring to this distance we had then first conquered it by our vision, and were made privy to the design of the architect; so when we behold the shadow of our earth on the moon's disk. When we climb a mountain and observe the lesser irregularities, we do not give credit to the comprehensive and general intelligence which shaped them; but when we see the outline in the horizon, we confess that the hand which moulded those opposite slopes, making one balance the other, worked round a deep centre, and was privy to the plan of the universe. The smallest of nature's works fits the farthest and widest view, as if it had been referred in its bearings to every point in space. It harmonizes with the horizon line and the orbits of the planets.

A horizon of mountains.

Sept. 2. A Green Meadow

I saw a green meadow in the midst of the woods to-day which looked as if Dame Nature had set her foot there, and it had bloomed in consequence. It was the print of her moccasin.

Sept. 3. Moonlight

Moonlight is the best restorer of antiquity. The houses in the village have a classical elegance as of the best days of Greece, and this half-finished church reminds me of the Parthenon, or whatever is most famous and excellent in art. So serene it stands, reflecting the moon, and intercepting the stars with its rafters, as if it were refreshed by the dews of the night equally with me. By day Mr. Hosmer, but by night Vitruvius rather. If it were always to stand in this mild and sombre light it would be finished already. It is in progress by day but completed by night, and already its designer is an old master. The projecting rafter so carelessly left on the tower, holding its single way through the sky, is quite architectural, and in the unnecessary length of the joists and flooring of the staging around the walls there is an artistic superfluity and grace. In these fantastic lines described upon the sky there is no trifling or conceit. Indeed, the staging for the most part is the only genuine native architecture and deserves to stand longer than the building it surrounds. In this obscurity there are no fresh colors to offend, and the light and shade of evening adorn the new equally with the old.

Dec. 15. All Wildness

I SEEM TO SEE somewhat more of my own kith and kin in the lichens on the rocks than in any books. It does seem as if mine were a peculiarly wild nature, which so yearns toward all wildness. I know of no redeeming qualities in me but a sincere love for some things, and when I am reproved I have to fall back on to this ground. This is my argument in reserve for all cases. My love is invulnerable. Meet me on that ground, and you will find me strong. When I am condemned, and condemn myself utterly, I think straightway, "But I rely on my love for some things." Therein I am whole and entire. Therein I am God-propped.

Dec. 23. A Celebrated Wood

A FOREST IS IN all mythologies a sacred place, as the oaks among the Druids and the grove of Egeria; and even in more familiar and common life a celebrated wood is spoken of with respect, as "Barnsdale Wood" and "Sherwood." Had Robin Hood no Sherwood to resort [to], it would be difficult to invest his story with the charms it has got. It is always the tale that is untold, the deeds done and the life lived in the unexplored secrecy of the wood, that charm us and make us children again,—to read his ballads, and hear of the greenwood tree.

1842

March 24. Successful Authors

THURSDAY. THOSE AUTHORS ARE successful who do not *write down* to others, but make their own taste and judgment their audience. By some strange infatuation we forget that we do not approve what yet we recommend to others. It is enough if I please myself with writing; I am then sure of an audience.

March 25. Artist Must Work

THE ARTIST MUST WORK with indifference. Too great interest vitiates his work.

1 8 4 5

Aug. 6.   Nature Akin to Art

ALL NATURE IS CLASSIC and akin to art. The sumach and pine and hickory which surround my house remind me of the most graceful sculpture. Sometimes their tops, or a single limb or leaf, seems to have grown to a distinct expression as if it were a symbol for me to interpret. Poetry, painting, and sculpture claim at once and associate with themselves those perfect specimens of the art of nature,—leaves, vines, acorns, pine cones, etc. The critic must at last stand as mute though contented before a true poem as before an acorn or a vine leaf. The perfect work of art is received again into the bosom of nature whence its material proceeded, and that criticism which can only detect its unnaturalness has no longer any office to fulfill. The choicest maxims that have come down to us are more beautiful or integrally wise than they are wise to our understandings. This wisdom which we are inclined to pluck from their stalk is the point only of a single association. Every natural form—palm leaves and acorns, oak leaves and sumach and dodder—are [*sic*] untranslatable aphorisms.

1 8 4 5 – 4 7

Feb. 22.   Surveyor of Forest Paths

FOR MANY YEARS I was self-appointed inspector of snow-storms and rain-storms, and did my duty faithfully, though I never received one cent for it.

Surveyor, if not of higher ways, then of forest paths and all across-lot routes, keeping many open ravines bridged and passable at all seasons, where the public heel had testified to the importance of the same, all not only without charge, but even at considerable risk and inconvenience. Many a mower would have forborne to complain had he been aware of the invisible public good that was in jeopardy.

1 8 3 7 – 4 7

?Date.   Picture Is a Glass

NOT ONLY HAS THE foreground of a picture its glass of transparent crystal spread over it, but the picture itself is a glass or transparent medium to a remoter background. We demand only of all pictures that they be perspicuous, that the laws of perspective have been truly observed. It is not the fringed foreground of the desert nor the intermediate oases that detain the eye and the imagination, but the infinite, level, and roomy horizon, where the sky meets the sand, and heavens and earth, the ideal and actual, are coincident, the background into which leads the path of the pilgrim.

Chapter II

Year
1850
Age
32–33

?Date.   *Imposing Horizons*

THE MOST IMPOSING HORIZONS are those which are seen from tops of hills rising out of a river valley. The prospect even from a low hill has something majestic in it in such a case. The landscape is a vast amphitheatre rising to its rim in the horizon. There is a good view of Lincoln lying high up in among the hills. You see that it is the highest town hereabouts, and hence its fruit. The river at this time looks as large as the Hudson. I think that a river-valley town is much the handsomest and largest-featured,—like Concord and Lancaster, for instance, natural centres.

June 20. I Have a Garden

AND THEN FOR MY afternoon walks I have a garden, larger than any
artificial garden that I have read of and far more attractive to me,—mile after mile
of embowered walks, such as no nobleman's grounds can boast, with animals
running free and wild therein as from the first,—varied with land and water
prospect, and, above all, so retired that it is extremely rare that I meet a single
wanderer in its mazes. No gardener is seen therein, no gates nor [sic]. You may
wander away to solitary bowers and brooks and hills.

July. Walk by Night

MANY MEN WALK BY day; few walk by night. It is a very different season.
Instead of the sun, there are the moon and stars; instead of the wood thrush, there
is the whip-poor-will; instead of butterflies, fireflies, winged sparks of fire! who
would have believed it? What kind of life and cool deliberation dwells in a spark
of fire in dewy abodes? Every man carries fire in his eye, or in his blood, or in his
brain. Instead of singing birds, the croaking of frogs and the intenser dream of
crickets. The potatoes stand up straight, the corn grows, the bushes loom, and,
in a moonlight night, the shadows of rocks and trees and bushes and hills are more
conspicuous than the objects themselves. The slightest inequalities in the ground
are revealed by the shadows; what the feet find comparatively smooth appears
rough and diversified to the eye. The smallest recesses in the rocks are dim and
cavernous; the ferns in the wood appear to be of tropical size; the pools seen
through the leaves become as full of light as the sky. "The light of day takes refuge
in their bosom," as the Purana says of the ocean. The woods are heavy and dark.
Nature slumbers. The rocks retain the warmth of the sun which they have absorbed all night.

July. Today's Indians

THE NAMES OF THOSE who bought these fields of the red men, the wild
men of the woods, are Buttrick, Davis, Barrett, Bulkley, etc., etc. (Vide History.)
Here and there still you will find a man with Indian blood in his veins, an eccentric
farmer descended from an Indian chief; or you will see a solitary pure-blooded
Indian, looking as wild as ever among the pines, one of the last of the Massachusetts tribes, stepping into a railroad car with his gun.

Still here and there an Indian squaw with her dog, her only companion, lives
in some lone house, insulted by school-children, making baskets and picking
berries her employment. You will meet her on the highway, with few children or
none, with melancholy face, history, destiny; stepping after her race; who had
stayed to tuck them up in their long sleep. For whom berries condescend to grow

I have not seen one on the Musketaquid for many a year, and some who came up in their canoes and camped on its banks a dozen years ago had to ask me where it came from. A lone Indian woman without children, accompanied by her dog, wearing the shroud of her race, performing the last offices for her departed race. Not yet absorbed into the elements again; a daughter of the soil; one of the nobility of the land. The white man an imported weed,—burdock and mullein, which displace the ground-nut.

July.   A Glorious Sunset

THERE WAS A GLORIOUS lurid sunset to-night, accompanied with many sombre clouds, and when I looked into the west with my head turned, the grass had the same fresh green, and the distant herbage and foliage in the horizon the same dark blue, and the clouds and sky the same bright colors beautifully mingled and dissolving into one another, that I have seen in pictures of tropical landscapes and skies. Pale saffron skies with faint fishes of rosy clouds dissolving in them. A bloodstained sky. I regretted that I had an impatient companion. What shall we make of the fact that you have only to stand on your head a moment to be enchanted with the beauty of the landscape?

July.   Concord Town

I CAN EASILY WALK ten, fifteen, twenty, any number of miles, commencing at my own door, without going by any house, without crossing a road except where the fox and the mink do. Concord is the oldest inland town in New England, perhaps in the States, and the walker is peculiarly favored here. There are square miles in my vicinity which have no inhabitant. First along by the river, and then the brook, and then the meadow and the woodside. Such solitude! From a hundred hills I can see civilization and abodes of man afar. These farmers and their works are scarcely more obvious than woodchucks.

July.   The Elm

THERE WAS REASON ENOUGH for the first settler's selecting the elm out of all the trees of the forest with which to ornament his villages. It is beautiful alike by sunlight and moonlight, and the most beautiful specimens are not the largest. I have seen some only twenty-five or thirty years old, more graceful and healthy, I think, than any others. It is almost become a villageous tree,—like martins and bluebirds.

Elm tree of old.

July. Air Painted Hillsides

I WALK OVER THE hills, to compare *great* things with *small,* as through a gallery of pictures, ever and anon looking through a gap in the wood, as through the frame of a picture, to a more distant wood or hillside, painted with several more coats of air. It is a cheap but pleasant effect. To a landscape in picture, glassed with air.

What is a horizon without mountains?

Aug. 31. The Sassafras

THE ODORIFEROUS SASSAFRAS, WITH its delicate green stem, its three-lobed leaf, tempting the traveller to bruise it, it sheds so rare a perfume on him, equal to all the spices of the East. Then its rare-tasting root bark, like nothing else, which I used to dig. The first navigators freighted their ships with it and deemed it worth its weight in gold.

Sept. Twilight Elms

IN THE TWILIGHT, WHEN you can only see the outlines of the trees in the horizon, the elm-tops indicate where the houses are. I have looked afar over fields and even over distant woods and distinguished the conspicuous graceful, sheaf-like head of an elm which shadowed some farmhouse. From the northwest (?) part of Sudbury you can see an elm on the Boston road, on the hilltop in the horizon in Wayland, five or six miles distant. The elm is a tree which can be distinguished farther off perhaps than any other.

Sept. Goldenrods and Asters

THE GOLDENRODS AND ASTERS impress me not like individuals but great families covering a thousand hills and having a season to themselves.

Sept. The Way a River Went

IT IS PLEASANT TO have been to a place by the way a river went.

River beginnings.

Oct. Withered Plants

I THOUGHT TO-DAY THAT it would be pleasing to study the dead and withered plants, the ghosts of plants, which now remain in the fields, for they fill almost as large a space to the eye as the green have done. They live not in memory only, but to the fancy and imagination.

Oct. 31. This Beautiful Day

WHY WAS THIS BEAUTIFUL day made, and no man to improve it? We went through Seven-Star (?) Lane to White Pond.

Looking through a stately pine grove, I saw the western sun falling in golden streams through its aisles. Its west side, opposite to me, was all lit up with golden light; but what was I to it? Such sights remind me of houses which we never inhabit,—that commonly I am not at home in the world. I see somewhat fairer than I enjoy or possess.

A fair afternoon, a celestial afternoon, cannot occur but we mar our pleasure by reproaching ourselves that we do not make all our days beautiful. The thought of what I am, of my pitiful conduct, deters me from receiving what joy I might from the glorious days that visit me. After the era of youth is passed, the knowledge of ourselves is an alloy that spoils our satisfactions.

I am wont to think that I could spend my days contentedly in any retired country house that I see; for I see it to advantage now and without incumbrance; I have not yet imported my humdrum thoughts, my prosaic habits, into it to mar the landscape. What is this beauty in the landscape but a certain fertility in me? I look in vain to see it realized but in my own life. If I could wholly cease to be ashamed of myself, I think that all my days would be fair.

Nov. 8.   Waiting for Winter

THE STILLNESS OF THE woods and fields is remarkable at this season of the year. There is not even the creak of a cricket to be heard. Of myriads of dry shrub oak leaves, not one rustles. Your own breath can rustle them, yet the breath of heaven does not suffice to. The trees have the aspect of waiting for winter. The autumnal leaves have lost their color; they are now truly sere, dead, and the woods wear a sombre color. Summer and harvest are over. The hickories, birches, chestnuts, no less than the maples, have lost their leaves. The sprouts, which had shot up so vigorously to repair the damage which the choppers had done, have stopped short for the winter. Everything stands silent and expectant. If I listen, I hear only the note of a chickadee,—our most common and I may say native bird, most identified with our forests,—or perchance the scream of a jay, or perchance from the solemn depths of these woods I hear tolling far away the knell of one departed. Thought rushes in to fill the vacuum. As you walk, however, the partridge still bursts away. The silent, dry, almost leafless, certainly fruitless woods. You wonder what cheer that bird can find in them. The partridge bursts away from the foot of a shrub oak like its own dry fruit, immortal bird! This sound still startles us. Dry goldenrods, now turned gray and white, lint our clothes as we walk. And the drooping, downy seed-vessels of the epilobium remind us of the summer. Perchance you will meet with a few solitary asters in the dry fields, with a little color left. The sumach is stripped of everything but its cone of red berries.

Nov. 9.   A New Prospect

IT IS A PLEASANT surprise to walk over a hill where an old wood has recently been cut off, and, on looking round, to see, instead of dense ranks of trees almost impermeable to light, distant well-known blue mountains in the horizon and perchance a white village over an expanded open country. I now take this in preference to all my old familiar walks. So a new prospect and walks can be created where we least expected it. The old men have seen other prospects from these hills than we do. There was the old Kettell place, now Watts's, which I surveyed for him last winter and lotted off, where twenty-five years ago

I played horse in the paths of a thick wood and roasted apples and potatoes in an old pigeon-place and gathered fruit at the pieapple tree. A week or two after I surveyed it, it now being rotten and going to waste, I walked there and was surprised to find the place and prospect which I have described.

Nov. 9. Pitch Pine Field

IT IS PLEASANT TO observe any growth in a wood. There is the pitch pine field northeast of Beck Stow's Swamp, where some years ago I went a-blackberrying and observed that the pitch pines were beginning to come in, and I have frequently noticed since how fairly they grew, dotting the plain as evenly as if dispersed by art. To-day I was aware that I walked in a pitch pine wood, which ere long, perchance, I may survey and lot off for a wood auction and see the choppers at their work. There is also the old pigeon-place field by the Deep Cut. I remember it as an open grassy field. It is now one of our most pleasant woodland paths. In the former place, near the edge of the old wood, the young pines line each side of the path like a palisade, they grow so densely.

Nov. 9. Stone Walls

I SOMETIMES SEE WELL-PRESERVED walls running straight through the midst of high and old woods, built, of course, when the soil was cultivated many years ago, and am surprised to see slight stones still lying one upon another, as the builder placed them, while this huge oak has grown up from a chance acorn in the soil.

Pasture and stone wall, Concord, Massachusetts.

Nov. 11. Time for Wild Apples

NOW IS THE TIME for wild apples. I pluck them as a wild fruit native to this quarter of the earth, fruit of old trees that have been dying ever since I was a boy and are not yet dead. From the appearance of the tree you would expect nothing but lichens to drop from it, but underneath your faith is rewarded by finding the ground strewn with spirited fruit. Frequented only by the woodpecker, deserted now by the farmer, who has not faith enough to look under the boughs. Food for walkers. Sometimes apples red inside, perfused with a beautiful blush, faery food, too beautiful to eat,—apple of the evening sky, of the Hesperides.

Wild apple grove.

Nov. 11. Dry Grass

THAT DELICATE, WAVING, FEATHERY dry grass which I saw yesterday is to be remembered with the autumn. The dry grasses are not dead for me. A beautiful form has as much life at one season as another.

Nov. 16. The Smallest Brook

I AM ACCUSTOMED TO regard the smallest brook with as much interest for the time being as if it were the Orinoco or Mississippi. What is the difference, I would like to know, but mere size? And when a tributary rill empties in, it is like the confluence of famous rivers I have read of. When I cross one on a fence, I love to pause in midpassage and look down into the water, and study its bottom, its little mystery. There is none so small but you may see a pickerel regarding you with a wary eye, or a pygmy trout glance from under the bank, or in spring, perchance, a sucker will have found its way far up its stream. You are sometimes astonished to see a pickerel far up some now shrunken rill, where it is a mere puddle by the roadside. I have stooped to drink at a clear spring no bigger than a bushel basket in a meadow, from which a rill was scarcely seen to dribble away, and seen lurking at its bottom two little pickerel not so big as my finger, sole monarchs of this their ocean, and who probably would never visit a larger water.

Snow laden brook.

Nov. 16. The Wild in Literature

IN LITERATURE IT IS only the wild that attracts us. Dullness is only another name for tameness. It is the untamed, uncivilized, free, and wild thinking in Hamlet, in the Iliad, and in all the scriptures and mythologies that delights us,—not learned in the schools, not refined and polished by art. A truly good book is something as wildly natural and primitive, mysterious and marvellous, ambrosial and fertile, as a fungus or a lichen. Suppose the muskrat or beaver were to turn his views [*sic*] to literature, what fresh views of nature would he present! The fault of our books and other deeds is that they are too humane, I want something speaking in some measure to the condition of muskrats and skunk-cabbage as well as of men,—not merely to a pining and complaining coterie of philanthropists.

Nov. 16. Wild Apples

THE ERA OF WILD apples will soon be over. I wander through old orchards of great extent, now all gone to decay, all of native fruit which for the most part went to the cider-mill. But since the temperance reform and the general introduction of grafted fruit, no wild apples, such as I see everywhere in deserted pastures, and where the woods have grown up among them, are set out. I fear that he who walks over these hills a century hence will not know the pleasure of knocking off wild apples. Ah, poor man! there are many pleasures which he will be debarred from! Notwithstanding the prevalence of the Baldwin and the Porter, I doubt if as extensive orchards are set out to-day in this town as there were a century ago, when these vast straggling cider-orchards were planted. Men stuck in a tree then by every wallside and let it take its chance. I see nobody planting trees to-day in such out of the way places, along almost every road and lane and wall-side, and at the bottom of dells in the wood. Now that they have grafted trees and pay a price for them, they collect them into a plot by their houses and fence them in.

Nov. 21. A White Pine Wood

SOME DISTANT ANGLE IN the sun where a lofty and dense white pine wood, with mingled gray and green, meets a hill covered with shrub oaks, affects me singularly, reinspiring me with all the dreams of my youth. It is a place far away, yet actual and where we have been. I saw the sun falling on a distant white pine wood whose gray and moss-covered stems were visible amid the green, in an angle where this forest abutted on a hill covered with shrub oaks. It was like looking into dreamland. It is one of the avenues to my future. Certain coincidences like this are accompanied by a certain flash as of hazy lightning, flooding all the world suddenly with a tremulous serene light which it is difficult to see long at a time.

I saw Fair Haven Pond with its island, and meadow between the island and the shore, and a strip of perfectly still and smooth water in the lee of the island, and two hawks, fish hawks perhaps, sailing over it. I did not see how it could be improved. Yet I do not see what these things can be. I begin to see such an object when I cease to *understand* it and see that I did not realize or appreciate it before, but I get no further than this. How adapted these forms and colors to my eye! A meadow and an island! What are these things? Yet the hawks and the ducks keep so aloof! and Nature is so reserved! I am made to love the pond and the meadow, as the wind is made to ripple the water.

Dec. 22. Thawed Apples

THE APPLES ARE NOW thawed. This is their first thawing. Those which a month ago were sour, crabbed, and uneatable are now filled with a rich, sweet cider which I am better acquainted with than with wine. And others, which have more substance, are a sweet and luscious food,—in my opinion of more worth than the pineapples which are imported from the torrid zone. Those which a month ago I tasted and repented of it, which the farmer willingly left on the tree, I am now glad to find have the property of hanging on like the leaves of the shrub oak. It is a way to keep cider sweet without boiling. Let the frost come to freeze them first solid as stones, and then the sun or a warm winter day—for it takes but little heat—to thaw them, and they will seem to have borrowed a flavor from heaven through the medium of the air in which they hang. I find when I get home that they have thawed in my pocket and the ice is turned to cider. But I suspect that

A piny view.

after the second freezing and thawing they will not be so good. I bend to drink the cup and save my lappets. What are the half-ripe fruits of the torrid south, to this fruit matured by the cold of the frigid north. There are those crabbed apples with which I cheated my companion, and kept a smooth face to tempt him to eat. Now we both greedily fill our pockets with them, and grow more social with their wine. Was there one that hung so high and sheltered by the tangled branches that our sticks could not dislodge it? It is a fruit never brought to market that I am aware of,—quite distinct from the apple of the markets, as from dried apple and cider. It is not every winter that produces it in perfection.

CHAPTER III
YEAR
1851
AGE
33–34

Jan. 10. A Genius for Sauntering

I HAVE MET WITH but one or two persons in the course of my life who understood the art of taking walks daily,—not [to] exercise the legs or body merely, nor barely to recruit the spirits, but positively to exercise both body and spirit, and to succeed to the highest and worthiest ends by the abandonment of all specific ends,—who had a genius, so to speak, for sauntering. And this word "saunter," by the way, is happily derived "from idle people who roved about the country [in the Middle Ages] and asked charity under pretence of going *à la Sainte Terre,*" to the Holy Land, till, perchance, the children exclaimed, "There goes a *Sainte-Terrer,*" a Holy-Lander. They who never go to the Holy Land in their walks, as they pretend, are indeed mere idlers and vagabonds.

Feb. Nature and Mythology

I DO NOT KNOW where to find in any literature, whether ancient or modern, any adequate account of that Nature with which I am acquainted. Mythology comes nearest to it of any.

Feb. Nature and Literature

IT IS REMARKABLE HOW few passages, comparatively speaking, there are in the best literature of the day which betray any intimacy with Nature.

Feb. 12. Trespassing

I TRUST THAT THE walkers of the present day are conscious of the blessings which they enjoy in the comparative freedom with which they can ramble over the country and enjoy the landscape, anticipating with compassion that future day when possibly it will be partitioned off into so-called pleasure-grounds, where only a few may enjoy the narrow and exclusive pleasure which is compatible with ownership,—when walking over the surface of God's earth shall be construed to mean trespassing on some gentleman's grounds, when fences shall be multiplied and man traps and other engines invented to confine men to the public road. I am thankful that we have yet so much room in America.

Feb. 13. Nature as Imitator

NATURE IS A GREAT imitator and loves to repeat herself. She wastes her wonders on the town. It impresses me as one superiority in her art, if art it may be called, that she does not require that man appreciate her, takes no steps to attract his attention.

Feb. 14. Fair Haven Pond

ONE AFTERNOON IN THE fall, November 21st, I saw Fair Haven Pond with its island and meadow; between the island and the shore, a strip of perfectly smooth water in the lee of the island; and two hawks sailing over it; and something more I saw which cannot easily be described, which made me say to myself that the landscape could not be improved. I did not see how it could be improved. Yet I do not know what these things can be; I begin to see such objects only when I leave off understanding them, and afterwards remember that I did not appreciate them before. But I get no further than this. How adapted these forms and colors to our eyes, a meadow and its islands! What are these things? Yet the hawks and the ducks keep so aloof, and nature is so reserved! We are made to love the river and the meadow, as the wind to ripple the water.

North end of Fair Haven Bay with view of hillside east of the bay
and marsh in the foreground near Concord, Massachusetts.

May 1. Heaven Intervenes

ALL DISTANT LANDSCAPES SEEN from hilltops are veritable pictures, which will be found to have no actual existence to him who travels to them. " 'Tis distance lends enchantment to the view." It is the bare landscape without this depth of atmosphere to glass it. The distant river-reach seen in the north from the Lincoln Hill, high in the horizon, like the ocean stream flowing round Homer's shield, the rippling waves reflecting the light, is unlike the same seen near at hand. Heaven intervenes between me and the object. By what license do I call it Concord River. It redeems the character of rivers to see them thus. They were worthy then of a place on Homer's shield.

As I looked to-day from Mt. Tabor in Lincoln to the Waltham hill, I saw the same deceptive slope, the near hill melting into the further inseparably, indistinguishably; it was one gradual slope from the base of the near hill to the summit of the further one, a succession of copse-woods, but I knew that there intervened a valley two or three miles wide, studded with houses and orchards and drained by a considerable stream. When the shadow of a cloud passed over the nearer hill, I could distinguish its shaded summit against the side of the other.

May 25. A Home Site

A FINE, FRESHENING AIR, a little hazy, that bathes and washes everything, saving the day from extreme heat. Walked to the hills south of Wayland by the road by Deacon Farrar's. First vista just beyond Merron's (?), looking west down a valley, with a verdant-columned elm at the extremity of the vale and the blue hills and horizon beyond. These are the resting-places in a walk. We love to see any part of the earth tinged with blue, cerulean, the color of the sky, the celestial color. I wonder that houses are not oftener located mainly that they may command particular rare prospects, every convenience yielding to this. The farmer would never suspect what it was you were buying, and such sites would be the cheapest of any. A site where you might avail yourself of the art of Nature for three thousand years, which could never be materially changed or taken from you, a noble inheritance for your children. The true sites for human dwellings are unimproved. They command no price in the market. Men will pay something to look into a travelling showman's box, but not to look upon the fairest prospects on the earth. A vista where you have the near green horizon contrasted with the distant blue one, terrestrial with celestial earth. The prospect of a vast horizon must be accessible in our neighborhood. Where men of enlarged views may be educated. An unchangeable kind of wealth, a *real* estate.

June 11. The Deep Cut

I SAW BY THE shadows cast by the inequalities of the clayey sand-bank in the Deep Cut that it was necessary to see objects by moonlight as well as sunlight, to get a complete notion of them. This bank had looked much more flat by day, when the light was stronger, but now the heavy shadows revealed its prominences. The prominences are light, made more remarkable by the dark shadows which they cast.

June 14. Shades of Night

HOW MODERATE, DELIBERATE, IS Nature! How gradually the shades of night gather and deepen, giving man ample leisure to bid farewell to-day, conclude his day's affairs, and prepare for slumber! The twilight seems out of proportion to the length of the day. Perchance it saves our eyes. Now for some hours the farmers have been getting home.

July 2. House Trees

MANY LARGE TREES, ESPECIALLY elms, about a house are a surer indication of old family distinction and worth than any evidence of wealth. Any evidence of care bestowed on these trees secures the traveller's respect as for a nobler husbandry than the raising of corn and potatoes.

July 5. Hubbard's Bridge

As WE COME OVER Hubbard's Bridge between 5 and 6 P.M., the sun getting low, a cool wind blowing up the valley, we sit awhile on the rails which are destined

Side view, the former Thoreau family home,
Concord, Massachusetts.

for the new railing. The light on the Indian hill is very soft and glorious, giving the idea of the most wonderful fertility. The most barren hills are gilded like waving grain-fields. What a paradise to sail by! The cliffs and woods up the stream are nearer and have more shadow and actuality about them. This retired bridge is a favorite spot with me. I have witnessed many a fair sunset from it.

July 6. June Is Past

THE RED CLOVER HEADS are now turned black. They no longer impart that rosaceous tinge to the meadows and fertile fields. It is but a short time that their rich bloom lasts. The white is black or withering also. Whiteweed still looks white in the fields. Blue-eyed grass is now rarely seen. The grass in the fields and meadows is not so fresh and fair as it was a fortnight ago. It is dryer and riper and ready for the mowers. Now June is past. June is the month for grass and flowers. Now grass is turning to hay, and flowers to fruits. Already I gather ripe blueberries on the hills. The red-topped grass is in its prime, tingeing the fields with red.

July 8. Rye as a Crop

HERE ARE SOME RICH rye-fields waving over all the land, their heads nodding in the evening breeze with an apparently alternating motion; *i. e.* they do not all bend at once by ranks, but separately, and hence this agreeable alternation. How rich a sight this cereal fruit, now yellow for the cradle,—*flavus!* It is an impenetrable phalanx. I walk for half a mile beside these Macedonians, looking in vain for an opening. There is no Arnold Winkelried to gather these spear-heads upon his breast and make an opening for me. This is food for man. The earth labors not in vain; it is bearing its burden. The yellow, waving, rustling rye extends far up and over the hills on either side, a kind of pinafore to nature, leaving only a narrow and dark passage at the bottom of a deep ravine. How rankly it has grown! How it hastes to maturity! I discover that there is such a goddess as Ceres. These long grain-fields which you must respect,—must go round,—occupying the ground like an army. The small trees and shrubs seen dimly in its midst are overwhelmed by the grain as by an inundation. They are seen only as indistinct forms of bushes and green leaves mixed with the yellow stalks. There are certain crops which give me the idea of bounty, of the *Alma Natura.* They are the grains. Potatoes do not so fill the lap of earth. This rye excludes everything else and takes possession of the soil. The farmer says, "Next year I will raise a crop of rye;" and he proceeds to clear away the brush, and either plows it, or, if it is too uneven or stony, burns and harrows it only, and scatters the seed with faith. And all winter the earth keeps his secret,—unless it did leak out somewhat in the fall,—and in the spring this early green on the hillsides betrays him. When I see this luxuriant crop spreading far and wide in spite of rock and bushes and unevenness of ground, I cannot help thinking that it must have been unexpected by the farmer himself, and regarded by him as a lucky accident for which to thank fortune. This, to reward a transient faith, the gods had given. As if he must have forgotten that he did it, until he saw the waving grain inviting his sickle.

Overturned boat by the Sudbury River,
near Concord, Massachusetts.

July 20.   River Interest

THE RIVER, TOO, STEADILY yields its crop. In louring days it is remarkable how many villagers resort to it. It is of more worth than many gardens. I meet one, late in the afternoon, going to the river with his basket on his arm and his pole in hand, not ambitious to catch pickerel this time, but he thinks he may perhaps get a mess of small fish. These [*sic*] kind of values are real and important, though but little appreciated, and he is not a wise legislator who underrates them and allows the bridges to be built low so as to prevent the passage of small boats. The town is but little conscious how much interest it has in the river, and might vote it away any day thoughtlessly. There is always to be seen either some unshaven wading man, an old mower of the river meadows, familiar with water, vibrating his long pole over the lagoons of the off-shore pads, or else some solitary fisher, in a boat behind the willows, like a mote in the sunbeams reflecting the light; and who can tell how many a mess of river fish is daily cooked in the town? They are an important article of food to many a poor family.

Little used road.

July 21.   Uninhabited Roads

8 A.M. — THE FORENOON IS FULLER of light. The butterflies on the flowers look like other and frequently larger flowers themselves. Now I yearn for one of those old, meandering, dry, uninhabited roads, which lead away from towns, which lead us away from temptation, which conduct to the outside of earth, over its uppermost crust; where you may forget in what country you are travelling; where no farmer can complain that you are treading down his grass, no gentleman who has recently constructed a seat in the country that you are trespassing; on which you can go off at half-cock and wave adieu to the village; along which you may travel like a pilgrim, going nowhither; where travellers are not too often to be met; where my spirit is free; where the walls and fences are not cared for; where your head is more in heaven than your feet are on earth; which have long reaches where you can see the approaching traveller half a mile off and be prepared for him; not so luxuriant a soil as to attract men; some root and stump fences which do not need attention; where travellers have no occasion to stop, but pass along and leave you to your thoughts; where it makes no odds

which way you face, whether you are going or coming, whether it is morning or evening, mid-noon or midnight; where earth is cheap enough by being public; where you can walk and think with least obstruction, there being nothing to measure progress by; where you can pace when your breast is full, and cherish your moodiness; where you are not in false relations with men, are not dining nor conversing with them; by which you may go to the uttermost parts of the earth. It is wide enough, wide as the thoughts it allows to visit you. Sometimes it is some particular half-dozen rods which I wish to find myself pacing over, as where certain airs blow; then my life will come to me, methinks; like a hunter I walk in wait for it. When I am against this bare promontory of a huckleberry hill, then forsooth my thoughts will expand. Is it some influence, as a vapor which exhales from the ground, or something in the gales which blow there, or in all things there brought together agreeably to my spirit? The walls must not be too high, imprisoning me, but low, with numerous gaps. The trees must not be too numerous, nor the hills too near, bounding the view, nor the soil too rich, attracting the attention to the earth. It must simply be the way and the life,—a way that was never known to be repaired, nor to need repair, within the memory of the oldest inhabitant. I cannot walk habitually in those ways that are liable to be mended; for sure it was the devil only that wore them. Never by the heel of thinkers (of thought) were they worn; the zephyrs could repair that damage. The saunterer wears out no road, even though he travel on it, and therefore should pay no highway, or rather *low* way, tax. He may be taxed to construct a higher way than men travel. A way which no geese defile, nor hiss along it, but only sometimes their wild brethren fly far overhead; which the kingbird and the swallow twitter over, and the song sparrow sings on its rails; where the small red butterfly is at home on the yarrow, and no boys threaten it with imprisoning hat. There I can walk and stalk and pace and plod. Which nobody but Jonas Potter travels beside me; where no cow but his is tempted to linger for the herbage by its side; where the guide-board is fallen, and now the hand points to heaven significantly,—to a Sudbury and Marlborough in the skies. That's a road I can travel, that the particular Sudbury I am bound for, six miles an hour, or two, as you please; and few there be that enter thereon. There I can walk, and recover the lost child that I am without any ringing of a bell; where there was nothing ever discovered to detain a traveller, but all went through about their business; where I never passed the time of day with any,—indifferent to me were the arbitrary divisions of time; where Tullus Hostilius might have disappeared,—at any rate has never been seen. The road to the Corner! the ninety and nine acres that you go through to get there! I would rather see it again, though I saw it this morning, than Gray's churchyard. The road whence you may hear a stake-driver, a whip-poor-will, a quail in a midsummer day, a—yes, a quail comes nearest to the *gum-c* bird heard there; where it would not be sport for a sportsman to go. And the mayweed looks up in my face,—not there; the pale lobelia, the Canada snapdragon, rather. A little hardhack and meadowsweet peep over the fence,—nothing more serious to obstruct the view,—and thimble-berries are the food of thought, before the drought, along by the walls.

July 22. Morning Fogs

THE SEASON OF MORNING fogs has arrived. I think it is connected with dog-days. Perhaps it is owing to the greater contrast between the night and the day, the nights being nearly as cold, while the days are warmer? Before I rise from my couch, I see the ambrosial fog stretched over the river, draping the trees. It is the summer's vapor bath. What purity in the color! It is almost musical; it is positively fragrant. How faery-like it has visited our fields. I am struck by its firm outlines, as distinct as a pillow's edge, about the height of my house. A great crescent over the course of the river from southwest to northeast. Already, 5.30 A.M., some parts of the river are bare. It goes off in a body down the river, before this air, and does not rise into the heavens. It retreats, and I do not see how it is dissipated. This slight, thin vapor which is left to curl over the surface of the still, dark water, still as glass, seems not [to] be the same thing,—of a different quality. I hear the cockerels crow through it, and the rich crow of young roosters, that sound indicative of the bravest, rudest health, hoarse without cold, hoarse with rude health. That crow is all-nature-compelling; famine and pestilence flee before it. These are our fairest days, which are born in a fog.

Aug. 5. What You See

AH, WHAT A POOR, dry compilation is the "Annual of Scientific Discovery!" I trust that observations are made during the year which are not chronicled there,—that some mortal may have caught a glimpse of Nature in some corner of the earth during the year 1851. One sentence of perennial poetry would make me forget, would atone for, volumes of mere science. The astronomer is as blind to the significant phenomena, or the significance of phenomena, as the wood-sawyer who wears glasses to defend his eyes from sawdust. The question is not what you look at, but what you see.

Aug. 21. Improvement of Mowing

MOWING TO SOME EXTENT improves the landscape to the eye of the walker. The aftermath, so fresh and green, begins now to recall the spring to my mind. In some fields fresh clover heads appear. This is certainly better than fields of lodged and withered grass.

Aug. 21. Taking Wide Views

THERE IS SOME ADVANTAGE, intellectually and spiritually, in taking wide views with the bodily eye and not pursuing an occupation which holds the body prone. There is some advantage, perhaps, in attending to the general features of the landscape over studying the particular plants and animals which inhabit it. A man may walk abroad and no more see the sky than if he walked under a shed. The poet is more in the air than the naturalist, though they may walk side by side. Granted that you are out-of-doors; but what if the outer door *is* open, if the inner door is shut! You must walk sometimes perfectly free, not prying nor inquisitive, not bent upon seeing things. Throw away a whole day for a single expansion, a single inspiration of air.

River scene with boat, Concord, Massachusetts.

Aug. 23. Man in a Boat

OUR LITTLE RIVER REACHES are not to be forgotten. I noticed that seen northward on the Assabet from the Causeway Bridge near the second stone bridge. There was [a] man in a boat in the sun, just disappearing in the distance round a bend, lifting high his arms and dipping his paddle as if he were a vision bound to land of the blessed,—far off, as in picture. When I see Concord to purpose, I see it as if it were not real but painted, and what wonder if I do not speak to *thee?*

Aug. 28. The Obscure Life

I OMIT THE UNUSUAL —the hurricanes and earthquakes—and describe the common. This has the greatest charm and is the true theme of poetry. You may have the extraordinary for your province, if you will let me have the ordinary. Give me the obscure life, the cottage of the poor and humble, the workdays of the world, the barren fields, the smallest share of all things but poetic perception. Give me but the eyes to see the things which you possess.

Aug. 31. River Scenery

THE ATTRACTIVE POINT IS that line where the water meets the land, not distinct, but known to exist. The willows are not the less interesting because of their nakedness below. How rich, like what we love to read of South American primitive forests, is the scenery of this river! What luxuriance of weeds, what depth of mud along its sides! These old antehistoric, geologic, antediluvian rocks which only primitive wading birds, still lingering among us, are worthy to tread. The season which we seem to *live* in anticipation of is arrived. The water, indeed, reflects heaven because my mind does; such is its own serenity, its transparency and stillness.

Aug. 31. The Hour of Sunset

WE COMMONLY SACRIFICE TO supper this serene and sacred hour. Our customs turn the hour of sunset to a trivial time, as at the meeting of two roads, one coming from the noon, the other leading to the night. It might be [well] if our repasts were taken out-of-doors, in view of the sunset and the rising stars; if there were two persons whose pulses beat together, if men cared for the κόυμος, or *beauty* of the world; if men were *social* in a high and rare sense; if they associated on high levels; if we took in with our tea a draught of the transparent, dew-freighted evening air; if, with our bread and butter, we took a slice of the red western sky; if the smoking, steaming urn were the vapor on a thousand lakes and rivers and meads.

The air of the valleys at this hour is the distilled essence of all those fragrances which during the day have been filling and have been dispersed in the atmosphere. The fine fragrances, perchance, which have floated in the upper atmospheres have settled to these low vales!

Sept. 2. Expressing Thoughts

WE CANNOT WRITE WELL or truly but what we write with gusto. The body, the senses, must conspire with the mind. Expression is the act of the whole man, that our speech may be vascular. The intellect is powerless to express thought without the aid of the heart and liver and of every member. Often I feel that my head stands out too dry, when it should be immersed. A writer, a man writing, is the scribe of all nature; he is the corn and the grass and the atmosphere writing. It is always essential that we love to do what we are doing, do it with a heart. The maturity of the mind, however, may perchance consist with a certain dryness.

Sept. 4. Avenues to Truth

IT IS WISE TO write on many subjects, to try many themes, that so you may find the right and inspiring one. Be greedy of occasions to express your thought.

Improve the opportunity to draw analogies. There are innumerable avenues to a perception of the truth. Improve the suggestion of each object however humble, however slight and transient the provocation. What else is there to be improved? Who knows what opportunities he may neglect? It is not in vain that the mind turns aside this way or that: follow its leading; apply it whither it inclines to go. Probe the universe in a myriad points. Be avaricious of these impulses. You must try a thousand themes before you find the right one, as nature makes a thousand acorns to get one oak. He is a wise man and experienced who has taken many views; to whom stones and plants and animals and a myriad objects have each suggested something, contributed something.

Sept. 7. Flower of the World

THE SCENERY, WHEN IT is truly seen, reacts on the life of the seer. How to live. How to get the most life. As if you were to teach the young hunter how to entrap his game. How to extract its honey from the flower of the world. That is my every-day business. I am as busy as a bee about it. I ramble over all fields on that errand, and am never so happy as when I feel myself heavy with honey and wax. I am like a bee searching the livelong day for the sweets of nature. Do I not impregnate and intermix the flowers, produce rare and finer varieties by transferring my eyes from one to another? I do as naturally and as joyfully, with my own humming music, seek honey all the day. With what honeyed thought any experience yields me I take a bee line to my cell. It is with flowers I would deal. Where is the flower, there is the honey,—which is perchance the nectareous portion of the fruit,—there is to be the fruit, and no doubt flowers are thus colored and painted to attract and guide the bee. So by the dawning or radiance of beauty are we advertised where is the honey and the fruit of thought, of discourse, and of action. We are first attracted by the beauty of the flower, before we discover the honey which is a foretaste of the future fruit.

Sept. 24. The Empurpled Hills

RETURNING OVER THE CAUSEWAY from Flint's Pond the other evening (22d), just at sunset, I observed that while the west was of a bright golden color under a bank of clouds,—the sun just setting,—and not a tinge of red was yet visible there, there was a distinct purple tinge in the nearer atmosphere, so that Annursnack Hill, seen through it, had an exceedingly rich empurpled look. It is rare that we perceive this purple tint in the air, telling of the juice of the wild grape and poke-berries. The empurpled hills! Methinks I have only noticed this in cooler weather.

Sept. 24. Abode of Man

WHAT CAN BE HANDSOMER for a picture than our river scenery now?
Take this view from the first Conantum Cliff. First this smoothly shorn meadow
on the west side of the stream, with all the swaths distinct, sprinkled with apple
trees casting heavy shadows black as ink, such as can be seen only in this clear
air, this strong light, one cow wandering restlessly about in it and lowing; then
the blue river, scarcely darker than and not to be distinguished from the sky, its
waves driven southward, or up-stream, by the wind, making it appear to flow that
way, bordered by willows and button-bushes; then the narrow meadow beyond,
with varied lights and shades from its waving grass, which for some reason has not
been cut this year, though so dry, now at length each grass-blade bending south
before the wintry blast, as if bending for aid in that direction; then the hill rising
sixty feet to a terrace-like plain covered with shrub oaks, maples, etc., now
variously tinted, clad all in a livery of gay colors, every bush a feather in its cap;
and further in the rear the wood-crowned Cliff some two hundred feet high, where
gray rocks here and there project from amidst the bushes, with its orchard on the
slope; and to the right of the Cliff the distant Lincoln hills in the horizon. The
landscape so handsomely colored, the air so clear and wholesome; and the surface
of the earth is so pleasingly varied, that it seems rarely fitted for the abode of man.

In Cohush Swamp the sumach leaves have turned a very deep red, but have
not lost their fragrance. I notice wild apples growing luxuriantly in the midst of
the swamp, rising red over the colored, painted leaves of the sumach, and reminding me that they were ripened and colored by the same influences,—some green,
some yellow, some red, like the leaves.

Sept. 29. By Walden

LOOKED ON WALDEN FROM the hill with the sawed pine stump on the
north side. Scared up three black ducks, which rose with a great noise of their
wings, striking the water. The hills this fall are unusually red, not only with the
huckleberry, but the sumach and the blackberry vines.

Walden plainly can never be spoiled by the woodchopper, for, do what you will
to the shore, there will still remain this crystal well. The intense brilliancy of the
red-ripe maples scattered here and there in the midst of the green oaks and
hickories on its hilly shore is quite charming. They are unexpectedly and incredibly brilliant, especially on the western shore and close to the water's edge, where,
alternating with yellow birches and poplars and green oaks, they remind me of a
line of soldiers, redcoats and riflemen in green mixed together.

The pine is one of the richest of trees to my eye. It stands like a great moss,
a luxuriant mildew,—the pumpkin pine,—which the earth produces without effort.

Visualization of Thoreau's cabin
and approach to the shore of Walden Pond.

Oct. 1.   Trembling Needles

THE SECOND GROWTH OF the white pine is probably softer and more beautiful than the primitive forest ever afforded. The primitive forest is more grand with its bare mossy stems and ragged branches, but exhibits no such masses of green needles trembling in the light.

Oct. 5.   Land in Motion

P.M.—TO THE HIGH OPEN land between Bateman's Pond and the lime-kiln.

It is a still, cloudy afternoon, rather cool. As I go past Cheney's boat-house, the river looks lighter than the sky. The butternuts have shed nearly all their leaves, and their nuts are seen black against the sky. The white oaks are turned a reddish brown in some valleys. The Norway cinquefoil and a smaller cinquefoil are still in blossom, and also the late buttercup. My companion remarked that the land (for the most part consisting of decayed orchards, huckleberry pastures, and forests) on both sides of the old Carlisle road, uneven and undulating like the road, appeared to be all in motion like the traveller, travelling on with him. Found a wild russet apple, very good, of peculiar form, flattened at the poles. Some red maples have entirely lost their leaves. The black birch is straw-colored.

Oct. 6. Celestial Waters

Monday. 12 m.—To Bedford line to set a stone by river on Bedford line.

The reach of the river between Bedford and Carlisle, seen from a distance in the road to-day, as formerly, has a singularly ethereal, celestial, or elysian look. It is of a light sky-blue, alternating with smoother white streaks, where the surface reflects the light differently, like a milk-pan full of the milk of Valhalla partially skimmed, more gloriously and heavenly fair and pure than the sky itself. It is something more celestial than the sky above it. I never saw any water look so celestial. I have often noticed it. I believe I have seen this reach from the hill in the middle of Lincoln. We have names for the rivers of hell, but none for the rivers of heaven, unless the Milky Way be one. It is such a smooth and shining blue, like a panoply of sky-blue plates. Our dark and muddy river has such a tint in this case as I might expect Walden or White Pond to exhibit, if they could be seen under similar circumstances, but Walden seen from Fair Haven is, if I remember, of a deep blue color tinged with green. Cerulean? Such water as that river reach appears to me of quite incalculable value, and the man who would blot that out of his prospect for a sum of money does not otherwise than to sell heaven.

Oct. 10. Freshly-Fallen Leaves

How agreeable to the eye at this season the color of new-fallen leaves (I am going through the young woods where the locusts grow near Goose Pond), sere and crisp! When freshly fallen, with their forms and their veins still distinct, they have a certain life in them still. The chestnut leaves now almost completely cover the ground under the trees, lying up light and deep, so clean and wholesome, whether to look at or handle or smell,—the tawny leaves, nature's color. They look as if they might all yield a wholesome tea. They are rustling down fast from the young chestnuts, leaving their bare and blackish-looking stems. You make a great noise now walking in the woods, on account of the dry leaves, especially chestnut and oak and maple, that cover the ground. I wish that we might make more use of leaves than we do. We wait till they are reduced to virgin mould. Might we not fill beds with them? or use them for fodder or litter? After they have been flattened by the snow and rain, they will be much less obvious. Now is the time to enjoy the dry leaves. Now all nature is a dried herb, full of medicinal odors. I love to hear of a preference given to one kind of leaves over another for beds. Some maples which a week ago were a mass of yellow foliage are now a fine gray smoke, as it were, and their leaves cover the ground.

Oct. 10. Amid the Witch-Hazels

The witch-hazel loves a hillside with or without wood or shrubs. It is always pleasant to come upon it unexpectedly as you are threading the woods in such places. Methinks I attribute to it some elvish quality apart from its fame. It affects a hillside partially covered with young copsewood. I love to behold its *gray speckled stems.* The leaf first green, then yellow for a short season, then, when it touches the ground, tawny leathercolor. As I stood amid the witch-hazels near Flint's Pond, a flock of a dozen chickadees came flitting and singing about me with great ado,—a most cheering and enlivening sound,—with incessant *day-day-day* and a fine wiry strain betweenwhiles, flitting ever nearer and nearer and nearer, inquisitively, till the boldest was within five feet of me; then suddenly, their curiosity satiated, they flit by degrees further away and disappear, and I hear with regret their retreating *day-day-days.*

Oct. 12. This Cloudy Afternoon

I LOVE VERY WELL this cloudy afternoon, so sober and favorable to reflection after so many bright ones. What if the clouds shut out the heavens, provided they concentrate my thoughts and make a more celestial heaven below! I hear the crickets plainer; I wander less in my thoughts, am less dissipated; am aware how shallow was the current of my thoughts before. Deep streams are dark, as if there were a cloud in their sky; shallow ones are bright and sparkling, reflecting the sun from their bottoms. The very wind on my cheek seems more fraught with meaning.

Many maples around the edges of the meadows are now quite bare, like smoke.

Oct. 31. The Wild Apples

THE WILD APPLES ARE now getting palatable. I find a few left on distant trees, which the farmer thinks it not worth his while to gather. He thinks that he has better in his barrels, but he is mistaken, unless he has a walker's appetite and imagination, neither of which can he have. These apples cannot be too knurly and rusty and crabbed (to look at). The knurliest will have some redeeming traits, even to the eyes. You will discover some evening redness dashed or sprinkled on some protuberance or in some cavity. It is rare that the summer lets an apple go without streaking or spotting it on some part of its sphere, though perchance one side may only seem to betray that it has once fallen in a brick-yard, and the other have been bespattered from a roily ink-bottle. Some red stains it will have, commemorating the mornings and evenings it has witnessed; some dark and rusty blotches, in memory of the clouds and foggy mildewy days that have passed over it; and a spacious field of green, reflecting the general face of nature,—green even as the fields; or yellowish ground, if it has a sunny flavor,—yellow as the harvests, or russet as the hills. The saunterer's apple not even the saunterer can eat in the house. The noblest of fruits is the apple. Let the most beautiful or swiftest have it.

Nov. 4. Saw Mill Brook

SAW MILL BROOK IS peculiar among our brooks as a mountain brook. For a short distance it reminds me of runs I have seen in New Hampshire. A brawling little stream tumbling through a rocky wood, ever down and down. Where the wood has been cleared, it is almost covered with the rubbish which the woodchoppers have left, the fine tree-tops, which no one cared to make into fagots. It was quite a discovery when I first came upon this brawling mountain stream in Concord woods. Rising out of an obscure meadow in the woods, for some fifty or sixty rods of its course it is a brawling mountain stream in our quiet Concord woods, as much obstructed by rocks—rocks out of all proportion to its tiny stream—as a brook can well be. And the rocks are bared throughout the wood on either side, as if a torrent had anciently swept through here; so unlike the after character of the stream. Who would have thought that, on tracing it up from where it empties into the larger Mill Brook in the open peat meadows, it would conduct him to such a headlong and impetuous youth. Perchance it should be called a "force." It suggests what various moods may attach to the same character. Ah, if I but knew that some minds which flow so muddily in the lowland portion of their course, when they cross the highways, tumbled thus impetuously and musically, mixed themselves with the air in foam, but a little way back in the woods! that these dark and muddy pools, where only the pout and the leech are to be found, issued from pure trout streams higher up! that the man's thoughts ever flowed as sparkling mountain water, that trout there loved to glance through his dimples, where the witch-hazel hangs over his stream!

This stream is here sometimes quite lost amid the rocks, which appear as if they had been arched over it, but which, in fact, it has undermined and found its way beneath, and they have merely fallen together archwise, as they were undermined.

It is truly a raw and gusty day, and I hear a tree creak sharply like a bird, a phœbe. The hypericums stand red or lake over the brook. The jays with their scream are at home in the scenery. I see where trees have spread themselves over the rocks in a scanty covering of soil, been undermined by the brook, then blown over and, as they fell, lifted and carried over with them all the soil, together with considerable rocks. So from time to time, by these natural levers, rocks are removed from the middle of the stream to the shore. The slender chestnuts, maples, elms, and white ash trees, which last are uncommonly numerous here, are now all bare of leaves, and a few small hemlocks, with their now thin but unmixed and fresh green foliage, stand over and cheer the stream and remind me of winter, the snows which are to come and drape them and contrast with their green, and the chickadees that are to flit and lisp amid them.

Ah, the beautiful tree, the hemlock, with its green canopy, under which little grows, not exciting the cupidity of the carpenter, whose use most men have not discovered! I know of some memorable ones worth walking many miles to see. These little cheerful hemlocks,—the lisp of chickadees seems to come from them now,—each standing with its foot on the very edge of the stream, reaching sometimes part way over its channel, and here and there one has lightly stepped across. These evergreens are plainly as much for shelter for the birds as for anything else. The fallen leaves are so thick they almost fill the bed of the stream and choke it. I hear the runnel gurgling underground. As if this puny rill had ever tossed these rocks about! these storied rocks with their fine lichens and sometimes red stains as of Indian blood on them! There are a few bright-green ferns lying flat by the sides of the brook, but it is cold, cold, withering to all else. A whitish lichen on the witch-hazel rings it here. I glimpse the frizzled tail of a red squirrel with a chestnut in its mouth on a white pine.

Nov. 9. Retired Pond

JAMES P. BROWN'S RETIRED pond, now shallow and more than half dried up, seems far away and rarely visited, known to few, though not far off. It is encircled by an amphitheatre of low hills, on two opposite sides covered with high pine woods, the other sides with young white oaks and white pines respectively. I am affected by beholding there reflected this gray day, so unpretendingly, the gray stems of the pine wood on the hillside and the sky,—that mirror, as it were a permanent picture to be seen there, a permanent piece of idealism. What were these reflections to the cows alone! Were these things made for cows' eyes mainly? You shall go over behind the hills, where you would suppose that otherwise there was no eye to behold, and find this piece of magic a constant phenomenon there. It is not merely a few favored lakes or pools that reflect the trees and skies, but the obscurest pond-hole in the most unfrequented dell does the same.

These reflections suggest that the sky underlies the hills as well as overlies them, and in another sense than in appearance. I am a little surprised on beholding this reflection, which I did not perceive for some minutes after looking into the pond, as if I had not regarded this as a constant phenomenon. What has become of Nature's common sense and love of facts, when in the very mud-puddles she reflects the skies and trees? Does that procedure recommend itself entirely to the common sense of men? Is that the way the *New England Farmer* would have arranged it?

Nov. 11. A Bright, Cold Day

2 P.M.—A BRIGHT, BUT COLD day, finger-cold. One must next wear gloves, put his hands in winter quarters. There is a cold, silvery light on the white pines as I go through J. P. Brown's field near Jenny Dugan's. I am glad of the shelter of the thick pine wood on the Marlborough road, on the plain. The roar of the wind over the pines sounds like the surf on countless beaches, an endless shore; and at intervals it sounds like a gong resounding through halls and entries, *i. e.* there is a certain resounding woodiness in the tone. How the wind roars among the shrouds of the wood! The sky looks mild and fair enough from this shelter. Every withered

blade of grass and every dry weed, as well as pine-needle, reflects light. The lately dark woods are open and light; the sun shines in upon the stems of trees which it has not shone on since spring. Around the edges of ponds the weeds are dead, and there, too, the light penetrates. The atmosphere is less moist and gross, and light is universally dispersed. We are greatly indebted to these transition seasons or states of the atmosphere, which show us thus phenomena which belong not to the summer or the winter of any climate. The brilliancy of the autumn is wonderful, this flashing brilliancy, as if the atmosphere were phosphoric.

Nov. 11. Says I to Myself

"SAYS I TO MYSELF" should be the motto of my journal.

It is fatal to the writer to be too much possessed by his thought. Things must lie a little remote to be described.

Nov. 12. A Thousand Themes

WRITE OFTEN, WRITE UPON a thousand themes, rather than long at a time, not trying to turn too many feeble somersets in the air,—and so come down upon your head at last. Antæus-like, be not long absent from the ground. Those sentences are good and well discharged which are like so many little resiliencies from the spring floor of our life,—a distinct fruit and kernel itself, springing from terra firma. Let there be as many distinct plants as the soil and the light can sustain.

Nov. 12. Walking with Minott

WALKING THROUGH EBBY HUBBARD'S wood this afternoon, with Minott, who was actually taking a walk for amusement and exercise, he said, on seeing some white pines blown down, that you might know that ground had been cultivated, by the trees being torn up so, for otherwise they would have rooted themselves more strongly. Saw some very handsome canoe birches there, the largest I know, a foot in diameter and forty or fifty feet high. The large ones have a reddish cast, perhaps from some small lichen. Their fringes and curls give them an agreeable appearance. Observed a peculiarity in some white oaks. Though they had a firm and close bark near the ground, the bark was very coarse and scaly, in loose flakes, above. Much coarser than the swamp white oak. Minott has a story for every woodland path. He has hunted in them all. Where we walked last, he had once caught a partridge by the *wing!*

Nov. 13. Hard Day, Hard Times

TO FAIR HAVEN HILL.

A cold and dark afternoon, the sun being behind clouds in the west. The landscape is barren of objects, the trees being leafless, and so little light in the sky for variety. Such a day as will almost oblige a man to eat his own heart. A day in which you must hold on to life by your teeth. You can hardly ruck up any skin on Nature's bones. The sap is down; she won't peel. Now is the time to cut timber for yokes and ox-bows, leaving the tough bark on,—yokes for your own neck. Finding yourself yoked to Matter and to Time. Truly a hard day, hard times these! Not a mosquito left. Not an insect to hum. Crickets gone into winter quarters. Friends long since gone there, and you left to walk on frozen ground, with your hands in your pockets. Ah, but is not this a glorious time for your deep inward fires? And will not your green hickory and white oak burn clear in this frosty air? Now is not your manhood taxed by the great Assessor? Taxed for having a soul, a ratable soul. A day when you cannot pluck a flower, cannot dig a parsnip, nor pull a turnip, for the frozen ground! What do the thoughts find to live on? What avails you now the fire you stole from heaven? Does not each thought become a vulture to gnaw your vitals? No Indian summer have we had this November. I see but few traces of the perennial spring. Now is there nothing, not even the cold beauty of ice crystals and snowy architecture, nothing but the echo of your steps over the frozen ground, no voice of birds nor frogs. You are dry as a farrow cow. The earth will not admit a spade. All fields lie fallow. Shall not your mind? True, the freezing ground is being prepared for immeasurable snows, but there are brave thoughts within you that shall remain to rustle the winter through like white oak leaves upon your boughs, or like scrub oaks that remind the traveller of a fire upon the hillsides; or evergreen thoughts, cold even in mid-summer, by their nature shall contrast the more fairly with the snow. Some warm springs shall still tinkle and fume, and send their column of vapor to the skies.

White Pines in silhouette.

Nov. 30. A Piny Precipice

SUNDAY. A RATHER COLD and windy afternoon, with some snow not yet melted on the ground. Under the south side of the hill between Brown's and Tarbell's, in a warm nook, disturbed three large gray squirrels and some partridges, who had all sought out this bare and warm place. While the squirrels hid themselves in the tree-tops, I sat on an oak stump by an old cellar-hole and mused. This squirrel is always an unexpectedly large animal to see frisking about. My eye wanders across the valley to the pine woods which fringe the opposite side, and in their aspect my eye finds something which addresses itself to my nature. Methinks that in my mood I was asking Nature to give me a sign. I do not know exactly what it was that attracted my eye. I experienced a transient gladness, at any rate, at something which I saw. I am sure that my eye rested with pleasure on the white pines, now reflecting a silvery light, the infinite stories of their boughs, tier above tier, a sort of basaltic structure, a crumbling precipice of pine horizontally stratified. Each pine is like a great green feather stuck in the ground. A myriad white pine boughs extend themselves horizontally, one above and behind another, each bearing its burden of silvery sunlight, with darker seams between them, as if it were a great crumbling piny precipice thus stratified. On this my eyes pastured, while the squirrels were up the trees behind me. That, at any rate, it was that I got by my afternoon walk, a certain recognition from the pine, some congratulation. Where is my home? It is indistinct as an old cellar-hole, now a faint indentation merely in a farmer's field, which he has plowed into and rounded off its edges years ago, and I sit by the old site on the stump of an oak which once grew there. Such is the nature where we have lived. Thick birch groves stand here and there, dark brown (?) now with white lines more or less distinct.

Dec. 30. Felling of a Pine

THIS AFTERNOON, BEING ON Fair Haven Hill, I heard the sound of a saw, and soon after from the Cliff saw two men sawing down a noble pine beneath about forty rods off. I resolved to watch it till it fell, the last of a dozen or more which were left when the forest was cut and for fifteen years have waved in solitary majesty over the sprout-land. I saw them like beavers or insects gnawing at the trunk of this noble tree, the diminutive manikins with their cross-cut saw which could scarcely span it. It towered up a hundred feet as I afterward found by measurement, one of the tallest probably in the township and straight as an arrow but slanting a little toward the hillside, its top seen against the frozen river and the hills of Conantum. I watch closely to see when it begins to move. Now the sawers stop, and with an axe open it a little on the side toward which it leans, that it may break the faster. And now their saw goes again. Now surely it is going; it is inclined one quarter of the quadrant, and, breathless, I expect its crashing fall. But no, I was mistaken; it has not moved an inch; it stands at the same angle a at first. It is fifteen minutes yet to its fall. Still its branches wave in the wind, as if it were destined to stand for a century, and the wind soughs through its needles as of yore; it is still a forest tree, the most majestic tree that waves over Musketaquid. The silvery sheen of the sunlight is reflected from its needles; it still affords an inaccessible crotch for the squirrel's nest; not a lichen has forsaken its mast-like stem, its raking mast,—the hill is the hulk. Now, now's the moment! The manikins at its base are fleeing from their crime. They have dropped the guilty saw and axe. How slowly and majestically it starts! as if it were only swayed by a summer breeze, and would return without a sigh to its location in the air. And now it fans the hillside with its fall, and it lies down to its bed in the valley, from which it is never to rise, as softly as a feather, folding its green mantle about it like a warrior, as if, tired of standing, it embraced the earth with silent joy, returning its elements to the dust again. But hark! there you only saw, but did not hear. There now comes up a deafening crash to these rocks, advertising you that even trees do not die without a groan. It rushes to embrace the earth, and mingle its elements with the dust. And now all is still once more and forever, both to eye and ear.

I went down and measured it. It was about four feet in diameter where it was sawed, about one hundred feet long. Before I had reached it the axemen had already half divested it of its branches. Its gracefully spreading top was a perfect wreck on the hillside as if it had been made of glass, and the tender cones of one year's growth upon its summit appealed in vain and too late to the mercy of the chopper. Already he has measured it with his axe, and marked off the mill-logs it will make. And the space it occupied in upper air is vacant for the next two centuries. It is lumber. He has laid waste the air. When the fish hawk in the spring revisits the banks of the Musketaquid, he will circle in vain to find his accustomed perch, and the hen-hawk will mourn for the pines lofty enough to protect her brood. A plant which it has taken two centuries to perfect, rising by slow stages into the heavens, has this afternoon ceased to exist. Its sapling top had expanded to this January thaw as the forerunner of summers to come. Why does not the village bell sound a knell? I hear no knell tolled. I see no procession of mourners in the streets, or the woodland aisles. The squirrel has leaped to another tree; the hawk has circled further off, and has now settled upon a new eyrie, but the woodman is preparing [to] lay his axe at the root of that also.

Dec. 31.   To Study Lichens

THERE IS A LOW mist in the woods. It is a good day to study lichens. The view so confined it compels your attention to near objects, and the white background reveals the disks of the lichens distinctly. They appear more loose, flowing, expanded, flattened out, the colors brighter for the damp. The round greenish-yellow lichens on the white pines loom through the mist (or are seen dimly) like shields whose devices you would fain read. The trees appear all at once covered with their crop of lichens and mosses of all kinds,—flat and tearful are some, distended by moisture. This is their solstice, and your eyes run swiftly through the mist to these things only. On every fallen twig, even, that has lain under the snows, as well as on the trees, they appear erect and now first to have attained their full expansion. Nature has a day for each of her creatures, her creations. To-day it is an exhibition of lichens at Forest Hall, the livid green of some, the fruit of others. They eclipse the trees they cover. And the red, club-pointed (baobab-tree-like) on the stumps, the *erythrean* stumps! Ah, beautiful is decay! True, as Thales said, the world was made out of water. That is the principle of all things.

CHAPTER IV

YEAR
1852
AGE
34–35

Jan. 11. The Traveler

THE QUESTION IS NOT where did the traveller go? what places did he see?—it would be difficult to choose between places—but who was the traveller? how did he travel? how genuine an experience did he get? For travelling is, in the main, like as if you stayed at home, and then the question is how do you live and conduct yourself at home? What I mean is that it might be hard to decide whether I would travel to Lake Superior, or Labrador, or Florida. Perhaps none would be worth the while, if I went by the usual mode. But if I travel in a simple, primitive, original manner, standing in a truer relation to men and nature, travel away from the old and commonplace, get some honest experience of life, if only out of my feet and homesickness, then it becomes less important whither I go or how far. I so see the world from a new and more commanding point of view. Perhaps it is easier to live a true and natural life while travelling,—as one can move about less awkwardly than he can stand still.

Jan. 17. Sky and Contemplation

IN PROPORTION AS I have celestial thoughts, is the necessity for me to be out and behold the western sky before sunset these winter days. That is the symbol of the unclouded mind that knows neither winter nor summer. What is your thought like? That is the hue, that the purity, and transparency, and distance from earthly taint of my inmost mind, for whatever we see without is a symbol of something within, and that which is farthest off is the symbol of what is deepest within. The lover of contemplation, accordingly, will gaze much into the sky.

Jan. 22. On Keeping a Journal

TO SET DOWN SUCH choice experiences that my own writings may inspire me and at last I may make wholes of parts. Certainly it is a distinct profession to rescue from oblivion and to fix the sentiments and thoughts which visit all men more or less generally, that the contemplation of the unfinished picture may suggest its harmonious completion. Associate reverently and as much as you can with your loftiest thoughts. Each thought that is welcomed and recorded is a nest egg, by the side of which more will be laid. Thoughts accidentally thrown together become a frame in which more may be developed and exhibited. Perhaps this is the main value of a habit of writing, of keeping a journal,—that so we remember our best hours and stimulate ourselves. My thoughts are my company. They have a certain individuality and separate existence, aye, personality. Having by chance recorded a few disconnected thoughts and then brought them into juxtaposition, they suggest a whole new field in which it was possible to labor and to think. Thought begat thought.

Jan. 22. Ebby Hubbard's Hillside

I LOVE TO LOOK at Ebby Hubbard's oaks and pines on the hillside from Brister's Hill. Am thankful that there is one old miser who will not sell nor cut his woods, though it is said that they are wasting. It is an ill wind that blows nobody any good.

Jan. 24. If Thou Art a Writer

IF THOU ART A writer, write as if thy time were short, for it is indeed short at the longest. Improve each occasion when thy soul is reached. Drain the cup of inspiration to its last dregs. Fear no intemperance in that, for the years will come when otherwise thou wilt regret opportunities unimproved. The spring will not last forever. These fertile and expanding seasons of thy life, when the rain reaches thy root, when thy vigor shoots, when thy flower is budding, shall be fewer and farther between.

Jan. 24. The Axe in Concord

THESE WOODS! WHY DO I not feel their being cut more sorely? Does it not affect me nearly? The axe can deprive me of much. Concord is sheared of its pride. I am certainly the less attached to my native town in consequence. One, and a main, link is broken. I shall go to Walden less frequently.

River scene near Concord, Massachusetts.

Jan. 25. Stems and Twigs

NOW WE ARE ON Fair Haven, still but a snow plain. Far down the river the shadows on Conantum are bluish, somewhat like the holes in the snow, perchance. The sun is half an hour high, perhaps. Standing near the outlet of the pond, I look up and down the river with delight, it is so warm and the air is, notwithstanding, so clear. When I invert my head and look at the woods half a mile down the stream, they suddenly sink lower in the horizon and are removed full two miles off; yet the air is so clear that I seem to see every stem and twig with beautiful distinctness. The fine tops of the trees are so relieved against the sky that I never cease to admire the minute subdivisions. It is the same when I look up the stream. A bare hickory under Lee's Cliff, seen against the sky, becomes an interesting, even beautiful, object to behold. I think where have I been staying all these days. I will surely come here again.

Jan. 26. Trees Against the Sky

A TREE SEEN AGAINST other trees is a mere dark mass, but against the sky it has parts, has symmetry and expression.

Whatever wit has been produced on the spur of the moment will bear to be reconsidered and reformed with phlegm. The arrow had best not be loosely shot. The most transient and passing remark must be reconsidered by the writer, made sure and warranted, as if the earth had rested on its axle to back it, and all the natural forces lay behind it. The writer must direct his sentences as carefully and leisurely as the marksman his rifle, who shoots sitting and with a rest, with patent sights and conical balls beside. He must not merely seem to speak the truth. He must really speak it. If you foresee that a part of your essay will topple down after the lapse of time, throw it down now yourself.

The thousand fine points and tops of the trees delight me; they are the plumes and standards and bayonets of a host that march to victory over the earth. The trees are handsome towards the heavens as well as up their boles; they are good for other things than boards and shingles.

Hedgerow silhouette.

Jan. 26. Pond as a Symbol

WOULD YOU SEE YOUR mind, look at the sky. Would you know your own moods, be weather-wise. He whom the weather disappoints, disappoints himself.

Let all things give way to the impulse of expression. It is the bud unfolding, the perennial spring. As well stay the spring. Who shall resist the thaw?

What if all the ponds were shallow? Would it not react on the minds of men?

If there were no physical deeps. I thank God that he made this pond deep and pure for a symbol.

Jan. 28. Teaching Children Colors

IT IS REMARKABLE THAT no pains is taken to teach children to distinguish colors. I am myself uncertain about the names of many.

Jan. 30. Cutting Off the Woods

DO NOTHING MERELY OUT of good resolutions. Discipline yourself only to yield to love; suffer yourself to be attracted. It is in vain to write on chosen themes. We must wait till they have kindled a flame in our minds. There must be the copulating and generating force of love behind every effort destined to be successful. The cold resolve gives birth to, begets, nothing. The theme that seeks me, not I it. The poet's relation to his theme is the relation of lovers. It is no more to be courted. Obey, report.

Though they are cutting off the woods at Walden, it is not all loss. It makes some new and unexpected prospects. We read books about logging in the Maine woods as if it were wholly strange to these parts. But I here witness almost exactly the same things, scenes that might be witnessed in Maine or New Hampshire: the logger's team, his oxen on the ice chewing the cud, the long pine tree, stripped of its branches, chained upon his sled, resting on a stout cross-bar or log and trailing behind, the smoke of his fire curling up blue amid the trees, the sound of the axe and of the teamsters' voices. A pretty forest scene, seeing oxen, so patient and stationary, good for pictures, standing on the ice,—a piece of still life. Oh, it is refreshing to see, to think of, these things after hearing of the discussions and politics of the day! The smoke I saw was quite blue. As I stood on the partially cleared bank at the east end of the pond, I looked south over the side of the hill into a deep dell still wooded, and I saw, not more than thirty rods off, a chopper at his work. I was half a dozen rods distant from the standing wood, and I saw him through a vista between two trees (it was now mainly an oak wood, the pine having been cut), and he appeared to me apparently half a mile distant, yet charmingly distinct, as in a picture of which the two trees were the frame. He was seen against the snow on the hillside beyond. I could distinguish each part of his dress perfectly, and the axe with distinct outline as he raised it above his head, the black iron against the snow, and could hear every stroke distinctly. Yet I should have deemed it ridiculous to have called to him, he appeared so distant. He appeared with the same distinctness as objects seen through a pinhole in a card. This was the effect rather than by comparison of him, his size, with the nearer trees, between which I saw him and which made the canopied roof of the grove far above his head. It was, perhaps, one of those coincidences and effects which have made men painters. I could not behold him as an actual man; he was more ideal than in any picture I have seen. He refused to be seen as actual. Far in the hollow, yet somewhat enlightened, aisles of this wooded dell. Some scenes will thus present themselves as picture. Those scenes which are picture, subjects for the pencil, are distinctly marked; they do not require the aid of genius to idealize them. They must be seen as ideal.

Jan. 30. Observing at Home

I AM AFRAID TO TRAVEL much or to famous places, lest it might completely dissipate the mind. Then I am sure that what we observe at home, if we observe anything, is of more importance than what we observe abroad. The far-fetched is of the least value. What we observe in travelling are to some extent the accidents of the body, but [what] we observe when sitting at home are, in the same proportion, phenomena of the mind itself. A wakeful night will yield as much thought as a long journey. If I try thoughts by their quality, not their quantity, I may find that a restless night will yield more than the longest journey.

Rocks, pines and clouds.

Feb. 5. Tiers of Pine Boughs

TIME NEVER PASSES SO rapidly and unaccountably as when I am engaged in recording my thoughts. The world may perchance reach its end for us in a profounder thought, and Time itself run down.

I suspect that the child plucks its first flower with an insight into its beauty and significance which the subsequent botanist never retains.

The trunks and branches of the trees are of different colors at different times and in different lights and weathers,—in sun, rain, and in the night. The oaks bare of leaves on Hubbard's hillside are now a light gray in the sun, and their boughs, seen against the pines behind, are a very agreeable maze. The stems of the white pines also are quite gray at this distance, with their lichens. I am detained to contemplate the boughs, feathery boughs, of the white pines, tier above tier, reflecting a silvery light, with intervals between them through which you look, if you so intend your eye, into the darkness of the grove. That is, you can see both the silvery-lighted and greenish bough and the shadowy intervals as belonging to one tree, or, more truly, refer the latter to the shade behind.

March 9. March Winds

CLOUDY BUT SPRINGLIKE. WHEN the frost comes out of the ground, there is a corresponding thawing of the man. The earth is now half bare. These March winds, which make the woods roar and fill the world with life and bustle, appear to wake up the trees out of their winter sleep and excite the sap to flow. I have no doubt they serve some such use, as well as to hasten the evaporation of the snow and water.

March 16. A Wilderness of Books

THE LIBRARY A WILDERNESS of books. Looking over books on Canada written within the last three hundred years, could see how one had been built upon another, each author consulting and referring to his predecessors. You could read most of them without changing your leg on the steps. It is necessary to find out exactly what books to read on a given subject. Though there may be a thousand books written upon it, it is only important to read three or four; they will contain all that is essential, and a few pages will show which they are. Books which are books are all that you want, and there are but half a dozen in any thousand. I saw that while we are clearing the forest in our westward progress, we are accumulating a forest of books in our rear, as wild and unexplored as any of nature's primitive wildernesses. The volumes of the Fifteenth, Sixteenth, and Seventeenth Centuries, which lie so near on the shelf, are rarely opened, are effectually forgotten and not implied by our literature and newspapers. When I looked into Purchas's Pilgrims, it affected me like looking into an impassable swamp, ten feet deep with sphagnum, where the monarchs of the forest, covered with mosses and stretched along the ground, were making haste to become peat. Those old books suggested a certain fertility, an Ohio soil, as if they were making a humus for new literatures to spring in. I heard the bellowing of bullfrogs and the hum of mosquitoes reverberating through the thick embossed covers when I had closed the book. Decayed literature makes the richest of all soils.

March 17. Returning to Consciousness

I CATCH MYSELF PHILOSOPHIZING most abstractly when first returning to consciousness in the night or morning. I make the truest observations and distinctions then, when the will is yet wholly asleep and the mind works like a machine without friction. I am conscious of having, in my sleep, transcended the limits of the individual, and made observations and carried on conversations which in my waking hours I can neither recall nor appreciate. As if in sleep our individual fell into the infinite mind, and at the moment of awakening we found ourselves on the confines of the latter. On awakening we resume our enterprise, take up our bodies and become limited mind again. We meet and converse with those bodies which we have previously animated. There is a moment in the dawn, when the darkness of the night is dissipated and before the exhalations of the day commence to rise, when we see things more truly than at any other time. The light is more trustworthy, since our senses are purer and the atmosphere is less gross. By afternoon all objects are seen in mirage.

April 1. Woods Odors and Colors

THE PREVAILING COLOR OF the woods at present, excepting the evergreens, is russet, a little more red or grayish, as the case may be, than the earth, for those are the colors of the withered leaves and the branches; the earth has the lighter hue of withered grass. Let me see how soon the woods will have acquired a new color. Went over the hill toward the eastern end of the pond. What is the significance of odors, of the odoriferous woods? Sweet and yellow birch, sassafras, fever-bush, etc., are an interesting clan to me. When we bruise them in our walk, we are suddenly exhilarated by their odor. This sweet scent soon evaporates, and you must break the twig afresh. If you cut it, it is not as if you break it. Some, like the sassafras, have brought a great price as articles of commerce. No wonder that men thought they might have some effect toward renovating their lives. Gosnold, the discoverer of Cape Cod, carried home a cargo of sassafras. What could be more grateful to the discoverer of a new country than a new fragrant wood?

April 1. Saw Mill Brook and Hemlocks

SAT AWHILE BEFORE SUNSET on the rocks in Saw Mill Brook. A brook need not be large to afford us pleasure by its sands and meanderings and falls and their various accompaniments. It is not so much size that we want as picturesque beauty and harmony. If the sound of its fall fills my ear it is enough. I require that the rocks over which it falls be agreeably disposed, and prefer that they be covered with lichens. The height and volume of the fall is of very little importance compared with the appearance and disposition of the rocks over which it falls, the agreeable diversity of still water, rapids, and falls, and of the surrounding scenery. I require that the banks and neighboring hillsides be not cut off, but excite a sense of at least graceful wildness. One or two small evergreens, especially hemlocks, standing gracefully on the brink of the rill, contrasting by their green with the surrounding deciduous trees when they have lost their leaves, and thus enlivening the scene and betraying their attachment to the water. It would be no more pleasing to me if the stream were a mile wide and the hemlocks five feet in diameter. I believe that there is a harmony between the hemlock and the water which it overhangs not explainable. In the first place, its green is especially grateful to the eye the greater part of the year in any locality, and in the winter, by its verdure overhanging and shading the water, it concentrates in itself the beauty of all fluviatile trees. It loves to stand with its foot close to the water, its roots running over the rocks of the shore, and two or more on opposite sides of a brook make the most beautiful frame to a waterscape, especially in deciduous woods, where the light is sombre and not too glaring. It makes the more complete frame because its branches, particularly in young specimens such as I am thinking of, spring from so near the ground, and it makes so dense a mass of verdure. There are many larger hemlocks covering the steep sidehill forming the bank of the Assabet, where they are successively undermined by the water, and they lean at every angle over the water. Some are almost horizontally directed, and almost every year one falls in and is washed away. The place is known as the "Leaning Hemlocks."

April 1. Saw Mill Run Falls

BUT TO RETURN TO Saw Mill Run. I love that the green fronds of the fern, pressed by the snow, lie on its rocks. It is a great advantage to take in so many parts at one view. We love to see the water stand, or seem to stand, at many different levels within a short distance, while we sit in its midst, some above, some below us, and many successive falls in different directions, meandering in the course of the fall, rather than one "chute,"—rather spreading and shoaling than contracting and deepening at the fall. In a small brook like this, there are many adjuncts to increase the variety which are wanting in a river, or, if present, cannot be attended to; even dead leaves and twigs vary the ripplings and increase the foam. And the very lichens on the rocks of the run are an important ornament, which in the great waterfall are wont to be overlooked. I enjoy this little fall on Saw Mill Run more than many a large one on a river that I have seen. The hornbeams and witch-hazel and canoe birches all come in for their share of attention. We get such a complete idea of the small rill with its overhanging shrubs as only a bird's-eye view from some eminence could give us of the larger stream. Perhaps it does not fall more than five feet within a rod and a half. I should not hear Niagara a short distance off. The never-ending refreshing sound! It suggests more thoughts than Montmorenci. A stream and fall which the woods imbosom. They are not in this proportion to a larger fall. They lie in a more glaring and less picturesque light. Even the bubbles are a study. It can be completely examined in its details. The consciousness of there being water about you at different levels is agreeable. The sun can break through and fall on it and vary the whole scene infinitely.

April 2.   Institutions of Man

I DO NOT VALUE any view of the universe into which man and the institutions of man enter very largely and absorb much of the attention. Man is but the place where I stand, and the prospect hence is infinite. It is not a chamber of mirrors which reflect me. When I reflect, I find that there is other than me. Man is a past phenomenon to philosophy. The universe is larger than enough for man's abode. Some rarely go outdoors, most are always at home at night, very few indeed have stayed out all night once in their lives, fewer still have gone behind the world of humanity, seen its institutions like toadstools by the wayside.

April 2.   Ascending Round Hill

WE LANDED NEAR A corn-field in the bay on the west side, below Sherman's Bridge, in order to ascend Round Hill, it still raining gently or with drops far apart. From the top we see smoke rising from the green pine hill in the southern part of Lincoln. The steam of the engine looked very white this morning against the oak-clad hillsides. The clouds, the showers, and the breaking away now in the west, all belong to the summer side of the year and remind me of long-past days. The prospect is often best from two thirds the way up a hill, where, looking directly down at the parts of the landscape—the fields and barns—nearest the base, you get the sense of height best, and see how the land slopes up to where you stand. From the top, commonly, you overlook all this, and get a sense of *distance* merely, with a break in the landscape by which the most interesting point is concealed. This hill with its adjuncts is now almost an island, surrounded by broad lakes. The south lakes reflect the most light at present, but the sober surface of the northern is yet more interesting to me.

April 3.   Clouds, Shade and Man's Eye

I HAVE OBSERVED MUCH snow lately on the north slopes where shrub oaks grow, where probably the ground is frozen, more snow, I think, than lies in the woods in such positions. It is even two or three feet deep in many such places, though few villagers would believe it. One side of the village street, which runs east and west, appears a month in advance of the other. I go down the street on the wintry side; I return through summer. How agreeable the contrasts of light and shade, especially when the successive swells of a hillside produce the shade! The clouds are important to-day for their shadows. If it were not for them, the landscape would be one glare of light without variety. By their motion they still more vary the scene.

Man's eye is so placed as to look straight forward on a level best, or rather down than up. His eye demands the sober colors of the earth for its daily diet. He does not look up at a great angle but with an effort. Many clouds go over without our noticing them, for it would not profit us much to notice it, but few cattle pass by in the street or the field without our knowing it.

April 4. A Dripping Fountain

IT IS REFRESHING TO stand on the face of the Cliff and see the water gliding over the surface of the almost perpendicular rock in a broad thin sheet, pulsing over it. It reflects the sun for half a mile like a patch of snow,—as you stand close by, bringing out the colors of the lichens like polishing or varnish. It is admirable, regarded as a dripping fountain. You have lichens and moss on the surface, and starting saxifrage, ferns still green, and huckleberry bushes in the crevices. The rocks never appear so diversified, and cracked, as if the chemistry of nature were now in full force. Then the drops, falling perpendicularly from a projecting rock, have a pleasing geometrical effect.

April 11. Nut Meadow Brook

THE SIGHT OF NUT Meadow Brook in Brown's land reminds me that the attractiveness of a brook depends much on the character of its bottom. I love just now to see one flowing through soft sand like this, where it wears a deep but irregular channel, now wider and shallower with distinct ripple-marks, now shelving off suddenly to indistinct depths, meandering as much up and down as from side to side, deepest where narrowest, and ever gullying under this bank or that, its bottom lifted up to one side or the other, the current inclining to one side. I stop to look at the circular shadows of the dimples over the yellow sand, and the dark-brown clams on their edges in the sand at the bottom. (I hear the sound of the piano below as I write this, and feel as if the winter in me were at length beginning to thaw, for my spring has been even more backward than nature's. For a month past life has been a thing incredible to me. None but the kind gods can make me sane. If only they will let their south winds blow on me! I ask to be melted. You can only ask of the metals that they be tender to the fire that *melts* them. To naught else can they be tender.) The sweet flags are now starting up under water two inches high, and minnows dart. A pure brook is a very beautiful object to study minutely. It will bear the closest inspection, even to the fine air-bubbles, like minute globules of quicksilver, that lie on its bottom. The minute particles or spangles of golden mica in these sands, when the sun shines on them, remind one of the golden sands we read of. Everything is washed clean and bright, and the water is the best glass through which to see it.

April 11. A River Is Best Seen

I SEE NOW THE mosses in pastures, bearing their light-colored capsules on the top of red filaments. When I reach the bridge, it is become a serene evening;

Windy day on the Sudbury River,
near Concord, Massachusetts.

the broad waters are more and more smooth, and everything is more beautiful in the still light. The view toward Fair Haven, whose woods are now cut off, is beautiful. No obvious sign of spring. The hill now dimly reflected; the air not yet quite still. The wood on Conantum abuts handsomely on the water and can ill be spared. The ground on which it stands is not level as seen from this point, but pleasantly varied and swelling, which is important. (Before my neighbor's pig is cold his boys have made a football of his bladder! So goes the world. No matter how much the boy snivels at first, he kicks the bladder with ecstasy.) This is the still evening hour. Insects in the air. The blackbirds whistle and sing *conqueree;* the robin peeps and sings; the bluebird warbles. The light of the setting sun on the pitch pines on Fair Haven and Bear Hill lights them up warmly, for the rays fall horizontally on them through the *mellow* evening atmosphere. They do not appear so bright to us at noon, nor do they now to the hawk that comes soaring sluggishly over them,—the brown and dusky bird seen even from beneath. Of course the pines seen from above have now more of the evening shades in them than seen from the earth on one side. The catkins of the willow are silvery. The shadow of the wood named above at the river end is indispensable in this scene; and, what is remarkable, I see where it has reached across the river and is creeping up the hill with dark pointed spears, though the intermediate river is all sunny, the reflection of the sunny hill covered with withered grass being seen through the invisible shadow. A river is best seen breaking through highlands, issuing from some narrow pass. It imparts a sense of power. The shadow at the end of the wood makes it appear grander in this case. The serenity and warmth are the main thing after the windy and cool days we have had. You may even hear a fish leap in the water now. The lowing of a cow advances me many weeks towards summer. The reflections grow more distinct every moment. At last the outline of the hill is as distinct below as above. And every object appears rhymed by reflection. By partly closing my eyes and looking through my eyelashes, the wood end appears thus:

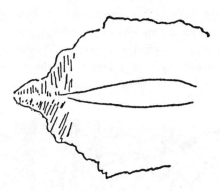

Now the shadow, reaching across the river, has crept so far up the hill that I see its reflection on the hillside in the water, and in this way it may at length connect itself with its source. Clouds are now distinctly seen in the water. The bridge is now a station for walkers. I parted with my companion here; told him not to wait for me. Maple in the swamp answers to maple, birch to birch. There is one clump of three birches particularly picturesque. In a few minutes the wind has thus gone down. At this season the reflections of deciduous trees are more picturesque and remarkable than when they are in leaf, because, the branches being seen, they make with their reflections a more wonderful rhyme. It is not mere mass or outline corresponding to outline, but a kind of geometrical figure. The maples look thus: The twilight must to the extent above mentioned be earlier to birds soaring in the sky; *i. e.* they see more decided shades of evening than a man looking east. The frogs peep thinly.

April 11. The Sandy Road

THE ROAD THROUGH THE pitch pine woods beyond J. Hosmer's is very pleasant to me, curving under the pines, without a fence,—the sandy road, with the pines close abutting on it, yellow in the sun and low-branched, with younger pines filling up all to the ground. I love to see a sandy road like this curving through a pitch pine wood where the trees closely border it without fences, a great cart-path merely. That is a pleasant part of the North River, under the black birches. The dog does not hesitate to take to the water for a stick, but the current carries him rapidly down. The lines of sawdust left at different levels on the shore is just hint enough of a sawmill on the stream above.

April 16. Sturdy Strength of Oaks

IT CLEARS UP (the rain) at noon, with a rather cool wind from the northwest and flitting clouds. The ground about one third covered with snow still. What variety in the trunks of oaks! How expressive of strength are some! There is one behind Hubbard's which expresses a sturdy strength, thus: with a protuberant ridge and seam toward the north. There is a still   more remarkable one in a different style near Derby's Bridge. The very emblem of sturdy resistance to tempests.

White Oak grove.

April 16. Our Overflowing River

I THINK OUR OVERFLOWING river far handsomer and more abounding in soft and beautiful contrasts than a merely broad river would be. A succession of bays it is, a chain of lakes, an endlessly scalloped shore, rounding wood and field. Cultivated field and wood and pasture and house are brought into ever new and unexpected positions and relations to the water. There is just stream enough for a flow of thought; that is all. Many a foreigner who has come to this town has worked for years on its banks without discovering which way the river runs.

April 17. Fence as a Frame

UP THE EAST BANK of river to Fair Haven at 2 P.M.

The farmers are in haste beginning their plowing. The season is remarkably backward. The wind is rising at last, and it is somewhat from the east-southeast, but it is the more fresh and life-giving. The water is over the Corner road since last night, higher than before this season, so that we (I and C.) go not that way. In that little pasture of Potter's under the oak, I am struck with the advantage of the fence in landscapes. Here is but a half-acre inclosed [sic], but the fence has the effect of confining the attention to this little undulation of the land and to make you consider it by itself, and the importance of the oak is proportionally increased. This formation of the surface would be lost in an un-fenced prairie, but the fence, which nearly enough defines it, frames it and pre-sents it as a picture.

April 19. A Grand Oak

That oak by Derby's is a grand object, seen from any side. It stands like an athlete and defies the tempests in every direction. It has not a weak point. It is an agony of strength. Its branches look like stereotyped gray lightning on the sky. But I fear a price is set upon its sturdy trunk and roots for ship-timber, for knees to make stiff the sides of ships against the Atlantic billows. Like an athlete, it shows its well-developed muscles.

April 21. Pine-Tree Shillings

As we stand by the monument on the Battle-Ground, I see a white pine dimly in the horizon just north of Lee's Hill, at 5.30 P.M., its upright stem and straight horizontal feathered branches, while at the same time I hear a robin sing. Each enhances the other. That tree seems the emblem of my life; it stands for the west, the wild. The sight of it is grateful to me as to a bird whose perch it is to be at the end of a weary flight. I [am] not sure whether the music I hear is most in the robin's song or in its boughs. My wealth should be all in pine-tree shillings. The pine tree that stands on the verge of the clearing, whose boughs point westward; which the village does not permit to grow on the common or by the roadside; which is banished from the village; in whose boughs the crow and the hawk have their nests.

April 23. Sky and Water Blue

Now that the sun shines and the sky is blue, the water is a dark blue which in the storm was light or whitish. It follows the sky's, though the sky is a lighter blue.

April 25. Blue Tints of the Sky

In the rear of the Major Heywood house, lay on the sere grass in a long pasture bounded by a pitch pine wood and heard the robin sing. What different tints of blue in the same sky! It requires to be parted by white clouds that the delicacy and depth of each part may appear. Beyond a narrow wisp or feather of mist, how different the sky! Sometimes it is full of light, especially toward the horizon. The sky is never seen to be of so deep and delicate a blue as when it is seen between downy clouds.

April 30. Far River-Reach

CROSSING THE TURNPIKE, WE entered Smith's highlands. Dodging behind a swell of land to avoid the men who were plowing, I saw unexpectedly (when I looked to see if we were concealed by the field) the blue mountains' line in the west (the whole intermediate earth and towns being concealed), this greenish field for a foreground sloping upward a few rods, and then those grand mountains seen over it in the background, so blue,—seashore, earth-shore,—and, warm as it is, covered with snow which reflected the sun. Then when I turned, I saw in the east, just over the woods, the modest, pale, cloud-like moon, two-thirds full, looking spirit-like on these daylight scenes. Such a sight excites me. The earth is worthy to inhabit. The far river-reach from this hill. It is not so placid a blue—as if with a film of azure over it—to-day, however. The more remote the water, the lighter the blue, perchance. It is like a lake in Tartary; there our camels will find water. Here is a rock made to sit on,—large and inviting, which you do not fear to crush. I hear the flicker and the huckleberry-bird. Yet no leaves apparent. This in some measure corresponds to the fine afternoon weather after the leaves have fallen, though there is a different kind of promise now than then. We are now going out into the field to work; then we were going into the house to think. I love to see alders and dogwood instead of peach trees. May we not see the melted snow lapsing over the rocks on the mountains in the sun, as well as snow? The white surfaces appear declivitous. While we sit here, I hear for the first time the flies buzz so dronishly in the air. I see travellers like mere dark objects in the yellow road afar,—the Turnpike. Hosmer's house and cottage under its elms and on the summit of green smooth slopes looks like a terrestrial paradise, the abode of peace and domestic happiness. Far over the woods westward, a shining vane, glimmering in the sun.

May 5. Recur to Experience

I SUCCEED BEST WHEN I *recur* to my experience not too late, but within a day or two; when there is some distance, but enough of freshness.

May 6. Fringe of Wood

IT IS PLEASANT WHEN the road winds along the side of a hill with a thin fringe of wood through which to look into the low land. It furnishes both shade and frame for your pictures,—as this Corner road.

May 16. New Leaves

TO-DAY THE CINQUEFOILS (the earliest one) on the hillsides shine in the sun. Their brightness becomes the day. That is a beautiful footpath through the pitch pines on the hillside north of this pond, over a carpet of tawny pine leaves, so slippery under your feet. Why do not men sprinkle these over their floors instead of sand? The sun on the young foliage of birches, alders, etc., on the opposite side of the pond has an enchanting effect. The sunshine has a double effect. The new leaves abet it, so fresh and tender, not apprehending their insect foes. Now the sun has come out after the May storm, how bright, how full of freshness and tender promise and fragrance is the new world! The woods putting forth new leaves; it is a memorable season. So hopeful! These young leaves have the beauty of flowers. The shrub oaks are just beginning to blossom. The forward leaves and shoots of the meadow-sweet, beneath the persistent dead flowers, make a very rich and conspicuous green now along the fences and walls. The conspicuous white flowers of the two kinds of shad-blossom spot the hillsides at a distance. This is the only bush or tree whose flowers are sufficiently common and large at this time (to-day), except the *Salix alba* and the peach (the choke-cherry is rare), to make a show now, as the apples will soon. I see dark pines in the distance in the sunshine, contrasting with the light fresh green of the deciduous trees.

May 18. The Earth Alive

THE LANDSCAPE IS MOST beautiful looking towards the sun (in the orchard on Fair Haven) at four. First, there is this green slope on which I sit, looking down between the rows of apple trees just being clothed with tender green,—sometimes underneath them to the sparkling water, or over through them, or seeing them against the sky. Secondly, the outline of this bank or hill is drawn against the water far below; the river still high, a beautifully bright sheen on the water there, though it is elsewhere a dull slaty-blue color, a sober rippled surface. A fine sparkling shimmer in front, owing to the remarkable clearness of the atmosphere (clarified by the May storm?). Thirdly, on either side of the wood beyond the river are patches of bright, tender, yellowish, velvety green grass in meadows and on hillsides. It is like a short furred mantle now and bright as if it had the sun on it. Those great fields of green affect me as did those early green blades by the Corner Spring,—like a fire flaming up from the earth. The earth proves itself well alive even in the skin. No scurf on it, only a browner color on the barren tops of hills. Fourthly, the forest, the dark-green pines, wonderfully distinct, near and erect, with their distinct dark stems, spiring tops, regularly disposed branches, and silvery light on their needles. They seem to wear an aspect as much fresher and livelier as the other trees,—though their growth can hardly be perceptible yet,—as if they had been washed by the rains and the air. They are now being invested with the light, sunny, yellowish-green of the deciduous trees. This tender foliage, putting so much light and life into the landscape, is the remarkable feature at this date. The week when the deciduous trees are generally and conspicuously expanding their leaves. The various tints of gray oaks and yellowish-green birches and aspens and hickories, and the red or scarlet tops where maple keys are formed (the blossoms are now over),—these last the high color (rosaceous?) in the bouquet. And fifthly, I detect a great stretch of high-backed, mostly bare, grassy pasture country between this and the Nashua, spotted with pines and forests, which I had formerly taken for forest uninterrupted. And finally, sixthly, Wachusett rising in the background, slightly veiled in bluish mist,— toward which all these seem to slope gradually upward,—and those grassy hillsides in the foreground, seen but as patches of bare grassy ground on a spur of that distant mountain.

June 5. Lupines

THE LUPINE IS now in its glory. It is the more important because it occurs in such extensive patches, even an acre or more together, and of such a pleasing variety of colors,—purple, pink, or lilac, and white,—especially with the sun on it, when the transparency of the flower makes its color changeable. It paints a whole hillside with its blue, making such a field (if not meadow) as Proserpine might have wandered in. Its leaf was made to be covered with dewdrops. I am quite excited by this prospect of blue flowers in clumps with narrow intervals. Such a profusion of the heavenly, the elysian, color, as if these were the Elysian Fields. They say the seeds look like babies' faces, and hence the flower is so named. No other flowers exhibit so much blue. That is the value of the lupine. The earth is blued with them. Yet a third of a mile distant I do not detect their color on the hillside. Perchance because it is the color of the air. It is not *distinct* enough. You passed along here, perchance, a fortnight ago, and the hillside was comparatively barren, but now you come and these glorious redeemers appear to have flashed out here all at once. Who planted the seeds of lupines in the barren soil? Who watereth the lupines in the fields?

June 12. The Landscape-Viewer

HEDGE-MUSTARD. (TURNED INTO the lane beyond Dennis's.) Some fields are almost wholly covered with sheep's-sorrel, now turned red,—its valves (?). It helps thus agreeably to paint the earth, contrasting even at a distance with the greener fields, blue sky, and dark or downy clouds. It is red, marbled, watered, mottled, or waved with greenish, like waving grain,—three or four acres of it. To the farmer or grazier it is a troublesome weed, but to the landscape-viewer an

*Landscape view through an old White Pine and hedgerow,
Concord, Massachusetts.*

agreeable red tinge laid on by the painter. I feel well into summer when I see this redness. It appears to be avoided by the cows.

The petals of the sidesaddle-flower, fully expanded, hang down. How complex it is, what with flowers and leaves! It is a wholesome and interesting plant to me, the leaf especially. Rye that has sown itself and come up scatteringly in bunches is now nearly ripe. They are beginning to cut rank grass on the village street. I should say the summer began with the leafiness,—umbrageous summer! The glory of Dennis's lupines is departed, and the white now shows in abundance beneath them. So I cannot walk longer in those fields of Enna in which Proserpine amused herself gathering flowers.

The steam whistle at a distance sounds even like the hum of a bee in a flower. So man's works fall into nature.

The flies hum at mid-afternoon, as if peevish and weary of the length of the days. The river is shrunk to summer width; on the sides smooth whitish water,—or rather it is the light from the pads;—in the middle, dark blue or slate, rippled.

The color of the earth at a distance where a wood has been cut off is a reddish brown. Nature has put no large object on the face of New England so glaringly white as a white house.

June 15. A Flowery Revolution

HOW RAPIDLY NEW FLOWERS unfold! as if Nature would get through her work too soon. One has as much as he can do to observe how flowers successively unfold. It is a flowery revolution, to which but few attend. Hardly too much attention can be bestowed on flowers. We follow, we march after, the highest color; that is our flag, our standard, our "color." Flowers were made to be seen, not overlooked. Their bright colors imply eyes, spectators. There have been many flower men who have rambled the world over to see them. The flowers robbed from an Egyptian traveller were at length carefully boxed up and forwarded to Linnæus, the man of flowers. The common, early cultivated red roses are certainly very handsome, so rich a color and so full of blossoms; you see why even blunderers have introduced them into their gardens.

June 18. A Meadow Rock

LOOKING AT A CLUMP of trees and bushes on the meadow, which is commonly flooded in the spring, I saw a middling-sized rock concealed by the leaves lying in the midst, and perceived that this had obtained a place, had made good the locality, for the maples and shrubs which had found a foothold about it. Here the reeds or tender plants were detained and protected. Now concealed by the beneficiaries it had protected? The boulder dropped once on a meadow makes at length a clump of trees there.

June 21. A Moral Test

NATURE HAS LOOKED UNCOMMONLY bare and dry to me for a day or two. With our senses applied to the surrounding world we are reading our own physical and corresponding moral revolutions. Nature was so shallow all at once I did not know what had attracted me all my life. I was therefore encouraged when, going through a field this evening, I was unexpectedly struck with the beauty of an apple tree. The perception of beauty is a moral test.

June 23. Agreeable Pastures

THESE ARE VERY AGREEABLE pastures to me; no house in sight, no cultivation. I sit under a large white oak, upon its swelling instep, which makes an admirable seat, and look forth over these pleasant rocky and bushy pastures, where for the most part there are not even cattle to graze them, but patches of huckleberry bushes, and birches, and pitch pines, and barberry bushes, and creeping juniper in great circles, its edges curving upward, and wild roses spotting the green with red, and numerous tufts of indigo-weed, and, above all, great gray boulders lying about far and near, with some barberry bush, perchance, growing half-way up them; and, between all, the short sod of the pasture here and there appears.

*Pasture and open field White Pine
near Concord, Massachusetts.*

June 23.   Upcountry Pastures

AS I WALK THROUGH these old deserted wild orchards, half pasture, half huckleberry-field, the air is filled with fragrance from I know not what source. How much purer and sweeter it must be than the atmosphere of the streets, rendered impure by the filth about our houses! It is quite offensive often when the air is heavy at night. The roses in the front yard do not atone for the sink and pigsty and cow-yard and jakes in the rear.

I sit on one of these boulders and look south to Ponkawtasset. Looking west, whence the wind comes, you do not see the under sides of the leaves, but, looking east, every bough shows its under side; those of the maples are particularly white. All leaves tremble like aspen leaves. Perhaps on those westward hills where I walked last Saturday the fields are somewhat larger than commonly with us, and I expand with a sense of freedom. The side of the hill commonly makes but one field. They begin to partake of the character of upcountry pastures a little more. Two or three large boulders, fifteen or twenty feet square, make a good foreground in this landscape, for the gray color of the rock contrasts well with the green of the surrounding and more distant hills and woods and fields. They serve instead of cottages for a wild landscape as perches or *points d'appui* for the eye.

The red color of cattle, also, is agreeable in a landscape; or let them be what color they may,—red, black, white, or mouse-color, or spotted, all which I have

Pasture and woods beyond.

seen this afternoon. The cows which, confined to the barn or barn-yard all winter, were covered with filth, after roaming in flowery pastures possess now clean and shining coats, and the cowy odor is without alloy. Indeed they make such an impression of neatness (I think of a white cow, spotted with red, and her two sizable calves of like color, which I saw this afternoon) that one who was unacquainted with etymology might be excused if he gave a new signification to the word neat as applied to cattle, and did not refer it to *knittan,* to butt (*i. e.* horned cattle).

It seems natural that rocks which have lain under the heavens so long should be gray, as it were an intermediate color between the heavens and the earth. The air is the thin paint in which they have been dipped and brushed with the wind. Water, which is more fluid and like the sky in its nature, is still more like it in color. Time will make the most discordant materials harmonize.

I see the silk-green-abdomened fly on cow-dung in the road.

There are some very handsome white pines and pine groves on the left of the road just before you enter the woods. They are of second growth, of course, broad and perfect, with limbs almost to the ground, and almost as broad as they are high, their fine leaves trembling with silvery light, very different from the tall masts of the primitive wood, naked of limbs beneath and crowded together. So soft, and with such a mass of foliage through which the wind soughs. But you must be careful how you sit beneath them on account of pitch. Somewhat of a conical form.

June 24. Learning by the Clouds

THE DRIFTING WHITE DOWNY clouds are to the landsman what sails on the sea are to him that dwells by the shore,—objects of a large, diffusive interest. When the laborer lies on the grass or in the shade for rest, they do not too much tax or weary his attention. They are unobtrusive. I have not heard that white clouds, like white houses, made any one's eyes ache. They are the flitting sails in that ocean whose bounds no man has visited. They are like all great themes, always at hand to be considered, or they float over us unregarded. Far away they float in the serene sky, the most inoffensive of objects, or, near and low, they smite us with their lightnings and deafen us with their thunder. We know no Ternate nor Tidore grand enough whither we can imagine them bound. There are many mare's-tails today, if that is the name. What could a man learn by watching the clouds? The objects which go over our heads unobserved are vast and indefinite. Even those clouds which have the most distinct and interesting outlines are commonly below the zenith, somewhat low in the heavens, and seen on one side. They are among the most glorious objects in nature. A sky without clouds is a meadow without flowers, a sea without sails. Some days we have the mackerel fleet. But our devilishly industrious laborers rarely lie in the shade. How much better if they were to take their nooning like the Italians, relax and expand and never do any work in the middle of the day, enjoy a little sabbath in the middle of the day.

June 27. Sympathy with Nature

A HEALTHY AND REFINED nature would always derive pleasure from the landscape. As long as the bodily vigor lasts, man sympathizes with nature.

July 5. The Wood Thrush

SOME BIRDS ARE POETS and sing all summer. They are the true singers. Any man can write verses during the love season. I am reminded of this while we rest in the shade on the Major Heywood road and listen to a wood thrush, now just before sunset. We are most interested in those birds who sing for the love of the music and not of their mates; who meditate their strains, and *amuse* themselves with singing; the birds, the strains, of deeper sentiment; not bobolinks, that lose their plumage, their bright colors, and their song so early.

The robin, the red-eye, the veery, the wood thrush, etc., etc.

The wood thrush's is no opera music; it is not so much the composition as the strain, the tone,—cool bars of melody from the atmosphere of everlasting morning or evening. It is the quality of the song, not the sequence. In the peawai's note here is some sultriness, but in the thrush's, though heard at noon, there is the liquid coolness of things that are just drawn from the bottom of springs. The

thrush alone declares the immortal wealth and vigor that is in the forest. Here i
a bird in whose strain the story is told, though Nature waited for the science o
æsthetics to discover it to man. Whenever a man hears it, he is young, and Natur
is in her spring. Wherever he hears it, it is a new world and a free country, and
the gates of heaven are not shut against him. Most other birds sing from the leve
of my ordinary cheerful hours—a carol; but this bird never fails to speak to me
out of an ether purer than that I breathe, of immortal beauty and vigor. He
deepens the significance of all things seen in the light of his strain. He sings to make
men take higher and truer views of things. He sings to amend their institutions
to relieve the slave on the plantation and the prisoner in his dungeon, the slave
in the house of luxury and the prisoner in his own low thoughts.

July 9. Low Hills

LOW HILLS, OR EVEN hillocks, which are stone-capped,—have rocky
summits,—as that near James Baker's, remind me of mountains, which, in fact
they are on a small scale. The brows of earth, round which the trees and bushe
trail like the hair of eyebrows, outside bald places, *templa,* primitive places, where
lichens grow. I have some of the same sensations as if I sat on the summit of the
Rocky Mountains. Some low places thus give a sense of elevation.

July 12. Fences and Walls

WHAT ART CAN SURPASS the rows of maples and elms and swamp white
oaks which the water plants along the river,—I mean in variety and graceful
ness,—conforming to the curves of the river.

Excepting those fences which are mere boundaries of individual property, the
walker can generally perceive the reason for those which he is obliged to get over
This wall runs along just on the edge of the hill and following all its windings, to
separate the more level and cultivatable summit from the slope, which is only fit
for pasture or wood-lot, and that other wall below divides the pasture or wood-lot
from the richer low grass ground or potato-field, etc. Even these crooked walls are
not always unaccountable and lawless.

July 17. Beck Stow's Swamp

BECK STOW'S SWAMP! WHAT an incredible spot to think of in town or
city! When life looks sandy and barren, is reduced to its lowest terms, we have
no appetite, and it has no flavor, then let me visit such a swamp as this, deep and
impenetrable, where the earth quakes for a rod around you at every step, with
its open water where the swallows skim and twitter, its meadow and cotton-grass
its dense patches of dwarf andromeda, now brownish-green, with clumps of blue
berry bushes, its spruces and its verdurous border of woods imbowering it on every

side. The trees now in the rain look heavy and rich all day, as commonly at twilight, drooping with the weight of wet leaves.

July 18. The Great Meadow

WE PUSH STILL FURTHER up the river into the great meadow, scaring the bitterns, the largest and the next in size. In many parts of the river the pickerel-weed is several rods wide, its blueness akin to the misty blue air which paints the hills. You thin it by rising in the boat; you thicken or deepen it by sitting low. (When we looked from the hills, there was a general sheeny light from the broad, level meadow, from the bent grass, watered, as it were, with darker streaks where a darker grass, the pipes, etc., bordered the (for the most part) concealed river.) The lilies are shut. First on the edge of the bright river in the sun, in this great meadow, are the pads, then the pontederia or polygonum, then the bulrushes standing in dense squadrons, or pipes or meadow-grass, then the broad heavens, in which small downy clouds are constantly forming and dissolving. No fear of rain. The sky is a pretty clear blue, yet not such a skimmed-milk blue, methinks, as in winter; some cream left in the milk. I cannot believe that any of these dissolving cloudlets will be rainbow-tinged or mother-o'-pearled. I observe that even in these meadows, where no willows nor button-bushes line the shore, there is still a pretty constant difference between the shores. The border of pontederia is rarely of equal depth on both sides at once, but it keeps that side in the meander where the sediment is deposited, the shortest course which will follow the shore,

 as I have dotted it, crossing from this side to that as the river meanders; for on the longest side the river is active, not passive, wearing into the bank, and runs there more swiftly. This is the longest line of blue that nature paints with flowers in our fields, though the lupines may have been more densely blue within a small compass. Thus by a natural law a river, instead of flowing straight through its meadows, meanders from side to side and fertilizes this side or that, and adorns its banks with flowers. The river has its active and its passive side, its right and left breast.

July 20. Sunset

SUNSET.—TO CLIFFS.

The clouds, as usual, are arranged with reference to the sunset. The sun is gone. An amber light and golden glow. The first redness is on clouds in the cast horizon. As we go by the farmhouses, the chickens are coming home to roost. The horns of the moon only three or four days old look very sharp, still cloud-like, in the midst of a blue space, prepared to shine a brief half-hour before it sets. The redness now begins to fade on eastern clouds, and the western cloudlets glow with burnished copper alloyed with gold. As we approach the woods, we perceive a fresh, cool evening scent from them. The squeak of the nighthawk is heard; the hum of mosquitoes in the woods; the song sparrow and the huckleberry-bird. The bat seen flying over the path. The western clouds grow more red or fiery, by fits and starts, and now, as suddenly, their glory departs, and they remain gray or greenish. We see from the hill darkness infolding the village, collected first in the elm-tops. If it were not for the light-colored barns and white houses, it would already be dark there. The redness of the clouds, or the golden or coppery or fuscous glow, appears to endure almost till starlight. Then the cloudlets in the west turn rapidly dark, the shadow of night advances in the east, and the first stars become visible. Then, and before the western clouds, the light behind them having faded, do or appear to disperse and contract and leave a clear sky, when I invert my head (on Fair Haven Hill), the dark cloudlets in the west horizon are like isles, like the tops of mountains cut off by the gross atmosphere.

July 23.   The Sunset and After

TWENTY MINUTES AFTER SEVEN, I sit at my window to observe the sun set. The lower clouds in the north and southwest grow gradually darker as the sun goes down, since we now see the side opposite to the sun, but those high overhead, whose under sides we see reflecting the day, are light. The small clouds low in the western sky were at first dark also, but, as the sun descends, they are lit up and aglow all but their cores. Those in the east, though we see their sunward sides, are a dark blue, presaging night, only the highest faintly glowing. A roseate redness, clear as amber, suffuses the low western sky about the sun, in which the small clouds are mostly melted, only their golden edges still revealed. The atmosphere there is like some kinds of wine, perchance, or molten cinnabar, if that is red, in which also all kinds of pearls and precious stones are melted. Clouds generally near the horizon, except near the sun, are now a dark blue. (The sun sets.) It is half past seven. The roseate glow deepens to purple. The low western sky is now, and has been for some minutes, a splendid map, where the fancy can trace islands, continents, and cities beyond compare. The glow forsakes the high eastern clouds, the uppermost clouds in the west now darken, the glow having forsaken them too; they become a dark blue, and anon their under sides reflect a deep red, like heavy damask curtains, after they had already been dark. The general redness gradually fades into a pale reddish tinge in the horizon, with a clear white light above it, in which the clouds grow more conspicuous and darker and darker blue, appearing to follow in the wake of the sun, and it is now a quarter to eight, or fifteen minutes after sunset, twenty-five minutes from the first. A quarter of an hour later, or half an hour after sunset, the white light grows cream-colored above the increasing horizon redness, passing through white into blue above. The western clouds, high and low, are now dark fuscous, not dark blue, but the eastern clouds are not so dark as the western. Now, about twenty minutes after the first glow left the clouds above the sun's place, there is a second faint fuscous or warm brown glow on the edges of the dark clouds there, sudden and distinct, and it fades again, and it is early starlight, but the tops of the eastern clouds still are white, reflecting the day. The cream-color grows more yellowish or amber. About three quarters of an hour after sunset the evening red is deepest, *i. e.* a general atmospheric redness close to the west horizon. There is more of it, after all, than I expected, for the day has been clear and rather cool, and the evening red is what was the blue haze by day. The moon, now in her first quarter, now begins to preside,—her light to prevail,—though for the most part eclipsed by clouds. As the light in the west fades, the sky there, seen between the clouds, has a singular clarity and serenity.

July 24. Weeds

I SYMPATHIZE WITH WEEDS perhaps more than with the crop they choke, they express so much vigor. They are the truer crop which the earth more willingly bears.

July 26. The Sunset Sky

THE GRANDEST PICTURE IN the world is the sunset sky. In your higher moods what man is there to meet? You are of necessity isolated. The mind that perceives clearly any natural beauty is in that instant withdrawn from human society. My desire for society is infinitely increased; my fitness for any actual society is diminished.

July 27. On Fair Haven Hill

I AM SURE THAT if I call for a companion in my walk I have relinquished in my design some closeness of communion with Nature. The walk will surely be more commonplace. The inclination for society indicates a distance from Nature. I do not design so wild and mysterious a walk.

The bigoted and sectarian forget that without religion or devotion of some kind nothing great was ever accomplished.

On Fair Haven Hill. The slight distraction of picking berries is favorable to a mild, abstracted, poetic mood, to sequestered or transcendental thinking. I return ever more fresh to my mood from such slight interruptions.

All the clouds in the sky are now close to the west horizon, so that the sun is nearly down before they are reached and lighted or gilded. Wachusett, free of clouds, has a fine purplish tinge, as if the juice of grapes had been squeezed over it, darkening into blue. I hear the scratching sound of a worm at work in this hardwood-pile on which I sit.

We are most disturbed by the sun's dazzle when it is lowest. Now the upper edge of that low blue bank is gilt where the sun has disappeared, leaving a glory in the horizon through which a few cloudy peaks send raylike shadows. Now a slight rosy blush is spreading north and south over the horizon sky and tingeing a few small scattered clouds in the east. A blue tinge southward makes the very edge of the earth there a mountain. That low bank of cloud in the west is now exactly the color of the mountains, a dark blue. We should think sacredly, with devotion. That is one thing, at least, we may do magnanimously. May not every man have some private affair which he can conduct greatly, unhurriedly? The river is silvery, as it were plated and polished smooth, with the slightest possible tinge of gold, to-night. How beautiful the meanders of a river, thus revealed! How beautiful hills and vales, the whole surface of the earth a succession of these great cups, falling away from dry or rocky edges to gelid green meadows and water in the midst, where night already is setting in! The thrush, now the sun is apparently set, fails not to sing. Have I heard the veery lately? All glow on the clouds is gone, except from one higher, small, rosy pink or flesh-colored isle. The sun is now probably set. There are no clouds on high to reflect a golden light into the river.

Aug. 2. Wachusett from Fair Haven Hill

WACHUSETT FROM FAIR HAVEN Hill looks like this:

the dotted line being the top of the surrounding forest. Even on the low principle that misery loves company and is relieved by the consciousness that it is shared by many, and therefore is not so insignificant and trivial, after all, this blue mountain outline is valuable. In many moods it is cheering to look across hence to that blue rim of the earth, and be reminded of the invisible towns and communities, for the most part also unremembered, which lie in the further and deeper hollows between me and those hills. Towns of sturdy uplandish fame, where some of the morning and primal vigor still lingers, I trust. Ashburnham, Rindge, Jaffrey, etc.,—it is cheering to think that it is with such communities that we survive or perish. Yes, the mountains do thus impart, in the mere prospect of them, some of the New Hampshire vigor. The melancholy man who had come forth to commit suicide on this hill might be saved by being thus reminded how many brave and contented lives are lived between him and the horizon. Those hills extend our plot of earth; they make our native valley or indentation in the earth so much the larger. There is a whitish line along the base of Wachusett more particularly, as if the reflection of bare cliffs there in the sun. Undoubtedly it is the slight vaporous haze in the atmosphere seen edgewise just above the top of the forest, though it is a clear day. It, this line, makes the mountains loom, in fact, a faint whitish line separating the mountains from their bases and the rest of the globe.

Aug. 3. Cow Paths

LOOKING DOWN INTO THE singular bare hollows from the back of hill near here, the paths made by the cows in the sides of the hills, going round the hollows, made gracefully curving lines in the landscape, ribbing it. The curves, both the rising and falling of the path and its winding to right and left, are agreeable.

Aug. 3. Slumbering Boulders

TOOK THAT INTERESTING VIEW from one of the boulder rocks toward Lincoln Hills, between Hubbard's Hill and Grove and Barrett's, whose back or north and wooded side is in front, a few oaks and elms in front and on the right, and some fine boulders slumbering in the foreground. It is a peculiar part of the town,—the old bridle-road plains further east. A great tract here of unimproved and unfrequented country, the boulders sometimes crowned with barberry bushes.

Clearing with boulders.

Aug. 7. A Passing Visit

F I WERE TO choose a time for a friend to make a passing visit to this world or the first time, in the full possession of all his faculties, perchance it would be t a moment when the sun was setting with splendor in the west, his light reflected ar and wide through the clarified air after a rain, and a brilliant rainbow, as now, 'erarching the eastern sky . Would he be likely to think this a vulgar place to live [sic], where one would weary of existence, and be compelled to devote his life to frivolity and dissipation? If a man travelling from world to world were to pass through this world at such a moment, would he not be tempted to take up his abode here?

Aug. 19. A Little Brook

HERE IS A LITTLE brook of very cold spring-water, rising a few rods distant, with a gray sandy and pebbly bottom, flowing through this dense swampy thicket, where, nevertheless, the sun falls in here and there between the leaves and shines on its bottom, meandering exceedingly, and sometimes running underground. The trilliums on its brink have fallen into it and bathe their red berries in the water, waving in the stream. The water has the coldness it acquired in the bowels of the earth. Here is a recess apparently never frequented. Thus this rill flowed here a thousand years ago, and with exactly these environments. It is a few rods of primitive wood, such as the bear and the deer beheld. It has a singular charm for me, carrying me back in imagination to those days. Yet a fisherman has once found out this retreat, and here is his box in the brook to keep his minnows in, now gone to decay. I love the rank smells of the swamp, its decaying leaves. The clear dark-green leaves of the fever-bush overhang the stream.

Aug. 23. These Hieroglyphics

NOW I SIT ON the Cliffs and look abroad over the river and Conantum hills. I live so much in my habitual thoughts, a routine of thought, that I forget there is any outside to the globe, and am surprised when I behold it as now,—yonder hills and river in the moonlight, the monsters. Yet it is salutary to deal with the surface of things. What are these rivers and hills, these hieroglyphics which my eyes behold? There is something invigorating in this air, which I am peculiarly sensible is a real wind, blowing from over the surface of a planet. I look out at my eyes, I come to my window, and I feel and breathe the fresh air. It is a fact equally glorious with the most inward experience. Why have we ever slandered the outward? The perception of surfaces will always have the effect of miracle to a sane sense. I can see Nobscot faintly.

Aug. 31. Evening on the River

I FLOAT SLOWLY DOWN from Fair Haven till I have passed the bridge. The sun, half an hour high, has come out again just before setting, with a brilliant warm light, and there is the slightest undulation discernible on the water, from the boat or other cause, as it were its imitation in glass. The reflections are perfect. A bright, fresh green on fields and trees now after the rain, springlike with the sense of summer past. The reflections are the more perfect for the blackness of the water. I see the down of a thistle, probably, in the air, descending to the water.

*Dusk on the Sudbury River
near Concord, Massachusetts.*

two or three rods off, which I mistake for a man in his shirt sleeves descending a distant hill, by an ocular delusion. How fair the smooth green swells of those low grassy hills on which the sunlight falls! Indian hills.

This is the most glorious part of this day, the serenest, warmest, brightest part, and the most suggestive. Evening is fairer than morning. It is chaste eve, for it has sustained the trials of the day, but to the morning such praise was inapplicable. It is incense-breathing. Morning is full of promise and vigor. Evening is pensive. The serenity is far more remarkable to those who are on the water. That part of the sky just above the horizon seen reflected, apparently, some rods off from the boat is as light a blue as the actual, but it goes on deepening as your eye draws nearer to the boat, until, when you look directly down at the reflection of the zenith, it is lost in the blackness of the water. It passes through all degrees of dark blue, and the threatening aspect of a cloud is very much enhanced in the reflection. As I wish to be on the water at sunset, I let the boat float.

Sept. 1. On Walden Pond

4 p.m.—To Walden.

Paddling over it, I see large schools of perch only an inch long, yet easily distinguished by their transverse bars. Great is the beauty of a wooded shore seen from the water, for the trees have ample room to expand on that side, and each puts forth its most vigorous bough to fringe and adorn the pond. It is rare that you see so natural an edge to the forest. Hence a pond like this, surrounded by hills wooded down to the edge of the water, is the best place to observe the tints of the autumnal foliage. Moreover, such as stand in or near to the water change earlier than elsewhere.

Sept. 1.   From Gilpin

THUS IT IS ONLY by emphasis and exaggeration that real effects are described. What Gilpin says in another place is perfectly applicable to this case, though he says that that which he is about to disclose is so bold a truth, "that it ought only, perhaps, to be opened to the initiated." "In the exhibition of distant mountains on paper, or canvas," says he, "unless you make them exceed their *real* or *proportional* size, they have no effect. It is inconceivable how objects lessen by distance. Examine any distance, closed by mountains, in a camera, and you will easily see what a poor, diminutive appearance the mountains make. By the power of perspective they are lessened to nothing. Should you represent them in your landscape in so diminutive a form, all dignity, and grandeur of idea would be lost."

Sept. 2.   The Scenery is Humble

THE SCENERY OF THIS small pond is humble though very beautiful, and does not approach to grandeur, nor can it much concern one who has not long frequented it, or lived by its shore.

Sept. 13.   The Earth Translated

IN MY RIDE I experienced the pleasure of coming into a landscape where there was more distance and a bluish tinge in the horizon. I am not contented long with such narrow valleys that all is greenness in them. I wish to see the earth translated, the green passing into blue. How this heaven intervenes and tinges our more distant prospects! The farther off the mountain which is the goal of our enterprise, the more of heaven's tint it wears. This is the chief value of a distance in landscapes.

I must walk more with free senses. It is as bad to *study* stars and clouds as flowers and stones. I must let my senses wander as my thoughts, my eyes see without looking. Carlyle said that how to observe was to look, but I say that it is rather to see, and the more you look the less you will observe. I have the habit of attention to such excess that my senses get no rest, but suffer from a constant strain. Be not preoccupied with looking. Go not to the object; let it come to you. When I have found myself ever looking down and confining my gaze to the flowers, I have thought it might be well to get into the habit of observing the clouds as a corrective; but no! that study would be just as bad. What I need is not to look at all, but a true sauntering of the eye.

Sept. 20.   Overlooking the Pond

ON HEYWOOD'S PEAK BY Walden.—The surface is not *perfectly* smooth on account of the zephyr, and the reflections of the woods are a little indistinct nd blurred. How soothing to sit on a stump on this height, overlooking the pond, nd study the dimpling circles which are incessantly inscribed and again erased n the smooth and otherwise invisible surface, amid the reflected skies! The reflected sky is of a deeper blue. How beautiful that over this vast expanse there can be no disturbance, but it is thus at once gently smoothed away and assuaged, as, when a vase of water is jarred, the trembling circles seek the shore and all is mooth again! Not a fish can leap or an insect fall on it but it is reported in lines of beauty, in circling dimples, as it were the constant welling up of its fountain, he gentle pulsing of its life, the heaving of its breast. The thrills of joy and those of pain are indistinguishable. How sweet the phenomena of the lake! Everything hat moves on its surface produces a sparkle. The peaceful pond! The works of men shine as in the spring. The motion of an oar or an insect produces a flash of ight; and if an oar falls, how sweet the echo!

Sept. 21. Maple a Fruit

P.M.—To Conantum.

The small skull-cap and cress and the mullein still in bloom. I see pigeon woodpeckers oftener now, with their light rears. Birches and elms begin to turn yellow, and ferns are quite yellow or brown in many places. I see many tall clustered bluish asters by the brooks, like the *A. undulatus.* The blue-stemmed goldenrod is abundant, bright and in its prime. The maples begin to be ripe. How beautiful when a whole maple on the edge of a swamp is like one great scarlet fruit, full of ripe juices! A sign of the ripening. Every leaf, from lowest limb to topmost spire, is aglow.

Sept. 26. Presiding Mountains

From Smith's Hill I looked toward the mountain line. Who can believe that the mountain peak which he beholds fifty miles off in the horizon, rising far and faintly blue above an intermediate range, while he stands on his trivial native hills or in the dusty highway, can be the same with that which he looked up at once near at hand from a gorge in the midst of primitive woods? For a part of two days I travelled across lots once, loitering by the way, through primitive wood and swamps over the highest peak of the Peterboro Hills to Monadnock, by ways from which all landlords and stage-drivers endeavored to dissuade us. It was not a month ago. But now that I look across the globe in an instant to the dim Monadnock peak, and these familiar fields and copsewoods appear to occupy the greater part of the interval, I cannot realize that Joe Eavely's house still stands there at the base of the mountain, and all that long tramp through wild woods with invigorating scents before I got to it. I cannot realize that on the tops of those cool blue ridges are in abundance berries still, bluer than themselves, as if they borrowed their blueness from their locality. From the mountains we do not discern our native hills; but from our native hills we look out easily to the far blue

mountains, which seem to preside over them. As I look northwestward to t
summit from a Concord cornfield, how little can I realize all the life that is passi
between me and it,—the retired up-country farmhouses, the lonely mills, wood
vales, wild rocky pastures, and new clearings on stark mountain-sides, and riv
murmuring through primitive woods! All these, and how much more, I *overloe*
I see the very peak,—there can be no mistake,—but how much I do not see, t
is between me and it! How much I overlook! In this way we see stars. What
it but a faint blue cloud, a mist that may vanish? But what is it, on the other ha
to one who has travelled to it day after day, has threaded the forest and climb
the hills that are between this and that, has tasted the raspberries or the blueb
ries that grow on it, and the springs that gush from it, has been wearied w
climbing its rocky sides, felt the coolness of its summit, and been lost in the clou
there?

Sept. 28. Some Wild Fruits

GRAPES ARE STILL ABUNDANT. I have only to shake the birches
bring down a shower of plums. But the flavor of none is quite equal to th
fragrance. Some soils, like this rocky one on the old Carlisle road, are so sui
to the apple that they spring up wild and bear well in the midst of pines, birch
maples, and oaks, their red and yellow fruit harmonizing with the autumnal ti
of the forest in which they grow. I am surprised to see rising amid the maples a
birches in a swamp the rounded tops of apple trees rosy with fair fruit.

A windy day. What have these high and roaring winds to do with the fall?
doubt they speak plainly enough to the sap that is in these trees, and perchar
they check its upward flow.

A very handsome *gray dotted* thorn near the black birch grove, six inches
diameter, with a top large in proportion, as large as a small apple tree, bristl
with many thorns from suckers about its trunk. This is a very handsome obje
and the largest thorn I have seen in Concord, almost bare of leaves and one m
of red fruit, five eighths of an inch in diameter, causing its slender branches
spread and droop gracefully. It reminds me of a wisp of straws tied together,
a dustbrush upright on its handle. It must be the same I have seen in Canada. T
same with that on Nawshawtuct. Probably most beautiful in fruit, not only
account of its color, but because this causes the branches to spread and cur
outward gracefully.

Oct. 12. Piled-up History

I AM STRUCK BY the superfluity of light in the atmosphere in the autun
as if the earth absorbed none, and out of this profusion of dazzling light came t
autumnal tints. Can it be because there is less vapor? The delicacy of the strat
cation in the white sand by the railroad, where they have been getting out sa

for the brick-yards, the delicate stratification of this great globe like the leaves of the choicest volume just shut on a lady's table. The piled-up history! I am struck by the slow and delicate process by which the globe was formed.

Oct. 13. Autumn-Tinted Woods

P.M.—TO CLIFFS.

Many maples have lost all their leaves and are shrunk all at once to handsome clean gray wisps on the edge of the meadows, where, crowded together, at a distance they look like smoke. This is a sudden and important change, produced mainly, I suppose, by the rain of Sunday, 10th. The autumnal tints have commonly already lost their brightness. It lasts but a day or two. Corn-spurry and spotted polygonum and polygala.

Fair Haven Pond, methinks, never looks so handsome as at this season. It is a sufficiently clear and warm, rather Indian-summer day, and they are gathering the apples in the orchard. The warmth is more required, and we welcome and appreciate it all. The shrub oak plain is now a deep red, with grayish, withered, apparently white oak leaves intermixed. The chickadees take heart, too, and sing above these warm rocks. Birches, hickories, aspens, etc., in the distance, are like innumerable small flames on the hillsides about the pond. The pond is now most beautifully framed with the autumn-tinted woods and hills. The water or lake, from however distant a point seen, is always the centre of the landscape. Fair Haven lies more open and can be seen from more distant points than any of our ponds. The air is singularly fine-grained; the sward looks short and firm. The mountains are more distinct from the rest of the earth and slightly impurpled. Seeming to lie up more. How peaceful great nature! There is no disturbing sound, but far amid the western hills there rises a pure white smoke in constant volumes.

Oct. 20. A Single Picture

MANY A MAN, WHEN I tell him that I have been on to a mountain, asks if I took a glass with me. No doubt, I could have seen further with a glass, and particular objects more distinctly,—could have counted more meeting-houses; but this has nothing to do with the peculiar beauty and grandeur of the view which an elevated position affords. It was not to see a few particular objects, as if they were near at hand, as I had been accustomed to see them, that I ascended the mountain, but to see an infinite variety far and near in their relation to each other, thus reduced to a single picture. The facts of science, in comparison with poetry, are wont to be as vulgar as looking from the mountain with a telescope. It is a counting of meeting-houses. At the public house, the mountain-house, they keep a glass to let, and think the journey to the mountain-top is lost, that you have got but half the view, if you have not taken a glass with you.

Oct. 22. Autumn Oaks

TO WALDEN.

Ebby Hubbard's oaks, now turned a sober and warm red and yellow, have a very rich crisp and curled look, especially against the green pines. This is when the ripe high-colored leaves have begun to curl and wither. Then they have a warm and harmonious tint. First they are ripened by the progress of the year, and the character of each appears in distinct colors. Then come the severe frosts and, dulling the brilliancy of most, produce a harmony of warm brown or red and yellow tinges throughout the forest, something like marbling and painting over it, making one shade run into another. The forest is the more rug-like.

Oct. 25. Hillside Hues

THE AUTUMNAL TINTS GROW gradually darker and duller, but not less rich to my eye. And now a hillside near the river exhibits the darkest, crispy reds and browns of every hue, all agreeably blended. At the foot, next the meadow, stands a front rank of smoke-like maples bare of leaves, intermixed with yellow birches. Higher up, red oaks of various shades of dull red, with yellowish, perhaps black oaks intermixed, and walnuts, now brown, and near the hilltop, or rising above the rest, perhaps, a still yellowish oak, and here and there amid the rest or in the foreground on the meadow, dull ashy salmon-colored white oaks large and small, all these contrasting with the clear liquid, sempiternal green of pines.

Nov. 1. Frame to a Landscape

DAY BEFORE YESTERDAY TO the Cliffs in the rain, misty rain. As I approached their edge, I saw the woods beneath, Fair Haven Pond, and the hills across the river,—which, owing to the mist, was as far as I could see, and seemed much further in consequence. I saw these between the converging boughs of two white pines a rod or two from me on the edge of the rock; and I thought that there was no frame to a landscape equal to this,—to see, between two near pine boughs, whose lichens are distinct, a distant forest and lake, the one frame, the other picture. In November, a man will eat his heart, if in any month. The birches have almost all lost their leaves. On the river this afternoon, the leaves, now crisp and curled, when the wind blows them on to the water become rude boats which float and sail about awhile conspicuously before they go to the bottom,—oaks, walnuts, etc.

Nov. 16. Muskrat-Houses

9 A.M.—SAIL UP RIVER TO Lee's Bridge.

Colder weather and very windy, but still no snow. A very little ice along the edges of the river, which does not all melt before night. Muskrat-houses completed. Interesting objects looking down a river-reach at this season, and our river should not be represented without one or two of these cones. They are quite conspicuous half a mile distant, and are of too much importance to be omitted in the river landscape.

Nov. 23. The Andromeda Ponds

HAVING DESCENDED THE CLIFF, I go along to the Andromeda Ponds. Sportsmen have already been out with their dogs, improving this first snow to track their game. The andromeda looks somewhat redder than before, a warm reddish brown, with an edging of yellowish sedge or coarse grass about the swamp, and red rustling shrub oak hills with a white ground rising around. These swamps, resorted to by the muskrat and ducks, most remind me of the Indian.

CHAPTER V

YEAR

1853

AGE

35–36

Jan. 3. Nature and Man

I LOVE NATURE PARTLY *because* she is not man, but a retreat from him. None of his institutions control or pervade her. There a different kind of right prevails. In her midst I can be glad with an entire gladness. If this world were all man, I could not stretch myself, I should lose all hope. He is constraint, she is freedom to me. He makes me wish for another world. She makes me content with this. None of the joys she supplies is subject to his rules and definitions.

Jan. 4. Yellow Birch Swamp

I MUST CALL THAT swamp of E. Hubbard's west of the Hunt Pasture, Yellow Birch Swamp. There are more of those trees than anywhere else in town that I know. How pleasing to stand beside a new or rare tree! And few are so handsome as this. Singularly allied to the black birch in its sweet checkerberry scent and its form, and to the canoe birch in its peeling or fringed and tasselled bark. The top is brush-like as the black birch; the bark an exquisite fine or delicate gold-color, curled off partly from the trunk, with vertical clear or smooth spaces, as if a plane had been passed up the tree. The sight of these trees affects me more than California gold. I measured one five feet and two inches in circumference at six feet from the ground. We have the silver and the golden birch. This is like a fair, flaxenhaired sister of the dark-complexioned black birch, with golden ringlets. How lustily it takes hold of the swampy soil, and braces itself! And here flows a dark cherry-wood or wine-colored brook over the iron-red sands in the sombre swamp,—swampy wine. In an undress, this tree. Ah, time will come when these will be all gone. Among the primitive trees. What sort of dryads haunt these? Blond nymphs.

March 21. Roads Lead Elsewhither

IT IS A GENIAL and reassuring day; the mere warmth of the west wind amounts almost to balminess. The softness of the air mollifies our own dry and congealed substance. I sit down by a wall to see if I can muse again. We become, as it were, pliant and ductile again to strange but memorable influences; we are led a little way by our genius. We are affected like the earth, and yield to the elemental tenderness; winter breaks up within us; the frost is coming out of me, and I am heaved like the road; accumulated masses of ice and snow dissolve, and thoughts like a freshet pour down unwonted channels. A strain of music comes to solace the traveller over earth's downs and dignify his chagrins, the petty men whom he meets are the shadows of grander to come. Roads lead elsewhither than to Carlisle and Sudbury. The earth is uninhabited but fair to inhabit, like the old Carlisle road. Is then the road so rough that it should be neglected? Not only narrow but rough is the way that leadeth to life everlasting. Our experience does not wear upon us. It is seen to be fabulous or symbolical, and the future is worth expecting. Encouraged, I set out once more to climb the mountain of the earth, for my steps are symbolical steps, and in all my walking I have not reached the top of the earth yet.

March 23. To Look at Nature

MAN CANNOT AFFORD TO be a naturalist, to look at Nature directly, but only with the side of his eye. He must look through and beyond her. To look at her is fatal as to look at the head of Medusa. It turns the man of science to stone. I feel that I am dissipated by so many observations. I should be the magnet in the midst of all this dust and filings. I knock the back of my hand against a rock, and as I smooth back the skin, I find myself prepared to study lichens there. I look upon man but as a fungus. I have almost a slight, dry headache as the result of all this observing. How to observe is how to behave. O for a little Lethe! To crown all, lichens, which are so thin, are described in the *dry* state, as they are most commonly, not most truly, seen. Truly, they are *dryly* described.

Without being the owner of any land, I find that I have a civil right in the river,—that, if I am not a landowner I am a water-owner. It is fitting, therefore, that I should have a boat, a cart, for this my farm. Since it is almost wholly given up to a few of us, while the other highways are much travelled, no wonder that I improve it. Such a one as I will choose to dwell in a township where there are most ponds and rivers and our range is widest. In relation to the river, I find my natural rights least infringed on. It is an extensive "common" still left. Certain savage liberties still prevail in the oldest and most civilized countries. I am pleased to find that, in Gilbert White's day, at least, the laborers in that part of England enjoyed certain rights of common in the royal forests,—so called, though no large wood,—where they cut their turf and other fuel, etc., etc., and obtained materials for broom-making, etc., when other labor failed. It is no longer so, according to his editor. Nobody legislates for me, for the way would be not to legislate at all.

March 29.   The Leaning Hemlocks

A PLEASANT SHORT VOYAGE is that to the Leaning Hemlocks on the Assabet, just round the Island under Nawshawtuct Hill. The river here has in the course of ages gullied into the hill, at a curve, making a high and steep bank, on which a few hemlocks grow and overhang the deep, eddying basin. For as long as I can remember, one or more of these has always been slanting over the stream at various angles, being undermined by it, until one after another, from year to year, they fall in and are swept away. This is a favorite voyage for ladies to make, down one stream and up the other, plucking the lilies by the way and landing on the Island, and concluding with a walk on Nawshawtuct Hill.

April 7.   Town Adorned by Its River

AS WE STAND ON Nawshawtuct at 5 P.M., looking over the meadows, I doubt if there is a town more adorned by its river than ours. Now the sun is low in the west, the northeasterly water is of a peculiarly ethereal light blue, more beautiful than the sky, and this broad water with innumerable bays and inlets running up into the land on either side and often divided by bridges and causeways, as if it were the very essence and richness of the heavens distilled and poured over the earth, contrasting with the clear russet land and the paler sky from which it has been subtracted,—nothing can be more elysian. Is not the blue more ethereal when the sun is at this angle? The river is but a long chain of flooded meadows. I think our most distant extensive low horizon must be that northeast from this hill over Ball's Hill,—to what town is it? It is down the river valley, partly at least toward the Merrimack, as it should be.

Concord River bridge, Concord, Massachusetts.

May 8. Long Row of Elms

A LONG ROW OF elms just set out by Wheeler from his gate to the old Lee place. The planting of so long a row of trees which are so stately and may endure so long deserves to be recorded. In many localities a much shorter row, or even a few scattered trees, set out sixty or a hundred years since, is the most conspicuous as well as interesting relic of the past in sight. Nothing more proves the civility of one's ancestors.

May 10. Nature My Language

HE IS THE RICHEST who has most use for nature as raw material of tropes and symbols with which to describe his life. If these gates of golden willows affect me, they correspond to the beauty and promise of some experience on which I am entering. If I am overflowing with life, am rich in experience for which I lack expression, then nature will be my language full of poetry,—all nature will *fable*, and every natural phenomenon be a myth. The man of science, who is not seeking for expression but for a fact to be expressed merely, studies nature as a dead language. I pray for such inward experience as will make nature significant.

Mountains and clouds.

May 10. Distant Mountains

FROM THE HILL, I look westward over the landscape. The deciduous woods are in their hoary youth, every expanding bud swaddled with downy webs. From this more eastern hill, with the whole breadth of the river valley on the west, the mountains appear higher still, the width of the blue border is greater,—not mere peaks, or a short and shallow sierra, but a high blue table-land with broad foundations, a deep and solid base or tablet, in proportion to the peaks that rest on it. As you ascend, the near and low hills sink and flatten into the earth; no sky is seen behind them; the distant mountains rise. The truly great are distinguished. Vergers, crests of the waves of earth, which in the highest break at the summit into granitic rocks over which the air beats. A part of their hitherto concealed base is seen blue. You see, not the domes only, but the body, the facade, of these terrene temples. You see that the foundation answers to the superstructure. Moral structures. (The sweet-fern leaves among odors now.) The successive lines of haze which divide the western landscape, deeper and more misty over each intervening valley, are not yet very dense; yet there is a light atmospheric line along the base of the mountains for their whole length, formed by this denser and grosser atmosphere through which we look next the earth, which almost melts them into the atmosphere, like the contact of molten metal with that which is unfused; but their pure, sublimed tops and main body rise, palpable skyland above it, like the waving signal of the departing who have already left these shores. It will be worth the while to observe carefully the direction and altitude of the mountains from the Cliffs. The value of the mountains in the horizon,—would not that be a good theme for a lecture? The text for a discourse on real values, and permanent; a sermon on the mount. They are stepping-stones to heaven,—as the rider has a horse-block at his gate,—by which to mount when we would commence our pilgrimage to heaven; by which we gradually take our departure from earth, from the time when our youthful eyes first rested on them,—from this bare actual earth, which has so little of the hue of heaven. They make it easier to die and easier to live. They let us off.

May 11. Partridge Drumming

I HEAR THE DISTANT drumming of a partridge. Its beat, however distant and low, falls still with a remarkably forcible, almost painful, impulse on the ear, like veritable little drumsticks on our tympanum, as if it were a throbbing or fluttering in our veins or brows or the chambers of the ear, and belonging to ourselves,—as if it were produced by some little insect which had made its way up into the passages of the ear, so penetrating is it. It is as palpable to the ear as the sharpest note of a fife. Of course, that bird can drum with its wings on a log which can go off with such a powerful whir, beating the air. I have seen a thoroughly frightened hen and cockerel fly almost as powerfully, but neither can sustain it long. Beginning slowly and deliberately, the partridge's beat sounds faster and faster from far away under the boughs and through the aisles of the wood until it becomes a regular roll, but is speedily concluded. How many things shall we not see and be and do, when we walk there where the partridge drums!

May 22. Pasture Scrub Apples

THE PASTURES ON THIS hill and its spurs are sprinkled profusely with thorny pyramidal apple scrubs, very thick and stubborn, first planted by the cows, then browsed by them and kept down stubborn and thorny for years, till, as they spread, their centre is protected and beyond reach and shoots up into a tree, giving a wine-glass form to the whole; and finally perchance the bottom disappears and cows come in to stand in the shade and rub against and redden the trunk. They must make fine dark shadows, these shrubs, when the sun is low; perfectly pyramidal they are now, many of them. You see the cow-dung everywhere now with a hundred little trees springing up in it. Thus the cows create their own shade and food.

May 25. Description of Species

WEDNESDAY. ELECTION DAY.—RAIN yesterday afternoon and to-day. Heard the popping of guns last night and this morning, nevertheless.

I quarrel with most botanists' description of different species, say of willows. It is a difference without a distinction. No stress is laid upon the peculiarity of the species in question, and it requires a very careful examination and comparison to detect any difference in the description. Having described you one species, he begins again at the beginning when he comes to the next and describes it *absolutely,* wasting time; in fact does not describe the species, but rather the genus or family; as if, in describing the particular races of men, you should say of each in its turn that it is but dust and to dust it shall return. The object should be to describe not those particulars in which a species resembles its genus, for they are many and that would be but a negative description, but those in which it is peculiar, for they are few and positive.

June 10.　Easterbrooks Country

WHAT SHALL THIS GREAT wild tract over which we strolled be called? Many farmers have pastures there, and wood-lots, and orchards. It consists mainly of rocky pastures. It contains what I call the Boulder Field, the Yellow Birch Swamp, the Black Birch Hill, the Laurel Pasture, the Hog-Pasture, the White Pine Grove, the Easterbrooks Place, the Old Lime-Kiln, the Lime Quarries, Spruce Swamp, the Ermine Weasel Woods; also the Oak Meadows, the Cedar Swamp, the Kibbe Place, and the old place northwest of Brooks Clark's. Ponkawtasset bounds it on the south. There are a few frog-ponds and an old mill-pond within it, and Bateman's Pond on its edge. What shall the whole be called? The old Carlisle road, which runs through the middle of it, is bordered on each side with wild apple pastures, where the trees stand without order, having, many if not most of them, sprung up by accident or from pomace sown at random, and are for the most part concealed by birches and pines. These orchards are very extensive, and yet many of these apple trees, growing as forest trees, bear good crops of apples. It is a paradise for walkers in the fall. There are also boundless huckleberry pastures as well as many blueberry swamps. Shall we call it the Easterbrooks Country? It would make a princely estate in Europe, yet it is owned by farmers, who live by the labor of their hands and do not esteem it much. Plenty of huckleberries and barberries here.

June 15.　A Clover Field

CLOVER NOW IN ITS prime. What more luxuriant than a clover-field? The poorest soil that is covered with it looks incomparably fertile. This is perhaps the most characteristic feature of June, resounding with the hum of insects. It is so massive, such a blush on the fields. The rude health of the sorrel cheek has given place to the blush of clover. Painters are wont, in their pictures of Paradise, to strew the ground too thickly with flowers. There should be moderation in all things. Though we love flowers, we do not want them so thick under our feet that we cannot walk without treading on them. But a clover-field in bloom is some excuse for them.

June 22. Song of the Wood Thrush

As I come over the hill, I hear the wood thrush singing his evening lay. This is the only bird whose note affects me like music, affects the flow and tenor of my thought, my fancy and imagination. It lifts and exhilarates me. It is inspiring. It is a medicative draught to my soul. It is an elixir to my eyes and a fountain of youth to all my senses. It changes all hours to an eternal morning. It banishes all trivialness. It reinstates me in my dominion, makes me the lord of creation, is chief musician of my court. This minstrel sings in a time, a heroic age, with which no event in the village can be contemporary. How can they be contemporary when only the latter is *temporary* at all? How can the infinite and eternal be contemporary with the finite and temporal? So there is something in the music of the cow-bell, something sweeter and more nutritious, than in the milk which the farmers drink. This thrush's song is a *ranz des vaches* to me. I long for wildness, a nature which I cannot put my foot through, woods where the wood thrush forever sings, where the hours are early morning ones, and there is dew on the grass, and the day is forever unproved, where I might have a fertile unknown for a soil about me. I would go after the cows, I would watch the flocks of Admetus there forever, only for my board and clothes. A New Hampshire everlasting and unfallen.

June 22. Wood Thrush's Strain

All that was ripest and fairest in the wilderness and the wild man is preserved and transmitted to us in the strain of the wood thrush. It is the mediator between barbarism and civilization. It is unrepentant as Greece.

July 24. A Table Constantly Spread

The berries of the *Vaccinium vacillans* are very abundant and large this year on Fair Haven, where I am now. Indeed these and huckleberries and blackberries are very abundant in this part of the town. Nature does her best to feed man. The traveller need not go out of the road to get as many as he wants; every bush and vine teems with palatable fruit. Man for once stands in such relation to Nature as the animals that pluck and eat as they go. The fields and hills are a table constantly spread. Wines of all kinds and qualities, of noblest vintage, are bottled up in the skins of countless berries, for the taste of men and animals. To men they seem offered not so much for food as for sociality, that they may picnic with Nature,—diet drinks, cordials, wines. We pluck and eat in remembrance of Her. It is a sacrament, a communion. The not-forbidden fruits, which no serpent tempts us to taste. Slight and innocent savors, which relate us to

Nature, make us her guests and entitle us to her regard and protection. It is a Saturnalia, and we quaff her wines at every turn. This season of berrying is so far respected that the children have a vacation to pick berries, and women and children who never visit distant hills and fields and swamps on any other errand are seen making haste thither now, with half their domestic utensils in their hands. The woodchopper goes into the swamp for fuel in the winter; his wife and children for berries in the summer.

Aug. 6. Sun Among Flowers

I SEE THE SUNFLOWER'S broad disk now in gardens, probably a few days,—a true sun among flowers, monarch of August. Do not the flowers of August and September generally resemble suns and stars?—sunflowers and asters and the single flowers of the goldenrod. I once saw one as big as a milk-pan, in which a mouse had its nest.

Aug. 19. A Memorable Day

HOW FRESHLY, BEAUTIFULLY GREEN the landscape after all these rains! The poke-berry ripe. Hear the incessant cricket of the fall now. Found a swamp full of high blueberries there, and from the hill near by looked to Nobscot, three or four miles distant. It was seen to advantage, rising green or with a glaucous tint above the slope of a near pasture which concealed all the intervening country. The great Sudbury meadows, looking north, appear elevated. Every blade and leaf has been washed by the rains, and the landscape is indescribably bright. It is light without heat, Septemberish, as if reflected from the earth, such as is common in the fall. The surface of the meadows and the whole earth is like that of a great reflector to the sun, but reflecting his light more than his heat.

It is a glorious and ever-memorable day. We observe attentively the first beautiful days in the spring, but not so much in the autumn. We might expect that the first fair days after so much rain would be remarkable. It is a day affecting the spirits of men, but there is nobody to enjoy it but ourselves. What do the laborer ox and the laborer man care for the beautiful days? Will the haymaker when he comes home to-night know that this has been such a beautiful day? This day itself has been the great phenomenon, but will it be reported in any journal, as the storm is, and the heat? It is like a great and beautiful flower unnamed. I see a man trimming willows on the Sudbury causeway and others raking hay out of the water in the midst of all this clarity and brightness, but are they aware of the splendor of this day? The mass of mankind, who live in houses or shops, or are *bent* upon their labor out of doors, know nothing of the beautiful days which are passing about and around them. Is not such a day worthy of a hymn? It is such a day as mankind might spend in praising and glorifying nature. It might be spent as a natural sabbath, if only all men would accept the hint, devoted to unwordly thoughts. The first bright day of the fall, the earth reflector. The dog-day mists are gone; the washed earth shines; the cooler air braces man. No summer day is so beautiful as the fairest spring and fall days.

Aug. 23. Ripe Purple Poke Stems

POKE STEMS ARE NOW ripe. I walked through a beautiful grove of them, six or seven feet high, on the side of Lee's Cliff, where they have ripened early. Their stems are a deep, rich purple with a bloom, contrasting with the clear green leaves. Every part but the leaves is a brilliant purple (lake (?)-purple); or, more strictly speaking, the racemes without the berries are a brilliant lake-red with crimson flame-like reflections. Hence the *lacca.* Its cylindrical racemes of berries of various hues from green to dark purple, six or seven inches long, are drooping on all sides, beautiful both with and without berries, all afire with ripeness. Its stalks, thus full of purple wine, are one of the fruits of autumn. It excites me to behold it. What a success is its! [sic] What maturity it arrives [at], ripening from leaf to root! May I mature as perfectly, root and branch, as the poke! Its stems are more beautiful than most flowers. It is the emblem of a successful life, a not premature death,—whose death is an ornament to nature. To walk amid these upright branching casks of purple wine, which retain and diffuse a sunset glow, for nature's vintage is not confined to the vine! I drink it with my eyes. Our poets have sung wine, the product of a foreign plant which they never saw, as if our own plants had no juice in them more than our poets. Here are berries enough to paint the western sky with and play the Bacchanal if you will. What flutes its ensanguined stems would make, to be used in the dance! It is a royal plant. I could spend the evening of the year musing amid the poke stems.

Oct. 20. The Great Harvest

I CANNOT EASILY DISMISS the subject of the fallen leaves. How densely they cover and conceal the water for several feet in width, under and amid the alders and button-bushes and maples along the shore of the river,—still light, tight, and dry boats, dense cities of boats, their fibres not relaxed by the waters, undulating and rustling with every wave, of such various pure and delicate, though fading, tints,—of hues that might make the fame of teas,—dried on great Nature's coppers. And then see this great fleet of scattered leaf boats, still tight and dry, each one curled up on every side by the sun's skill, like boats of hide, scarcely moving in the sluggish current,—like the great fleets with which you mingle on entering some great mart, some New York which we are all approaching together. Or else they are slowly moving round in some great eddy which the river makes, where the water is deep and the current is wearing into the bank. How gently each has been deposited on the water! No violence has been used toward them yet. But next the shore, as thick as foam they float, and when you turn your prow that way, list! what a rustling of the crisped waves! Wet grounds about the edges of swamps look dry with them, and many a wet foot you get in consequence.

Consider what a vast crop is thus annually shed upon the earth. This, more than any mere grain or seed, is the great harvest of the year. This annual decay and death, this dying by inches, before the whole tree at last lies down and turns to soil. As trees shed their leaves, so deer their horns, and men their hair or nails. The year's great crop. I am more interested in it than in the English grass alone or in the corn. It prepares the virgin mould for future cornfields on which the earth fattens. They teach us how to die. How many flutterings before they rest quietly in their graves! A myriad wrappers for germinating seeds. By what subtle chemistry they will mount up again, climbing by the sap in the trees. The ground is all parti-colored with them.

Oct. 30. Fall Has Ended

WHAT WITH THE RAINS and frosts and winds, the leaves have fairly fallen now. You may say the fall has ended. Those which still hang on the trees are withered and dry. I am surprised at the change since last Sunday. Looking at the distant woods, I perceive that there is no yellow nor scarlet there now. They are (except the evergreens) a mere dull, dry red. The autumnal tints are gone. What life remains is merely at the foot of the leaf-stalk. The woods have for the most part acquired their winter aspect, and coarse, rustling, light-colored withered grasses skirt the river and the wood-side. This is November. The landscape prepared for winter, without snow. When the forest and fields put on their sober winter hue, we begin to look more to the sunset for color and variety.

Nov. 6. Mingling of Wood and Water

CLIMBED THE WOODED HILL by Holden's spruce swamp and got a novel view of the river and Fair Haven Bay through the almost leafless woods. How much handsomer a river or lake such as ours, seen thus through a foreground of scattered or else partially leafless trees, though at a considerable distance this side of it, especially if the water is open, without wooded shores or isles! It is the most perfect and beautiful of all frames, which yet the sketcher is commonly careful to brush aside. I mean a pretty thick foreground, a view of the distant water through the near forest, through a thousand little vistas, as we are rushing toward the former,—that intimate mingling of wood and water which excites an expectation which the near and open view rarely realizes. We prefer that some part be concealed, which our imagination may navigate.

Nov. 12. My Native Region

I CANNOT BUT REGARD it as a kindness in those who have the steering of me that, by the want of pecuniary wealth, I have been nailed down to this my native region so long and steadily, and made to study and love this spot of earth more and more. What would signify in comparison a thin and diffused love and knowledge of the whole earth instead, got by wandering? The traveller's is but a barren and comfortless condition.

Nov. 22. A Leaf Specimen

I WAS JUST THINKING it would be fine to get a specimen leaf from each changing tree and shrub and plant in autumn, in September and October, when it had got its brightest characteristic color, the intermediate ripeness in its transition from the green to the russet or brown state, outline and copy its color exactly with paint in a book,—a book which should be a memorial of October, be entitled October Hues or Autumnal Tints. I remember especially the beautiful yellow of the *Populus grandidentata* and the tint of the scarlet maple. What a memento such a book would be, beginning with the earliest reddening of the leaves, woodbine and ivy, etc., etc., and the lake of radical leaves, down to the latest oaks! I might get the impression of their veins and outlines in the summer with lampblack, and after color them.

Nov. 30. A Pine Grove

I DO NOT KNOW so fine a pine grove as that of Mason's. The young second-growth white pines are peculiarly soft, thick, and bushy there. They branch directly at the ground and almost horizontally, for the most part four or five large stems springing from the ground together, as if they had been broken down by cattle originally. But the result is a very dark and dense, almost impenetrable, but peculiarly soft and beautiful grove, which any gentleman might covet on his estate.

Nov. 30. Meanders in the Road

WE RETURNED BY THE bridle-road across the pastures. When I returned to town the other night by the Walden road through the meadows from Brister's Hill to the poorhouse, I fell to musing upon the origin of the meanders in the road; for when I looked straight before or behind me, my eye met the fences at a short distance, and it appeared that the road, instead of being built in a straight line across the meadows, as one might have expected, pursued a succession of curves like a cow-path. In fact, it was just such a meandering path as an eye of taste requires, and the landscape-gardener consciously aims to make, and the wonder is that a body of laborers left to themselves, without instruments or geometry, and perchance intending to make a straight road,—in short, that circumstances ordinarily,—will so commonly make just such a meandering road as the eye requires. A man advances in his walk somewhat as a river does, meanderingly, and such, too, is the progress of the race. The law that plants the rushes in waving lines along the edge of a pond, and that curves the pondshore itself, incessantly beats against the straight fences and highways of men and makes them conform to the line of beauty which is most agreeable to the eye at last.

Dec. 11.   Nerves of the Eye Unused

R. W. E. TOLD ME THAT W. H. Channing conjectured that the landscape looked fairer when we turned our heads, because we beheld it with nerves of the eye unused before. Perhaps this reason is worth more for suggestion than explanation. It occurs to me that the reflection of objects in still water is in a similar manner fairer than the substance, and yet we do not employ unused nerves to behold it. Is it not that we let much more light into our eyes,—which in the usual position are shaded by the brows,—in the first case by turning them more to the sky, and in the case of the reflections by having the sky placed under our feet? *i.e.* in both cases we see terrestrial objects with the sky or heavens for a background or field. Accordingly they are not dark and terrene, but lit and elysian.

Dec. 26.   Snow on the Trees

MONDAY. THIS FORENOON IT snowed pretty hard for some hours, the first snow of any consequence thus far. It is about three inches deep. I go out at 2.30, just as it ceases. Now is the time, before the wind rises or the sun has shone, to go forth and see the snow on the trees. The clouds have lifted somewhat, but are still spitting snow a little. The vapor of the steam-engine does not rise high in the misty air. I go around Walden *via* the almshouse. The branches of deciduous trees,—oaks and maples, etc.,—especially the gray oaks of Hubbard's Close on the side-hill, support long lightning-like arms of snow, many times their own thickness. It has fallen so gently that it forms an upright wall on the slenderest twig. The agreeable maze which the branches make is more obvious than ever. And every twig thus laden is as still as the hillside itself. The pitch pines are covered with rich globular masses. The effect of the snow is to press down the forest, confound it with the grasses, and create a new surface to the earth above, shutting us in with it, and we go along somewhat like moles through our galleries. The sight of the pure and trackless road up Brister's Hill, with branches and trees supporting snowy burdens bending over it on each side, would tempt us to begin life again. The ice is covered up, and skating gone. The bare hills are so white that I cannot see their outlines against the misty sky. The snow lies handsomely on the shrub oaks, like a coarse braiding in the air. They have so many small and zigzag twigs that it comes near to filling up with a light snow to that depth. The hunters are already out with dogs to follow the first beast that makes a track.

CHAPTER VI

YEAR
1854
AGE
36-37

Jan. 7.　Winter Observations

P.M.—TO MINISTERIAL SWAMP.

The bare larch trees there, so slender and tall, where they grow close together, all beaded or studded with buds, or rather stubs, which look like the dry sterile blossoms. How much fuller, or denser and more flourishing, in winter is the white spruce than the white pine! It has two hues, I believe, the glaucous or bluish and the green, melting into each other. It has not shed all its seeds yet. Now that the snow has lain more than a week, it begins to be spotted and darkened in the woods, with various dry leaves and scales from the trees. The wind and thaw have brought down a fresh crop of dry pine and spruce needles. The little roundish and stemmed scales of the alder catkins spot it thickly. The bird-shaped scales of the white birch are blown more than twenty rods from the trees. I see also the wings of pine seeds,—the seed being gone,—which look exactly like the wings of ants. Also, in the pastures, the fine star-shaped fuzz of the gray goldenrod, somewhat like a spider with many legs.

Jan. 8. Art of Sketching Landscape

SUNDAY. GILPIN, IN HIS essay on the "ART OF SKETCHING LANDSCAPE," says: "When you have finished your sketch therefore with Indian ink, as far as you propose, tinge the whole over with some light horizon hue. It may be the rosy tint of morning; or the more ruddy one of evening; or it may incline more to a yellowish, or a greyish cast. . . . By washing this tint over your *whole drawing,* you lay a foundation for harmony."

I have often been attracted by this harmonious tint in his and other drawings, and sometimes, especially, have observed it in nature when at sunset I inverted my head. We love not so well the landscape represented as in broad noon, but in a morning or evening twilight, those seasons when the imagination is most active, the more hopeful or pensive seasons of the day. Our mood may then possess the whole landscape, or be in harmony with it, as the hue of twilight prevails over the whole scene. Are we more than crepuscular in our intellectual and spiritual life? Have we awakened to broad noon? The morning hope is soon lost in what becomes the routine of the day, and we do not recover ourselves again until we land on the pensive shores of evening, shores which skirt the great western continent of the night. At sunset we look into the west.

Young White Spruce.

Jan. 8. The White Spruce

THE LOWER TWO-THIRDS OF the white spruce has its branches retraced or turned downward, and then curving upward at the extremities, as much as the white pine commonly slants upwards. Above it is so thick that you cannot see through it.

Jan. 31. I Go A-Budding

THE PITCH PINES ARE yellowish, the white incline to bluish. In the winter, when there are no flowers and leaves are rare, even large buds are interesting and somewhat exciting. I go a-budding like a partridge. I am always attracted at this season by the buds of the swamp-pink, the poplars, and the sweet-gale.

Jan. 31. Winter Thoughts

WE TOO HAVE OUR thaws. They come to our January moods, when our ice cracks, and our sluices break loose. Thought that was frozen up under stern experience gushes forth in feeling and expression. There is a freshet which carries away dams of accumulated ice. Our thoughts hide unexpressed, like the buds under their downy or resinous scales; they would hardly keep a partridge from starving. If you would know what are my winter thoughts look for them in the partridge's crop. They are like the laurel buds,—some leaf, some blossom buds,—which, though food for such indigenous creatures, will not expand into leaves and flowers until summer comes.

Feb. 3. The Hollowell Farm

THE ATTRACTIONS OF THE Hollowell Farm were: its complete retirement, being at least two miles from the village, half a mile from any neighbor, and separated from the highway by a broad field; its bounding on the river; the pleasing ruin of the house and barn; the hollow and lichen-covered apple trees gnawed by rabbits; above all the recollection I had of it from my earliest voyages up the river, when the house was concealed behind a dense grove of red maples, which then stood between it and the river, through which I once heard the house-dog bark; and in general the slight improvements that had been made upon it. These were the motives that swayed, though I did not mention them to the proprietor. To enjoy these things I was ready to carry it on and do all those things which I now see had no other motive or excuse but that I might pay for it and be unmolested in my possession of it; though I knew all the while that it would yield the most abundant crop of the kind I wanted if I could only afford to let it alone. Though it afforded no western prospect, the dilapidated fences were picturesque. I was in some haste to buy, before the proprietor finished getting out some rocks, cutting down some hollow apple trees, and grubbing up some young birches which had sprung up in the pasture, all which in my eyes very much enhanced its value.

Feb. 5. A True Expression

I FEAR ONLY LEST my expressions may not be extravagant enough,—may not wander far enough beyond the narrow limits of our ordinary insight and faith, so as to be adequate to the truth of which I have been convinced. I desire to speak somewhere without bounds, in order that I may attain to an expression in some degree adequate to truth of which I have been convinced. From a man in a waking moment, to men in their waking moments. Wandering toward the more distant boundaries of a wider pasture. Nothing is so truly bounded and obedient to law as music, yet nothing so surely breaks all petty and narrow bonds. Whenever I hear any music I fear that I may have spoken tamely and within bounds. And I am convinced that I cannot exaggerate enough even to lay the foundation of a true expression. As for books and the adequateness of their statements to the truth, they are as the tower of Babel to the sky.

Feb. 12. A Little Hollow

HERE IS A LITTLE hollow which, for a short time every spring, gives passage to the melting snow, and it was consequently wet there late into the spring. I remember well when a few little alder bushes, encouraged by the moisture, first sprang up in it. They now make a perfect little grove, fifteen feet high, and maybe half a dozen rods long, with a rounded outline, as if they were one mass of moss, with the wrecks of ferns in their midst and the sweet-fern about its edge. And so, perchance, a swamp is beginning to be formed. The shade and the decaying vegetation may at last produce a spongy soil, which will supply a constant rill. Has not something like this been the history of the alder swamp and brook a little further along? True, the first is on a small scale and rather elevated, part way up the hill; and ere long trout begin to glance in the brook, where first was merely a course for melted snow which turned the dead grass-blades all one way,—which combed the grassy tresses down the hill.

Feb. 19. Lichens and Print

MUCH STUDY A WEARINESS of the flesh, eh? But did not they intend that we should read and ponder, who covered the whole earth with alphabets,—primers or bibles,—coarse or fine print? The very débris of the cliffs—the stivers [?] of the rocks—are covered with geographic lichens: no surface is permitted to be bare long. As by an inevitable decree, we have come to times at last when our very waste paper is printed. Was not He who creates lichens the abettor of Cadmus when he invented letters? Types almost arrange themselves into words and sentences as dust arranges itself under the magnet. Print! it is a closehugging lichen that forms on a favorable surface, which paper offers. The linen gets itself wrought into paper that the song of the shirt may be printed on it. Who placed us with eyes between a microscopic and a telescopic world?

Feb. 22. Fungus Covered Stump

SAW IN SLEEPY HOLLOW a small hickory stump, about six inches in diameter and six inches high, so completely, regularly, and beautifully covered by that winkle-like fungus in concentric circles and successive layers that the core was concealed and you would have taken it for some cabbage-like plant. This was the way the wound was healed. The cut surface of the stump was completely and thickly covered.

April 8. New Points of View

I FIND THAT I can criticise my composition best when I stand at a little distance from it,—when I do not see it, for instance. I make a little chapter of contents which enables me to recall it page by page to my mind, and judge it more impartially when my manuscript is out of the way. The distraction of surveying enables me rapidly to take new points of view. A day or two surveying is equal to a journey.

May 6. How Far You Travel

P.M.—TO EPIGÆA *VIA* CLAMSHELL HILL.

There is no such thing as pure *objective* observation. Your observation, to be interesting, *i. e.* to be significant, must be *subjective.* The sum of what the writer of whatever class has to report is simply some human experience, whether he be poet or philosopher or man of science. The man of most science is the man most alive, whose life is the greatest event. Senses that take cognizance of outward things merely are of no avail. It matters not where or how far you travel,—the farther commonly the worse,—but how much alive you are. If it is possible to conceive of an event outside to humanity, it is not of the slightest significance, though it were the explosion of a planet. Every important worker will report what life there is in him. It makes no odds into what seeming deserts the poet is born. Though all his neighbors pronounce it a Sahara, it will be a paradise to him; for the desert which we see is the result of the barrenness of our experience.

May 22. Earth a Paradise

I REST IN THE orchard, doubtful whether to sit in shade or sun. Now the springing foliage is like a sunlight on the woods. I was first attracted and surprised when I looked round and off to Conantum, at the smooth, lawn-like green fields and pasturing cows, bucolical, reminding me of new butter. The air so clear—as not in summer—makes all things shine, as if all surfaces had been washed by the rains of spring and were not yet soiled or begrimed or dulled. You see even to the mountains clearly. The grass so short and fresh, the tender yellowish-green and silvery foliage of the deciduous trees lighting up the landscape, the birds now most musical, the sorrel beginning to redden the fields with ruddy health,—all these things make earth now a paradise. How many times I have been surprised thus, on turning about on this very spot, at the fairness of the earth!

July 18.   Up-Country Eden

I FOUND SO MANY berries on that rocky road, between and about the careless farmers' houses and walls, that the soil seemed more fertile than where I live. Every bush and bramble bears its fruit; the sides of the road are a fruit garden; blackberries, huckleberries, thimbleberries, fresh and abundant, no signs of drought; all fruits in abundance; the earth teems. What are the virtues of the inhabitants that they are thus blessed? Do the rocks hold moisture, or are there no fingers to pluck them? I seem to have wandered into a land of greater fertility, some up-country Eden. Are not these the delectable hills? It is a land flowing with milk and honey. Great shining blackberries peep out at me from under the leaves upon the rocks. There the herbage never withers. There are abundant dews.

July 26.   Lately Shorn Fields

ONE REASON WHY THE lately shorn fields shine so and reflect so much light is that a lighter-colored and tender grass, which has been shaded by the crop taken off, is now exposed, and also a light and fresh grass is springing up there. Yet I think it is not wholly on this account, but in a great measure owing to a clearer air after rains which have succeeded to misty weather. I am going over the hill through Ed. Hosmer's orchard, when I observe this light reflected from the shorn fields, contrasting affectingly with the dark smooth Assabet, reflecting the now dark shadows of the woods. The fields reflect light quite to the edge of the stream. The peculiarity of the stream is in a certain languid or stagnant smoothness of the water, and of the bordering woods in a dog-day density of shade reflected darkly in the water. Alternate cornel berries, a day or two.

Aug. 9.   "Walden" Published

WEDNESDAY.— TO BOSTON.
   "Walden" published. Elder-berries. Waxwork yellowing.

*Evening reflections by the shore of Walden Pond
and cove near the site of Thoreau's cabin,
Concord, Massachusetts.*

Aug. 14. To Float a Stream

I NOW, STANDING ON the shore, see that in sailing or floating down a smooth stream at evening it is an advantage to the fancy to be thus slightly separated from the land. It is to be slightly removed from the commonplace of earth. To float thus on the silver-plated stream is like embarking on a train of thought itself. You are surrounded by water, which is full of reflections; and you see the earth at a distance, which is very agreeable to the imagination.

Aug. 15. Terrace Above Terrace

LOOKING FROM THIS STRAWBERRY Hill to the long range behind William Brown's, northeast by east, I see that it and other hills are marked finely by many parallel lines, apparently the edges of so many terraces, arranging the crops and trees in dark lines, as if they were the traces of so many lake-shores. Methinks this is an almost universal phenomenon. When farthest inland we are surrounded by countless shores or beaches, terrace above terrace. It is the parallelism of green trees, bushes, and crops which betrays them at a distance.

Aug. 19. The Dog-Days

P.M.—TO FLINT'S POND *VIA* railroad with Mr. Loomis.
  The hills and fields generally have such a russet, withered, wintry look that the meadows by the railroad appear to have got an exceedingly fresh and tender green.

The near meadow is very beautiful now, seen from the railroad through this dog-day haze, which softens to velvet its fresh green of so many various shades, blending them harmoniously,—darker and lighter patches of grass and the very light yellowish-green of the sensitive fern which the mowers have left. It has an indescribable beauty to my eye now, which it could not have in a clear day. The haze has the effect both of a wash or varnish and of a harmonizing tint. It destroys the idea of definite distance which distinctness suggests. It is as if you had painted a meadow of fresh grass springing up after the mower,—here a dark green, there lighter, and there again the yellowish onoclea,—then washed it over with some gum like a map and tinted the paper of a fine misty blue. This is an effect of the dog-days.

Aug. 22. Direction of a Walk

WALKING MAY BE A science, so far as the direction of a walk is concerned. I go again to the Great Meadows, to improve this remarkably dry season and walk where in ordinary times I cannot go. There is, no doubt, a particular season of the year when each place may be visited with most profit and pleasure, and it may be worth the while to consider what that season is in each case.

Sept. 7. Double Sunset

IT IS JUST AFTER sundown. The moon not yet risen, one star, Jupiter (?), visible, and many bats over and about our heads, and small skaters creating a myriad dimples on the evening waters. We see a muskrat crossing, and pass a white cat on the shore. There are many clouds about and a beautiful sunset sky, a yellowish (dunnish?) golden sky, between them in the horizon, looking up the river. All this is reflected in the water. The beauty of the sunset is doubled by the reflection. Being on the water we have double the amount of lit and dun-colored sky above and beneath. An elm in the yellow twilight looks very rich, as if moss- or ivy-clad, and a dark-blue cloud extends into the dun-golden sky, on which there is a little fantastic cloud like a chicken walking up the point of it, with its neck outstretched. The reflected sky is more dun and richer than the real one. Take a glorious sunset sky and double it, so that it shall extend downward beneath the horizon as much as above it, blotting out the earth, and [let] the lowest half be of the deepest tint, and every beauty more than before insisted on, and you seem withal to be floating directly into it. This seems the first autumnal sunset. The small skaters seem more active than by day, or their slight dimpling is more obvious in the lit twilight. A stray white cat sits on the shore looking over the water. This is her hour. A nighthawk dashes past, low over the water. This is what we had.

Sept. 7. To Hear and See at Night

NIGHT IS THE TIME to hear; our ears took in every sound from the meadows and the village. At first we were disturbed by the screeching of the locomotive and rumbling of the cars, but soon were left to the fainter natural sounds,—the creaking of the crickets, and the little *Rana palustris* (I am not sure that I heard it the latter part of the evening), and the shrilling of other crickets (?), the occasional faint lowing of a cow and the distant barking of dogs, as in a whisper. Our ears drank in every sound. I heard once or twice a dumping frog. This was while we lay off Nut Meadow Brook waiting for the moon to rise. She burned her way slowly through the small but thick clouds, and, as fast as she triumphed over them and rose over them, they appeared pale and shrunken, like the ghosts of their former selves. Meanwhile we measured the breadth of the clear cope over our heads, which she would ere long traverse, and, while she was concealed, looked up to the few faint stars in the zenith which is ever lighted. C. thought that these few faint lights in the ever-lit sky, whose inconceivable distance was enhanced by a few downy wisps of cloud, surpassed any scene that earth could show.

Sept. 14. Looming Pines

THE SUN SOON AFTER rising has gone into a mackerel sky this morning, and, as I come down the hill, I observe a singular mirage (?). There is a large dense field of mackerel sky with a straight and distinct edge parallel with the southeast horizon and lifted above it, apparently about double the height of the highest hills there; beneath this a clear sky, and lower still some level bars of mist, which cut off the top of Pine Hill, causing it to loom. The top, fringed with pines on account of the intervening lower mist, is seen as it were above the clouds, appears much too high, being referred to a far greater distance than the reality. Our humble scenery appears on a grand scale. I see the fair forms of mighty pines standing along a mountain ridge above the clouds and overlooking from a vast distance our low valley. I think that the image is not really elevated, but the bars of mist below make me refer it to too great a distance and therefore it is seen as higher. The appearance of those fine-edged pines, a narrow strip of a mountain ridge half a mile in length, is stupendous and imposing. It is as if we lived in a valley amid the Himmalaya Mountains, a vale of Cashmere.

Sept. 21. Insect Damaged Leaves

I AM SURPRISED TO see how many leaves in the woods have been apparently eaten through on the edges by some insect, leaving only a faded network of veins there, contrasting with the green centres. In some places almost every leaf of the young white oaks (and black or shrub oak) and chestnuts has this very handsome and regular pale edging as of lace-work. It is about one twelfth of an inch in diameter, and is exceedingly regular, following strictly the outline of the leaf, however cut or lobed, by nature or accident, and preserving the same width. As these leaves (of young oaks, etc.) are commonly several together in one plane disposed ray-wise,—rosettes,—the effect of this edging is enhanced. These young leaves are still of a clear and delicate and now somewhat precious green. The extreme edge is left firm and entire, and the pulp of the leaf is eaten through only just within it.

Sept. 22. Lesson by Moonlight

BY MOONLIGHT ALL IS simple. We are enabled to erect ourselves, our minds, on account of the fewness of objects. We are no longer distracted. It is simple as bread and water. It is simple as the rudiments of an art,—a lesson to be taken before sunlight, perchance, to prepare us for that.

Sept. 24. A Fall Aspect

THE FIRST FALL IS so gradual as not to make much impression, but the last suddenly and conspicuously gives a fall aspect to the scenery of the river. The button-bushes thus withered, covered still with the gray, already withered mikania, suddenly paint with a rich brown the river's brim. It is like the crust, the edging, of a boy's turnover done brown. And the black willows, slightly faded and crisped with age or heat, enhance my sense of the year's maturity. There, where the land appears to lap over the water by a mere edging, these thinner portions are first done brown. I float over the still liquid middle.

Sept. 24. A Changing Sunset

THERE WAS A SPLENDID sunset while I was on the water, beginning at the Clamshell reach. All the lower edge of a very broad dark-slate cloud which reached up backward almost to the zenith was lit up through and through with a dun golden fire, the sun being below the horizon, like a furze plain densely on fire, a short distance above the horizon, for there was a clear, pale robin's-egg sky beneath, and some little clouds on which the light fell high in the sky but nearer, seen against the upper part of the distant uniform dark-slate one, were of a fine grayish silver color, with fine mother-o'-pearl tints unusual at sunset (?). The furze gradually burnt out on the lower edge of the cloud, changed into a smooth, hard pale pink vermilion, which gradually faded into a gray satiny pearl, a fine Quaker-color. All these colors were prolonged in the rippled reflection to five or six times their proper length. The effect was particularly remarkable in the case of the reds, which were long bands of red perpendicular in the water.

The Sudbury River near Concord, Massachusetts.

Sept. 26. Along the Riverside

IT IS A WARM and very pleasant afternoon, and I walk along the riverside in Merrick's pasture. I hear a faint jingle from some sparrows on the willows, etc.,—tree or else song sparrows. Many swamp white oak acorns have turned brown on the trees. Some single red maples are very splendid now, the whole tree bright-scarlet against the cold green pines; now, when very few trees are changed, a most remarkable object in the landscape; seen a mile off. It is too fair to be believed, especially seen against the light.

Sept. 30. Acorn of Art

THE CONVENTIONAL ACORN OF art is of course of no particular species, but the artist might find it worth his while to study Nature's varieties again.

Dec. 21. The Finest Days

WE ARE TEMPTED TO call these the finest days of the year. Take Fair Haven Pond, for instance, a perfectly level plain of white snow, untrodden as yet by any fisherman, surrounded by snow-clad hills, dark evergreen woods, and reddish oak leaves, so pure and still. The last rays of the sun falling on the Baker Farm reflect a clear pink color. I see the feathers of a partridge strewn along on the snow a long distance, the work of some hawk perhaps, for there is no track

CHAPTER VII

YEAR
1855
AGE
37–38

Feb. 19. My Lectures

MANY WILL COMPLAIN OF my lectures that they are transcendental. "Can't understand them." "Would you have us return to the savage state?" etc., etc. A criticism true enough, it may be, from their point of view. But the fact is, the earnest lecturer can speak only to his like, and the adapting of himself to his audience is a mere compliment which he pays them. If you wish to know how I think, you must endeavor to put yourself in my place. If you wish me to speak as if I were you, that is another affair.

Oct. 18. Some Path, However Narrow

PURSUE SOME PATH, HOWEVER narrow and crooked, in which you can walk with love and reverence. Wherever a man separates from the multitude and goes his own way, there is a fork in the road, though the travellers along the highway see only a gap in the paling.

Oct. 18. Beauty in Decay

HOW MUCH BEAUTY IN decay! I pick up a white oak leaf, dry and stiff, but yet mingled red and green, October-like, whose pulpy part some insect has eaten beneath, exposing the delicate network of its veins. It is very beautiful held up to the light,—such work as only an insect eye could perform. Yet, perchance, to the vegetable kingdom such a revelation of ribs is as replusive as the skeleton in the animal kingdom. In each case it is some little gourmand, working for another end, that reveals the wonders of nature. There are countless oak leaves in this condition now, and also with a submarginal line of network exposed.

Oct. 21. Handsome Wild Apples

ALMOST ALL WILD APPLES are handsome. Some are knurly and peppered all over or on the stem side with fine crimson spots on a yellowish-white ground; others have crimson blotches or eyes, more or less confluent and fiery when wet,—for apples, like shells and pebbles, are handsomest in a wet day. Taken from under the tree on the damp sward, they shrivel and fade. Some have these spots beneath a reddened surface with obscure rays. Others have hundreds of fine blood-red rays, running regularly, though broken, from the stem dimple to the blossom, like meridian lines, on a straw-colored ground,—perfect spheres. Others are a deep, dark red, with very obscure yet darker rays; others a uniform clear, bright red, approaching to scarlet.

Oct. 22. Shrubs in Autumn Color

I THINK THAT THE trees generally have not worn very brilliant colors this month, but I find to-day that many small shrubs which have been protected by the forest are remarkably fair and bright. They, perhaps, have not felt the drought nor been defaced by insects. They are the best preserved and the most delicately tinted. I see the maple viburnum leaves a dark, dull spotted crimson toward the edges, like some wild apples. I distinguish it from the red maple at first only by its downy feeling beneath and the simple form of some leaves. These have also a short petiole and not a sharp sinus. Then there is the more or less crimson *nudum* viburnum, passing from scarlet through crimson to black-spotted and crimson in its decay. The blackness spreads very fast in one night. The glossy scarlet blueber

ries and the redder huckleberries; the scarlet choke-berry, or vermilion; some red
maples which are yellow with only scarlet eyes. But still, in the shade and shelter
of the woods as fair as anything, the leaves of the wild cherry, so clear of injury
from insects, passing from green through yellow or a cherry red to the palest and
purest imaginable cherry-color, the palest fawn with a mere tinge of cherry, with
their fine overlapping serrations. Those great twisted yellow leaves of hickory
sprouts, yellow and green, from which I used to drink. And here is a very handsome orange-red high blackberry leaf, with its five leafets all perfect; most are
dark-red. But all these, like shells and pebbles must be seen on their own seashore.
There are two seasons when the leaves are in their glory, their green and perfect
youth in June and this their ripe old age. Some of the very young oak leaves have
the deepest lustreless or inward scarlet of any. Most of the reddish oak leaves now
in the woods are spotted, mildewed as it were, by the drip from above.

Oct. 22.   Some Brilliant Leaves

THE STREETS ARE STREWN with buttonwood leaves, which rustle under
your feet, and the children are busy raking them into heaps, some for bonfires.
The large elms are bare; not yet the buttonwoods. The sugar maples on the
Common stand dense masses of rich yellow leaves with a deep scarlet blush,—far
more than blush. They are remarkably brilliant this year on the exposed surfaces.
The last are as handsome as any trees in the street. I am struck with the handsome
form and clear, though very pale, say lemon, yellow of the black birch leaves on
sprouts in the woods, finely serrate and distinctly *plaited* from the midrib. I
plucked three leaves from the end of a red maple shoot, an underwood, each
successively smaller than the last, the brightest and clearest scarlet that I ever saw.
These and the birch attracted universal admiration when laid on a sheet of white
paper and passed round the supper table, and several inquired particularly where
I found them. I never saw such colors painted. They were without spot; ripe
leaves. The small willows two or three feet high by the roadside in woods have
some rich, deep chrome-yellow leaves with a gloss. The sprouts are later to ripen
and richer-colored.

Oct. 23.   Stone Cast Against Trees

NOW IS THE TIME for chestnuts. A stone cast against the trees shakes them
down in showers upon one's head and shoulders. But I cannot excuse myself for
using the stone. It is not innocent, it is not just, so to maltreat the tree that feeds
us. I am not disturbed by considering that if I thus shorten its life I shall not enjoy
its fruit so long, but am prompted to a more innocent course by motives purely
of humanity. I sympathize with the tree, yet I heaved a big stone against the
trunks like a robber,—not too good to commit murder. I trust that I shall never
do it again. These gifts should be accepted, not merely with gentleness, but with
a certain humble gratitude. The tree whose fruit we would obtain should not be

too rudely shaken even. It is not a time of distress, when a little haste and violence even might be pardoned. It is worse than boorish, it is criminal, to inflict an unnecessary injury on the tree that feeds or shadows us. Old trees are our parents and our parents' parents, perchance. If you would learn the secrets of Nature, you must practice more humanity than others. The thought that I was robbing myself by injuring the tree did not occur to me, but I was affected as if I had cast a rock at a sentient being,—with a duller sense than my own, it is true, but yet a distant relation. Behold a man cutting down a tree to come at the fruit! What is the moral of such an act?

Oct. 24. Rain-Downed Leaves

RAINED LAST NIGHT AND all this day for the most part, bringing down the leaves, buttonwoods and sugar maples, in the street. The rich yellow and scarlet leaves of the sugar maple on the Common, which now thickly cover the grass in great circles about the trees, half having fallen, look like the reflection of the trees in water, and light up the Common, reflecting light even to the surrounding houses. The gentle touch of the rain brings down more leaves than the wind.

Oct. 27. Wild Apples for the Walker

I TRY ONE OF the wild apples in my desk. It is remarkable that the wild apples which I praise as so spirited and racy when eaten in the fields and woods when brought into the house have a harsh and crabbed taste. As shells and pebbles must be beheld on the seashore, so these October fruits must be tasted in a bracing walk amid the somewhat bracing airs of late October. To appreciate their wild and sharp flavors, it seems necessary that you be breathing the sharp October or November air. The outdoor air and exercise which the walker gets give a different tone to his palate, and he craves a fruit which the sedentary would call harsh and crabbed even. The palate rejects a wild apple eaten in the house—so of haws and acorns—and demands a tamed one, for here you miss that October air which is the wine it is eaten with. I frequently pluck wild apples of so rich and spicy a flavor that I wonder all orchardists do not get a scion from them, but when I have brought home my pockets full, and taste them in the house, they are unexpectedly harsh, crude things. They must be eaten in the fields, when your system is all aglow with exercise, the frosty weather nips your fingers (in November), the wind rattles the bare boughs and rustles the leaves, and the jay is heard screaming around.

So there is one thought for the field, another for the house. I would have my thoughts, like wild apples, to be food for walkers, and will not warrant them to be palatable if tasted in the house.

To appreciate the flavor of those wild apples requires vigorous and healthy senses, papillæ firm and erect on the tongue and palate, not easily tamed and flattened. Some of those apples might be labelled, "To be eaten in the wind."

Oct. 29.   Farmer Neglected Apples

THERE IS A WILD apple on the hill which has to me a peculiarly pleasant bitter tang, not perceived till it is three quarters tasted. It remains on the tongue. As you cut it, it smells exactly like a squash-bug. I like its very acerbity. It is a sort of triumph to eat and like it, an ovation. In the fields alone are the sours and bitters of nature appreciated; just as the woodchopper eats his meal in a sunny glade in middle of a winter day, with contentment, in a degree of cold which, experienced in the house, would make the student miserable,—basks in a sunny ray and dreams of summer, in a degree of cold which, felt in a chamber, would make a student wretched. They who are abroad at work are not cold; it is they who sit shivering in houses. As with cold and heat, so with sweet and sour. This natural raciness, sours and bitters, etc., which the diseased palate refuses, are the true casters and condiments. What is sour in the house a bracing walk makes sweet. Let your condiments be in the condition of your senses. Apples which the farmer neglects and leaves out as unsalable, and unpalatable to those who frequent the markets, are choicest fruit to the walker. When the leaves fall, the whole earth is a cemetery pleasant to walk in. I love to wander and muse over them in their graves, returning to dust again. Here are no lying nor vain epitaphs. The scent of their decay is pleasant to me. I buy no lot in the cemetery which my townsmen have just *consecrated* with a poem and an auction, paying so much for a choice. *Here* is room enough for me. The swamp white oak has a fine, firm, leathery leaf with a silver under side, half of them now turned up. Oaks are now fairly brown; very few still red. Water milkweed discounts.

Nov. 1.   Indian-Summer Day

THURSDAY. P.M.—UP ASSABET, a-wooding.

After a rain-threatening morning it is a beautiful Indian-summer day, the most remarkable hitherto and equal to any of the kind. Yet we kept fires in the forenoon, the warmth not having got into the house. It is akin to sin to spend such a day in the house. The air is still and warm. This, too, is the *recovery* of the year,—as if the year, having nearly or quite accomplished its work, and abandoned all design, were in a more favorable and poetic mood, and thought rushed in to fill the vacuum.

Nov. 7.   Open to Impressions

I FIND IT GOOD to be out this still, dark, mizzling afternoon; my walk or voyage is more suggestive and profitable than in bright weather. The view is contracted by the misty rain, the water is perfectly smooth, and the stillness is favorable to reflection. I am more open to impressions, more sensitive (not calloused or indurated by sun and wind), as if in a chamber still. My thoughts are concentrated; I am all compact. The solitude is real, too, for the weather keeps other men at home. This mist is like a roof and walls over and around, and I walk with a domestic feeling. The sound of a wagon going over an unseen bridge is louder than ever, and so of other sounds. I am *compelled* to look at near objects. All things have a soothing effect; the very clouds and mists brood over me. My power of observation and contemplation is much increased. My attention does not wander. The world and my life are simplified. What now of Europe and Asia?

Dec. 11. Eternal Beauty of Nature

IF ANY PART OF nature excites our pity, it is for ourselves we grieve, for there is eternal health and beauty. We get only transient and partial glimpses of the beauty of the world. Standing at the right angle, we are dazzled by the colors of the rainbow in colorless ice. From the right point of view, every storm and every drop in it is a rainbow. Beauty and music are not mere traits and exceptions. They are the rule and character. It is the exception that we see and hear. Then I try to discover what it was in the vision that charmed and translated me. What if we could daguerreotype our thoughts and feelings! for I am surprised and enchanted often by some quality which I cannot detect. I have seen an attribute of another world and condition of things. It is a wonderful fact that I should be affected, and thus deeply and powerfully, more than by aught else in all my experience,—that this fruit should be borne in me, sprung from a seed finer than the spores of fungi, floated from other atmospheres! finer than the dust caught in the sails of vessels a thousand miles from land! Here the invisible seeds settle, and spring, and bear flowers and fruits of immortal beauty.

Dec. 14. A Hemlock in Winter

HOW SNUG AND WARM a hemlock looks in the winter! That by the azalea looks thus: There is a tendency in the limbs to arrange themselves ray-wise about a regular- point one third from the base to the top. What singular ity in the outline of a tree!

Dec. 16. Revelations in the Mist

STEADY, GENTLE, WARM RAIN all the forenoon, and mist and mizzling in the afternoon, when I go round by Abel Hosmer's and back by the railroad.

The mist makes the near trees dark and noticeable, like pictures, and makes the houses more interesting, revealing but one at a time. The old apple trees are very important to this landscape, they have so much body and are so dark. It is very pleasing to distinguish the dim outline of the woods, more or less distant, through the mist, sometimes the merest film and suspicion of a wood. On one side it is the plump and rounded but soft masses of pitch pines, on another the brushy tops of maples, birches, etc. Going by Hosmer's, the very heaps of stones in the pasture are obvious as cairns in one of Ossian's landscapes.

Dec. 23. Old Root Fences

I ADMIRE THOSE OLD root fences which have almost entirely disappeared from tidy fields,—white pine roots got out when the neighboring meadow was a swamp,—the monuments of many a revolution. These roots have not penetrated into the ground, but spread over the surface, and, having been cut off four or five feet from the stump, were hauled off and set up on their edges for a fence. The roots are not merely interwoven, but grown together into solid frames, full of loopholes like Gothic windows of various sizes and all shapes, triangular and oval and harp-like, and the slenderer parts are dry and resonant like harp-strings. They are rough and unapproachable, with a hundred snags and horns which bewilder and balk the calculation of the walker who would surmount them. The part of the trees above ground presents no such fantastic forms. Here is one seven paces, or more than a rod, long, six feet high in the middle, and yet only one foot thick, and two men could turn it up, and in this case the roots were six or nine inches thick at the extremities. The roots of pines growing in swamps grow thus in the form of solid frames or rackets, and those of different trees are interwoven with all so that they stand on a very broad foot and stand or fall together to some extent before the blasts, as herds meet the assault of beasts of prey with serried front. You have thus only to dig into the swamp a little way to find your fence,—post, rails, and slats already solidly grown together and of material more durable than any timber. How pleasing a thought that a field should be fenced with the roots of the trees got out in clearing the land a century before! I regret them as mementoes of the primitive forest. The tops of the same trees made into fencing-stuff would have decayed generations ago. These roots are singularly unobnoxious to the effects of moisture.

Dec. 23. Colors of the Earth

I SIT ON THE hillside near the wall corner, in the further Conantum field, as I might in an Indian-summer day in November or October. These are the colors of the earth now: all land that has been some time cleared, except it is subject to the plow, is russet, the color of withered herbage and the ground finely commixed, a lighter straw-color where are rank grasses next water; sprout-lands, the pale leather-color of dry oak leaves; pine woods, green; deciduous woods (bare twigs and stems and withered leaves commingled), a brownish or reddish gray; maple swamps, smoke-color; land just cleared, dark brown and earthy; plowed land, dark brown or blackish; ice and water, slate-color or blue; andromeda swamps, dull red and dark gray; rocks, gray.

Chapter VIII

Year
1856
Age
38–39

Jan. 22. The Venerable Old Elm

MOST WERE NOT AWARE of the size of the great elm till it was cut down. I surprised some a few days ago by saying that when its trunk should lie prostrate it would be higher than the head of the tallest man in the town, and that two such trunks could not stand in the chamber we were then in, which was fifteen feet across; that there would be ample room for a double bedstead on the trunk, nay, that the very dinner-table we were sitting at, with our whole party of seven, chairs and all, around it, might be set there. On the decayed part of the butt end there were curious fine black lines, giving it a geographical look, here and there, half a dozen inches long, sometimes following the line of the rings; the boundary of a part which had reached a certain stage of decay. The force on the pulleys broke off more than a foot in width in the middle of the tree, much decayed.

I have attended the felling and, so to speak, the funeral of this old citizen of the town,—I who commonly do not attend funerals,—as it became me to do. I was the chief if not the only mourner there. I have taken the measure of his grandeur; have spoken a few words of eulogy at his grave, remembering the maxim *de mortuis nil nisi bonum* (in this case *magnum*). But there were only the choppers and the passers-by to hear me. Further the town was not represented; the fathers of the town, the selectmen, the clergy were not there. But I have not known a fitter occasion for a sermon of late. Travellers whose journey was for a short time delayed by its prostrate body were forced to pay it some attention and respect, but the axe-boys had climbed upon it like ants, and commenced chipping at it before it had fairly ceased groaning. There was a man already bargaining for some part. How have the mighty fallen! Its history extends back over more than half the whole history of the town. Since its kindred could not conveniently attend, I attended. Methinks its fall marks an epoch in the history of the town. It has passed away together with the clergy of the old school and the stage-coach which used to rattle beneath it. Its virtue was that it steadily grew and expanded from year to year to the very last. How much of old Concord falls with it! The town clerk will not chronicle its fall. I will, for it is of greater moment to the town than that of many a human inhabitant would be. Instead of erecting a monument to it, we take all possible pains to obliterate its stump, the only monument of a tree which is commonly allowed to stand. Another link that bound us to the past is broken. How much of old Concord was cut away with it! A few such elms would alone constitute a township. They might claim to send a representative to the General Court to look after their interests, if a fit one could be found, a native American one in a true and worthy sense, with catholic principles. Our town has lost some of its venerableness. No longer will our eyes rest on its massive gray trunk, like a vast Corinthian column by the wayside; no longer shall we walk in the shade of its lofty, spreading dome. It is as if you had laid the axe at the feet of some venerable Buckley or Ripley. You have laid the axe, you have made fast your tackle, to one of the king-posts of the town. I feel the whole building wracked by it. Is it not sacrilege to cut down the tree which has so long looked over Concord beneficently?

Supposing the first fifteen feet to average six feet in diameter, they would contain more than three cords and a foot of wood; but probably not more than three cords.

With what feelings should not the citizens hear that the biggest tree in the town has fallen! A traveller passed through the town and saw the inhabitants cutting it up without regret.

Jan. 24.   Stately Elms

I HAVE SEEN MANY a collection of stately elms which better deserved to be represented at the General Court than the manikins beneath,—than the barroom and victualling cellar and groceries they overshadowed. When I see their magnificent domes, miles away in the horizon, over intervening valleys and forests, they suggest a village, a community, there. But, after all, it is a secondary consideration whether there are human dwellings beneath them; these may have long since passed away. I find that into my idea of the village has entered more of the elm than of the human being. They are worth many a political borough. They constitute a borough. The poor human representative of his party sent out from beneath their shade will not suggest a tithe of the dignity, the true nobleness and comprehensiveness of view, the sturdiness and independence, and the serene beneficence that they do. They look from township to township. A fragment of their bark is worth the backs of all the politicians in the union. They are free-soilers in their own broad sense. They send their roots north and south and east and west into many a conservative's Kansas and Carolina, who does not suspect such underground railroads,—they improve the subsoil he has never disturbed,—and many times their length, if the support of their principles requires it. They battle with the tempests of a century. See what scars they bear, what limbs they lost before we were born! Yet they never adjourn; they steadily vote for their principles, and send their roots further and wider from the *same centre.* They die at their posts, and they leave a tough butt for the choppers to exercise themselves about, and a stump which serves for their monument. They attend no caucus, they make no compromise, they use no policy. Their one principle is growth. They combine a true radicalism with a true conservatism. Their radicalism is not cutting away of roots, but an infinite multiplication and extension of them under all surrounding institutions. They take a firmer hold on the earth that they may rise higher into the heavens. Their conservative heartwood, in which no sap longer flows, does not impoverish their growth, but is a firm column to support it; and when their expanding trunks no longer require it, it utterly decays. Their conservatism is a dead but solid heart-wood, which is the pivot and firm column of support to all this growth, appropriating nothing to itself, but forever by its support assisting to extend the area of their radicalism. Half a century after they are dead at the core, they are preserved by radical reforms. They do not, like men, from radicals turn conservative. Their conservative part dies out first; their radical and growing part survives. They acquire new States and Territories, while the old dominions decay, and become the habitation of bears and owls and coons.

Feb. 14.   Willows, Emblem of Joy

I WAS STRUCK TO-DAY by the size and continuousness of the natural willow hedge on the east side of the railroad causeway, at the foot of the embankment, next to the fence. Some twelve years ago, when that causeway was built through the meadows, there were no willows there or near there, but now, just at the foot of the sand-bank, where it meets the meadow, and on the line of the fence, quite a dense willow hedge has planted itself. I used to think that the seeds were brought with the sand from the Deep Cut in the woods, but there is no golden willow there; but now I think that the seeds have been blown hither from a distance, and lodged against the foot of the bank, just as the snow-drift accumulates there, for I see several ash trees among them, which have come from an ash ten rods east in the meadow, though none has sprung up elsewhere. There are also a few alders, elms, birch, poplars, and some elder. For years a willow might not have been persuaded to take root in that meadow; but run a barrier like this through it, and in a few years it is lined with them. They plant themselves here solely, and not in the open meadow, as exclusively as along the shores of a river. The sand-bank is a shore to them, and the meadow a lake. How impatient, how rampant, how precocious these osiers! They have hardly made two shoots from the sand in as many springs, when silvery catkins burst out along them, and anon golden blossoms and downy seeds, spreading their race with incredible rapidity. Thus they multiply and clan together. Thus they take advantage even of the railroad, which elsewhere disturbs and invades their domains. May I ever be in as good spirits as a willow! How tenacious of life! How withy! How soon it gets over its hurts! They never despair. Is there no moisture longer in nature which they can transmute into sap? They are emblems of youth, joy, and everlasting life. Scarcely is their growth restrained by winter, but their silvery down peeps forth in the warmest days in January (?). The very trees and shrubs and weeds, if we consider their origin, have drifted thus like snow against the fences and hillsides. Their growth is protected and favored there. Soon the alders will take their places with them. This hedge is, of course, as straight as the railroad or its bounding fence.

June 3. Conversation with Hosmer

TUESDAY. SURVEYING FOR JOHN Hosmer beyond pail-factory.

Hosmer says that seedling white birches do not grow larger than your arm, but cut them down and they spring up again and grow larger.

While clearing a line through shrub oak, which put his eyes out, he asked, "What is shrub oak made for?" R. Hoar, I believe, bought that (formerly) pine lot of Loring's which is now coming up shrub oak. Hosmer says that he will not see any decent wood there as long as he lives. H. says he had a lot of pine in Sudbury, which being cut, shrub oak came up. He cut and burned and raised rye, and the next year (it being surrounded by pine woods on three sides) a dense growth of pine sprang up.

As I have said before, it seems to me that the squirrels, etc., disperse the acorns, etc., amid the pines, they being a covert for them to lurk in, and when the pines are cut the fuzzy shrub oaks, etc., have the start. If you cut the shrub oak soon, probably pines or birches, maples, or other trees which have light seeds will spring next, because squirrels, etc., will not be likely to carry acorns into open land. If the pine wood had been surrounded by white oak, probably that would have come up after the pine.

July 30. A Perfect Dog-Day

THIS IS A PERFECT dog-day. The atmosphere thick, mildewy, cloudy. It is difficult to dry anything. The sun is obscured, yet we expect no rain. Bad hay weather. The streams are raised by the showers of yesterday and day before, and I see the farmers turning their black-looking hay in the flooded meadows with a fork. The water is suddenly clear, as if clarified by the white of an egg or lime. I think it must be because the light is reflected downward from the overarching dog-day sky. It assists me very much as I go looking for the ceratophyllum, potamogetons, etc. All the secrets of the river bottom are revealed. I look down into sunny depths which before were dark. The wonderful clearness of the water, enabling you to explore the river bottom and many of its secrets now, exactly as if the water had been clarified. This is our compensation for a heaven concealed. The air is close and still.

Aug. 1. Moisture Reigns

SINCE JULY 30TH, INCLUSIVE, we have had perfect dog-days without interruption. The earth has suddenly [become] invested with a thick musty mist. The sky has become a mere fungus. A thick blue musty veil of mist is drawn before the sun. The sun has not been visible, except for a moment or two once or twice a day, all this time, nor the stars by night. Moisture reigns. You cannot dry a napkin at the window, nor press flowers without their mildewing. You imbibe so much moisture from the atmosphere that you are not so thirsty, nor is bathing so grateful as a week ago. The burning heat is tempered, but as you lose sight of the sky and imbibe the musty, misty air, you exist as a vegetable, a fungus. Unfortunate those who have not got their hay. I see them wading in overflowed meadows and pitching the black and mouldy swaths about in vain that they may dry. In the meanwhile, vegetation is becoming rank, vines of all kinds are rampant. Squashes and melons *are said* to grow a foot in a night. But weeds grow as fast. The corn unrolls. Berries abound and attain their full size. Once or twice in the day there is an imperfect gleam of yellow sunlight for a moment through some thinner part of the veil, reminding us that we have not seen the sun so long, but no blue sky is revealed. The earth is completely invested with cloudlike wreaths of vapor (yet fear no rain and need no veil), beneath which flies buzz hollowly and torment, and mosquitoes hum and sting as if they were born of such an air. The drooping spirits of mosquitoes revive, and they whet their stings anew. Legions of buzzing flies blacken the furniture. (For a week *at least* have heard that snapping sound under pads.) We have a dense fog every night, which lifts itself but a short distance during the day. At sundown I see it curling up from the river and meadows. However, I love this moisture in its season. I believe it is good to breathe, wholesome as a vapor bath. Toadstools shoot up in the yards and paths.

Aug. 4.   Profusion of Berry Species

Conantum hillside is now literally black with berries. What a profusion of this kind of food Nature provides, as if to compensate for the scarcity last year! Fortunate that these cows in their pasture do not love them, but pass them by. The blackberries are already softening, and of all kinds there are many, many more than any or all creatures can gather. They are literally five or six species deep. First, away down in the shade under all you find, still fresh, the great very light blue (*i.e.* with a very thick blue bloom) *Vaccinium Pennsylvanicum* in heavy clusters, that early ambrosial fruit, delicate-flavored, thin-skinned, and cool,—Olympian fruit; then, next above, the still denser bunches and clusters of *V. vacillans,* of various varieties, firm and sweet, solid food; and, rising above these, large blue and also shining black huckleberries *(Gaylussacia resinosa)* of various flavors and qualities; and over all runs rampant the low blackberry *(Rubus Canadensis),* weighing down the thicket with its wreaths of black fruit. Also here and there the high blackberry, just beginning, towers over all. You go daintily wading through this thicket, picking, perchance, only the biggest of the blackberries—as big as your thumb—and clutching here and there a handful of huckleberries or blueberries, but never, perchance, suspecting the delicious cool blue-bloomed ones under all. This favorable moist weather has expanded some of the huckleberries to the size of bullets. Each patch, each bush, seems fuller and blacker than the last. Such a profusion, yet you see neither birds nor beasts eating them, unless ants and the huckleberry-bug! I carried my hands full of bushes to the boat, and, returning, the two ladies picked fully three pints from these alone, casting the bare bushes into the stream.

Aug. 26.   A Weather-Painted House

I rest and take my lunch on Lee's Cliff, looking toward Baker Farm. What is a New England landscape this sunny August day? A weather-painted house and barn, with an orchard by its side, in midst of a sandy field surrounded by green woods, with a small blue lake on one side. A sympathy between the color of the weather-painted house and that of the lake and sky. I speak not of a country road between its fences, for this house lies off one, nor do I commonly approach them from this side. The weather-painted house. This is the New England color, homely but fit as that of a toadstool. What matter though this one has not been inhabited for thirty years? Methinks I hear the crow of a cock come up from its barn-yard.

Aug. 26. Bee Tree Hill Asters

SAILED ACROSS TO BEE Tree Hill. This hillside, laid bare two years ago and partly last winter, is almost covered with the *Aster macrophyllus,* now in its prime. It grows large and rank, two feet high. On one I count seventeen central flowers withered, one hundred and thirty in bloom, and half as many buds. As I looked down from the hilltop over the sprout-land, its rounded grayish tops amid the bushes I mistook for gray, lichenclad rocks, such was its profusion and harmony with the scenery, like hoary rocky hilltops amid bushes. There were acres of it, densely planted. Also erechthites as abundant and rank in many places there as if it had been burnt over! So it does not necessarily imply fire. I thought I was looking down on gray, lichen-clad rocky summits on which a few bushes thinly grew. These rocks were asters, single ones a foot over, many prostrate, and making a gray impression. Many leaves of shrubs are crisp and withered and fallen there, though as yet no drought nor frost. Nothing but rain can have done it.

Aug. 30. Afternoon A-Cranberrying

I HAVE COME OUT this afternoon a-cranberrying, chiefly to gather some of the small cranberry, *Vaccinium Oxycoccus,* which Emerson says is the common cranberry of the north of Europe. This was a small object, yet not to be postponed, on account of imminent frosts, *i. e.,* if I would know this year the flavor of the European cranberry as compared with our larger kind. I thought I should like to have a dish of this sauce on the table at Thanksgiving of my own gathering. I could hardly make up my mind to come this way, it seemed so poor an object to spend the afternoon on. I kept foreseeing a lame conclusion,—how I should cross the Great Fields, look into Beck Stow's, and then retrace my steps no richer than before. In fact, I expected little of this walk, yet it did pass through the side of my mind that somehow, on this very account (my small expectation), it would turn out well, as also the advantage of having some purpose, however small, to be accomplished,—of letting your deliberate wisdom and foresight in the house to some extent direct and control your steps. If you would really take a position outside the street and daily life of men, you must have deliberately planned your course, you must have business which is not your neighbors' business, which they cannot understand. For only absorbing employment prevails, succeeds, takes up space, occupies territory, determines the future of individuals and states, drives Kansas out of your head, and actually and permanently occupies the only desirable and free Kansas against all border ruffians. The attitude of resistance is one of weakness, inasmuch as it only faces an enemy; it has its back to all that is truly attractive. You shall have your affairs, I will have mine. You will spend this afternoon in setting up your neighbor's stove, and be paid for it; I will spend it in gathering the few berries of the *Vaccinium Oxycoccus* which Nature produces here, before it is too late, and *be paid for it also* after another fashion. I have always reaped unexpected and incalculable advantages from carrying out at last, however tardily, any little enterprise which my genius suggested to me long ago as a thing to be done,—some step to be taken, however slight, out of the usual course.

How many schools I have thought of which I might go to but did not go to! expecting foolishly that some greater advantage or schooling would come to me! It is these comparatively cheap and private expeditions that substantiate our existence and batten our lives, as, where a vine touches the earth in its undulating course, it puts forth roots and thickens its stock. Our employment generally is tinkering, mending the old worn-out teapot of society. Our stock in trade is solder. Better for me, says my genius, to go cranberrying this afternoon for the *Vaccinium Oxycoccus* in Gowing's Swamp, to get but a pocketful and learn its peculiar flavor, aye, and the flavor of Gowing's Swamp and of *life* in New England, than to go consul to Liverpool and get I don't know how many thousand dollars for it, with no such flavor. Many of our days should be spent, not in vain expectations and lying on our oars, but in carrying out deliberately and faithfully the hundred little purposes which every man's genius must have suggested to him. Let not your life be wholly without an object, though it be only to ascertain the flavor of a cranberry, for it will not be only the quality of an insignificant berry that you will have tasted, but the flavor of your life to that extent, and it will be such a sauce as no wealth can buy.

Both a conscious and an unconscious life are good. Neither is good exclusively, for both have the same source. The wisely conscious life springs out of an unconscious suggestion. I have found my account in travelling in having prepared beforehand a list of questions which I would get answered, not trusting to my interest at the moment, and can then travel with the most profit. Indeed, it is by obeying the suggestions of a higher light within you that you escape from yourself and, in the transit, as it were see with the unworn sides of your eye, travel totally new paths. What is that pretended life that does not take up a claim, that does not occupy ground, that cannot build a causeway to its objects, that sits on a bank looking over a bog, singing its desires?

Aug. 30. So Wild a Place

I SEEMED TO HAVE reached a new world, so wild a place that the very huckleberries grew hairy and were inedible. I feel as if I were in Rupert's Land, and a slight cool but agreeable shudder comes over me, as if equally far away from human society. What's the need of visiting far-off mountains and bogs, if a half-hour's walk will carry me into such wildness and novelty? But why should not as wild plants grow here as in Berkshire, as in Labrador? Is Nature so easily tamed? Is she not as primitive and vigorous here as anywhere? How does this particular acre of secluded, unfrequented, useless (?) quaking bog differ from an acre in Labrador? Has any white man ever settled on it? Does any now frequent it? Not even the Indian comes here now. I see that there are some square rods within twenty miles of Boston just as wild and primitive and unfrequented as a square rod in Labrador, as unaltered by man. Here grows the hairy huckleberry as it did in Squaw Sachem's day and a thousand years before, and concerns me perchance more than it did her. I have no doubt that for a moment I experience exactly the same sensations as if I were alone in a bog in Rupert's Land, and it saves me the trouble of going there; for what in any case makes the difference between being here and being there but many such little differences of flavor and roughness put together? Rupert's Land is recognized as much by one sense as another. I felt a shock, a thrill, an agreeable surprise in one instant, for, no doubt, all the possible inferences were at once drawn, with a rush, in my mind,—I could be in Rupert's Land and supping at home within the hour! This beat the railroad. I recovered from my surprise without danger to my sanity, and permanently annexed Rupert's Land. That wild hairy huckleberry, inedible as it was, was equal to a domain secured to me and reaching to the South Sea. That was an unexpected harvest. I hope you have gathered as much, neighbor, from your corn and potato fields. I have got in my huckleberries. I shall be ready for Thanksgiving. It is in vain to dream of a wildness distant from ourselves. There is none such. It is the bog in our brain and bowels, the primitive vigor of Nature in us, that inspires that dream. I shall never find in the wilds of Labrador any greater wildness than in some recess in Concord, *i.e.* than I import into it. A little more manhood or virtue will make the surface of the globe anywhere thrillingly novel and wild. That alone will provide and pay the fiddler; it will convert the district road into an untrodden cranberry bog, for it restores all things to their original primitive flourishing and promising state.

Sept. 1. Delicate Tints of Fungi

WE GO ADMIRING THE pure and delicate tints of fungi on the surface of the damp swamp there, following up along the north side of the brook past the right of the old camp. There are many very beautiful lemon-yellow ones of various forms, some shaped like buttons, some becoming finely scalloped on the edge, some club-shaped and hollow, of the most delicate and rare but decided tints, contrasting well with the decaying leaves about them. There are others also pure white, others a wholesome red, others brown, and some even a light indigo-blue above and beneath and throughout. When colors come to be taught in the schools, as they should be, both the prism (or the rainbow) and these fungi should be used by way of illustration, and if the pupil does not learn colors, he may learn fungi, which perhaps is better. You almost envy the wood frogs and toads that hop amid such gems,—some pure and bright enough for a breastpin. Out of every crevice between the dead leaves oozes some vehicle of color, the unspent wealth of the year, which Nature is now casting forth, as if it were only to empty herself.

Sept. 14. Flowering of the Ditches

P.M.—To Hubbard's Close and Cardinal Ditch.

Now for the *Aster Tradescanti* along low roads, like the Turnpike, swarming with butterflies and bees. Some of them are pink. How ever unexpected are these later flowers! You thought that Nature had about wound up her affairs. You had seen what she could do this year, and had not noticed a few weeds by the roadside, or mistook them for the remains of summer flowers now hastening to their fall; you thought you knew every twig and leaf by the roadside, and nothing more was to be looked for there; and now, to your surprise, these ditches are crowded with millions of little stars. They suddenly spring up and face you, with their legions on each side the way, as if they had lain in ambuscade there. The flowering of the ditches. Call them travellers' thoughts, numerous though small, worth a penny at least, which, sown in spring and summer, in the fall spring up unobserved at first, successively dusted and washed, mingled with nettles and beggar-ticks as a highway harvest. A starry meteoric shower, a milky way, in the flowery kingdom in whose aisles we travel. Let the traveller bethink himself, elevate and expand his thoughts somewhat, that his successors may oftener hereafter be cheered by the sight of an *Aster Novæ-Angliæ* or *spectabilis* here and there, to remind him that a poet or philosopher has passed this way. The gardener with all his assiduity does not raise such a variety, nor so many successive crops on the same space, as Nature in the very roadside ditches. There they have stood, begrimed with dust and the wash of the road so long, and made acquaintance with passing sheep and cattle and swine, gathering a trivial experience, and now at last the fall rains have come to wash off some of that dust, and even they exhibit these dense flowery panicles as the result of all that experience, as pure for an hour as if they grew by some wild brook-side.

Oct. 18. My Work is Writing

Men commonly exaggerate the theme. Some themes they think are significant and others insignificant. I feel that my life is very homely, my pleasures very cheap. Joy and sorrow, success and failure, grandeur and meanness, and indeed most words in the English language do not mean for me what they do for my neighbors. I see that my neighbors look with compassion on me, that they think it is a mean and unfortunate destiny which makes me to walk in these fields and woods so much and sail on this river alone. But so long as I find here the only real elysium, I cannot hesitate in my choice. My work is writing, and I do not hesitate, though I know that no subject is too trivial for me, tried by ordinary standards; for, ye fools, the theme is nothing, the life is everything. All that interests the reader is the depth and intensity of the life excited. We touch our subject but by a point which has no breadth, but the pyramid of our experience, or our interest in it, rests on us by a broader or narrower base. That is, man is all in all, Nature nothing, but as she draws him out and reflects him. Give me simple, cheap, and homely themes.

Oct. 19. View of Wachusett

I RETURN BY THE west side of Lee's Cliff hill, and sit on a rounded rock there, covered with fresh-fallen pine-needles, amid the woods, whence I see Wachusett. How little unevenness and elevation is required for Nature's effects! An elevation one thousand or fifteen hundred feet above the plain is seen from all eminences and level open plains, as from over the opening made by a pond, within thirty miles. Nature is not obliged to lift her mountains very high in the horizon, after all, to make them visible and interesting.

Dec. 1. The Shrub Oak

A RIDGE OF EARTH, with the red cockscomb lichen on it, peeps out still at the rut's edge. The dear wholesome color of shrub oak leaves, so clean and firm, not decaying, but which have put on a kind of immortality, not wrinkled and thin like the white oak leaves, but full-veined and plump, as nearer earth. Well-tanned leather on the one side, sun-tanned, color of colors, color of the cow and the deer, silver-downy beneath, turned toward the late bleached and russet fields. What are acanthus leaves and the rest to this? Emblem of my winter condition. I love and could embrace the shrub oak with its scanty garment of leaves rising above the snow, lowly whispering to me, akin to winter thoughts, and sunsets, and to all virtue. Covert which the hare and the partridge seek, and I too seek. What cousin of mine is the shrub oak? How can any man suffer long? For a sense of want is a prayer, and all prayers are answered. Rigid as iron, clean as the atmosphere, hardy as virtue, innocent and sweet as a maiden is the shrub oak. In proportion as I know and love it, I am natural and sound as a partridge. I felt a positive yearning toward one bush this afternoon. There was a match found for me at last. I fell in love with a shrub oak. Tenacious of its leaves, which shrivel not but retain a certain wintry life in them, firm shields, painted in fast colors a rich brown. The deer mouse, too, knows the shrub oak and has its hole in the snow by the shrub oak's stem.

Dec. 1. Amid the Shrub Oaks

NO, I AM A stranger in your towns. I am not at home at French's, or Lovejoy's, or Savery's. I can winter more to my mind amid the shrub oaks. I have made arrangements to stay with them.

The shrub oak, lowly, loving the earth and spreading over it, tough, thick-leaved; leaves firm and sound in winter and rustling like leather shields; leaves fair and wholesome to the eye, clean and smooth to the touch. Tough to support the snow, not broken down by it. Well-nigh useless to man. A sturdy phalanx, hard to break through. Product of New England's surface. Bearing many striped acorns.

Dec. 1. Well Named Shrub Oak

WELL NAMED *SHRUB OAK.* Low, robust, hardy, indigenous. Well known to the striped squirrel and the partridge and rabbit. The squirrel nibbles its nuts sitting upon an old stump of its larger cousins. What is Peruvian bark to your bark? How many rents I owe to you! how many eyes put out! how many bleeding fingers! How many shrub oak patches I have been through, stooping, winding my way, bending the twigs aside, guiding myself by the sun, over hills and valleys and plains, resting in clear grassy spaces! I love to go through a patch of shrub oak in a bee-line, where you tear your clothes and put your eyes out.

Dec. 3. The Pine Forest's Edge

FOR YEARS MY APPETITE was so strong that I fed—I browsed—on the pine forest's edge seen against the winter horizon. How cheap my diet still! Dry sand that has fallen in railroad cuts and slid on the snow beneath is a condiment to my walk. I ranged about like a gray moose, looking at the spiring tops of the trees, and fed my imagination on them,—far-away, ideal trees not disturbed by the axe of the wood-cutter, nearer and nearer fringes and eyelashes of my eye. Where was the sap, the fruit, the value of the forest for me, but in that line where it was relieved against the sky? That was my wood-lot; that was my lot in the woods. The silvery needles of the pine straining the light.

Dec. 4. Variety Without Diversity

IN THE SPROUT-LAND by the road, in the woods this side of C. Miles's, much gray goldenrod is mixed with the shrub oak. It reminds me of the color of the rabbits which run there. Thus Nature feeds her children chiefly with color. I have no doubt that it is an important relief to the eyes which have long rested on snow, to rest on brown oak leaves and the bark of trees. We want the greatest variety within the smallest compass, and yet without glaring diversity, and we have it in the colors of the withered oak leaves. The white, so curled and shrivelled and *pale;* the black (?), more flat and glossy and darker brown; the red, much like the black, but *perhaps* less dark, and less deeply cut. The scarlet still occasionally retains some blood in its veins.

Dec. 5. Born in the Nick of Time

MY THEMES SHALL NOT be far-fetched. I will tell of homely every-day phenomena and adventures. Friends! Society! It seems to me that I have an abundance of it, there is so much that I rejoice and sympathize with, and men, too, that I never speak to but only know and think of. What you call bareness and poverty is to me simplicity. God could not be unkind to me if he should try. I love the winter, with its imprisonment and its cold, for it compels the prisoner to try new fields and resources. I love to have the river closed up for a season and a pause put to my boating, to be obliged to get my boat in. I shall launch it again in the spring with so much more pleasure. This is an advantage in point of abstinence and moderation compared with the seaside boating, where the boat ever lies on the shore. I love best to have each thing in its season only, and enjoy doing without it at all other times. It is the greatest of all advantages to enjoy no advantage at all. I find it invariably true, the poorer I am, the richer I am. What you consider my disadvantage, I consider my advantage. While you are pleased to get knowledge and culture in many ways, I am delighted to think that I am getting rid of them. I have never got over my surprise that I should have been born into the most estimable place in all the world, and in the very nick of time, too.

Dec. 6. Decaying Leaves

HOW HANDSOME EVERY ONE of these leaves that are blown about the snow-crust or lie neglected beneath, soon to turn to mould! Not merely a matted mass of fibres like a sheet of paper, but a perfect organism and system in itself, so that no mortal has ever yet discerned or explored its beauty.

Dec. 6. Buds as Concentrated Summer

ON ALL SIDES, IN swamps and about their edges and in the woods, the bare shrubs are sprinkled with buds, more or less noticeable and pretty, their little gemmæ or gems, their most vital and attractive parts now, almost all the greenness and color left, greens and salads for the birds and rabbits. Our eyes go searching along the stems for what is most vivacious and characteristic, the concentrated summer gone into winter quarters. For we are hunters pursuing the summer on snow-shoes and skates, all winter long. There is really but one season in our hearts.

Dec. 7. The Seasons Repeated

THAT GRAND OLD POEM called Winter is round again without any connivance of mine. As I sit under Lee's Cliff, where the snow is melted, amid sere pennyroyal and frost-bitten catnep, I look over my shoulder upon an arctic scene. I see with surprise the pond a dumb white surface of ice speckled with snow, just as so many winters before, where so lately were lapsing waves or smooth reflecting water. I see the holes which the pickerel-fisher has made, and I see him, too, retreating over the hills, drawing his sled behind him. The water is already skimmed over again there. I hear, too, the familiar belching voice of the pond. It seemed as if winter had come without any interval since midsummer, and I was prepared to see it flit away by the time I again looked over my shoulder. It was as if I had dreamed it. But I see that the farmers have had time to gather their harvests as usual, and the seasons have revolved as slowly as in the first autumn of my life. The winters come now as fast as snowflakes. It is wonderful that old men do not lose their reckoning. It was summer, and now again it is winter. Nature loves this rhyme so well that she never tires of repeating it. So sweet and whole-some is the winter, so simple and moderate, so satisfactory and perfect, that her children will never weary of it. What a poem! an epic in blank verse, enriched with a million tinkling rhymes. It is solid beauty. It has been subjected to the vicissi-tudes of millions of years of the gods, and not a single superfluous ornament remains. The severest and coldest of the immortal critics have shot their arrows at and pruned it till it cannot be amended.

Dec. 9.   A Progressive Sunset

I PERCEIVE THAT MORE or other things are seen in the reflection than in the substance. As I look now over the pond westward, I see in substance the now bare outline of Fair Haven Hill a mile beyond, but in the reflection I see not this, only the tops of some pines, which stand close to the shore but are invisible against the dark hill beyond, and these are indefinitely prolonged into points of shadow.

The sun is set, and over the valley, which looks like an outlet of Walden toward Fair Haven, I see a burnished bar of cloud stretched low and level, as if it were the bar over that passageway to Elysium, the last column in the train of the sun.

When I get as far as my bean-field, the reflected white in the winter horizon of this perfectly cloudless sky is being condensed at the horizon's edge, and its hue deepening into a dun golden, against which the tops of the trees—pines and elms—are seen with beautiful distinctness, and a slight blush begins to suffuse the eastern horizon, and so the picture of the day is done and set in a gilded frame.

Dec. 10.   A Rude Sketch

IT IS REMARKABLE HOW suggestive the slightest drawing as a memento of things seen. For a few years past I have been accustomed to make a rude sketch in my journal of plants, ice, and various natural phenomena, and though the fullest accompanying description may fail to recall my experience, these rude outline drawings do not fail to carry me back to that time and scene. It is as if I saw the same thing again, and I may again attempt to describe it in words if I choose.

Dec. 17.   The Shrub Oak Leaf

NOW YOU HAVE THE foliage of summer painted in brown. Go through the shrub oaks. All growth has ceased; no greenness meets the eye, except what there may be in the bark of this shrub. The green leaves are all turned to brown, quite dry and sapless. The little buds are sleeping at the base of the slender shrunken petioles. Who observed when they passed from green to brown? I do not remember the transition; it was very gradual. But these leaves still have a kind of life in them. They are exceedingly beautiful in their withered state. If they hang on, it is like the perseverance of the saints. Their colors are as wholesome, their forms as perfect, as ever. Now that the crowd and bustle of summer is passed, I have leisure to admire them. Their figures never weary my eye. Look at the few broad scallops in their sides. When was that pattern first cut? With what a free stroke the curve was struck! With how little, yet just enough, variety in their forms! Look at the fine bristles which arm each pointed lobe, as perfect now as when the wild bee hummed about them, or the chewink scratched beneath them. What pleasing and harmonious colors within and without, above and below! The smooth, delicately brown-tanned upper surface, acorn-color, the very pale (some silvery or ashy) ribbed under side. How poetically, how like saints or innocent and beneficent beings, they give up the ghost! How spiritual! Though they have lost their sap, they have not given up the ghost. Rarely touched by worm or insect, they are as fair as ever.

Chapter IX

Year
1857

Age
39–40

March 24.   Steps in Describing

IF YOU ARE DESCRIBING any occurrence, or a man, make two or more distinct reports at different times. Though you may think you have said all, you will to-morrow remember a whole new class of facts which perhaps interested most of all at the time, but did not present themselves to be reported. If we have recently met and talked with a man, and would report our experience, we commonly make a very partial report at first, failing to seize the most significant, picturesque, and dramatic points; we describe only what we have had time to digest and dispose of in our minds, without being conscious that there were other things really more novel and interesting to us, which will not fail to recur to us and impress us suitably at last. How little that occurs to us in any way are we prepared at once to appreciate! We discriminate at first only a few features, and we need to reconsider our experience from many points of view and in various moods, to preserve the whole fruit of it.

March 27.   Two Journal Reports

I WOULD FAIN MAKE two reports in my Journal, first the incidents and observations of to-day; and by to-morrow I review the same and record what was omitted before, which will often be the most significant and poetic part. I do not know at first what it is that charms me. The men and things of to-day are wont to lie fairer and truer in to-morrow's memory.

April 23.   Love for Nature

IT IS VERY RARE that I hear one express a strong and imperishable attachment to a particular scenery, or to the whole of nature,—I mean such as will control their whole lives and characters. Such seem to have a true home in nature, a hearth in the fields and woods, whatever tenement may be burned. The soil and climate is warm to them. They alone are naturalized, but most are tender and callow creatures that wear a house as their outmost shell and must get their lives insured when they step abroad from it. They are lathed and plastered in from all natural influences, and their delicate lives are a long battle with the dyspepsia. The others are fairly rooted in the soil, and are the noblest plant it bears, more hardy and natural than sorrel. The dead earth seems animated at the prospect of their coming, as if proud to be trodden on by them. It recognizes its lord. Children of the Golden Age. Hospitals and almshouses are not their destiny. When I hear of such an attachment in a reasonable, a divine, creature to a particular portion of the earth, it seems as if then first the earth succeeded and rejoiced, as if it had been made and existed only for such a use. These various soils and reaches which the farmer plods over, which the traveller glances at and the geologist dryly describes, then first flower and bear their fruit. Does he chiefly own the land who coldly uses it and gets corn and potatoes out of it, or he who loves it and gets inspiration from it? How rarely a man's love for nature becomes a ruling principle with him, like a youth's affection for a maiden, but more enduring! All nature is my bride. That nature which to one is a stark and ghastly solitude is a sweet, tender, and genial society to another.

May 20.   Pines Fill the Pastures

HOW SUDDENLY, AFTER ALL, pines seem to shoot up and fill the pastures! I wonder that the farmers do not earlier encourage their growth. To-day, perchance, as I go through some run-out pasture, I observe many young white pines dotting the field, where last year I had noticed only blackberry vines; but

Pasture with pines.

I see that many are already destroyed or injured by the cows which have dived into them to scratch their heads or for sport (such is their habit; they break off the leading shoot and bend down the others of different evergreens), or perchance where the farmer has been mowing them down, and I think the owner would rather have a pasture here than a wood-lot. A year or two later, as I pass through the same field, I am surprised to find myself in a flourishing young wood-lot, from which the cows are now carefully fenced out, though there are many open spaces, and I perceive how much further advanced it would have been if the farmer had been more provident and had begun to abet nature a few years earlier. It is surprising by what leaps—two or three feet in a season—the pines stretch toward the sky, affording shelter also to various hardwoods which plant themselves in their midst.

May 29. Thunder-Shower Cliff Retreat

FAIR HAVEN LAKE NOW, at 4.30 P.M., is perfectly smooth, reflecting the darker and glowing June clouds as it has not before. Fishes incessantly dimple it here and there, and I see afar, approaching steadily but diagonally toward the shore of the island, some creature on its surface, maybe a snake,—but my glass shows it to be a muskrat, leaving two long harrow-like ripples behind. Soon after, I see another, quite across the pond on the Baker Farm side, and even distinguish that to be a muskrat. The fishes, methinks, are busily breeding now. These things I see as I sit on the top of Lee's Cliff, looking into the light and dark eye of the lake. The heel of that summer-shower cloud, seen through the trees in the west, has extended further south and looks more threatening than ever. As I stand on the rocks, examining the blossoms of some forward black oaks which close over-

Rock retreat at Lee's Cliff,
near Concord, Massachusetts.

hang it, I think I hear the sound of flies against my hat. No, it is scattered raindrops, though the sky is perfectly clear above me, and the cloud from which they come is yet far on one side. I see through the tree-tops the thin vanguard of the storm scaling the celestial ramparts, like eager light infantry, or cavalry with spears advanced. But from the west a great, still, ash-colored cloud comes on. The drops fall thicker, and I seek a shelter under the Cliffs. I stand under a large projecting portion of the Cliff, where there is ample space above and around, and I can move about as perfectly protected as under a shed. To be sure, fragments of rock look as if they would fall, but I see no marks of recent ruin about me.

Soon I hear the low all-pervading hum of an approaching hummingbird circling above the rock, which afterward I mistake several times for the gruff voices of men approaching, unlike as these sounds are in some respects, and I perceive the resemblance even when I know better. Now I am sure it is a hummingbird, and now that it is two farmers approaching. But presently the hum becomes more sharp and thrilling, and the little fellow suddenly perches on an ash twig within a rod of me, and plumes himself while the rain is fairly beginning. He is quite out of proportion to the size of his perch. It does not acknowledge his weight.

I sit at my ease and look out from under my lichenclad rocky roof, half-way up the Cliff, under freshly leafing ash and hickory trees on to the pond, while the rain is falling faster and faster, and I am rather glad of the rain, which affords me

this experience. The rain has compelled me to find the cosiest and most homelik
part of all the Cliff. The surface of the pond, though the rain dimples it all alik
and I perceive no wind, is still divided into irregular darker and lighter spaces, wit
distinct boundaries, as it were *watered* all over. Even now that it rains very har
and the surface is all darkened, the boundaries of those spaces are not quit
obliterated. The countless drops seem to spring again from its surface like stalag
mites.

A mosquito, sole living inhabitant of this antrum, settles on my hand. I find her
sheltered with me a sweet-briar growing in a cleft of the rock above my head
where perhaps some bird or squirrel planted it. Mulleins beneath. *Galium Aparine*
just begun to bloom, growing next the rock; and, in the earth-filled clefts, colum
bines, some of whose cornucopias strew the ground. *Ranunculus bulbosus* i
bloom; saxifrage; and various ferns, as spleenwort, etc. Some of these plants ar
never rained on. I perceive the buttery-like scent of barberry bloom from over th
rock, and now and for some days the bunches of effete white ash anthers stre
the ground.

It lights up a little, and the drops fall thinly again, and the birds begin to sing
but now I see a new shower coming up from the southwest, and the wind seem
to have changed somewhat. Already I had heard the low mutterings of its thun
der—for this is a thunder-shower—in the midst of the last. It seems to have shifte
its quarters merely to attack me on a more exposed side of my castle. Two foe
appear where I had expected none. But who can calculate the tactics of the storm
It is a first regular summer thunder-shower, preceded by a rush of wind, and
begin to doubt if my quarters will prove a sufficient shelter. I am fairly besiege
and know not when I shall escape. I hear the still roar of the rushing storm a
a distance, though no trees are seen to wave. And now the forked flashes descend
ing to the earth succeed rapidly to the hollow roars above, and down comes th
deluging rain. I hear the alarmed notes of birds flying to a shelter. The air at lengt
is cool and chilly, the atmosphere is darkened, and I have forgotten the smoot
pond and its reflections. The rock feels cold to my body, as if it were a differen
season of the year. I almost repent of having lingered here; think how far I shoul
have got if I had started homeward. But then what a condition I should have bee
in! Who knows but the lightning will strike this cliff and topple the rocks dow
on me? The crashing thunder sounds like the overhauling of lumber on heaven'
loft. And now, at last, after an hour of steady confinement, the clouds grow thi
again, and the birds begin to sing. They make haste to conclude the day with thei
regular evening songs (before the rain is fairly over) according to the program. Th
pepe on some pine tree top was heard almost in the midst of the storm. One o
two bullfrogs trump. They care not how wet it is. Again I hear the still rushing
all-pervading roar of the withdrawing storm, when it is at least half a mile off
wholly beyond the pond, though no trees are seen to wave. It is simply the soun
of the countless drops falling on the leaves and the ground. You were not awar
what a sound the rain made. Several times I attempt to leave my shelter, bu

eturn to it. My first stepping abroad seems but a signal for the rain to commence again. Not till after an hour and a half do I escape. After all, my feet and legs re drenched by the wet grass.

June 16. Slanting Rail Fences

A.M.—I GO ALONG the sandy road through a region of small hills about half mile from the sea, between slight gray fences, either post and rail, or slanting ails,   a foot apart, resting on two crossed stakes, the ails ⟋⟋⟋⟋⟋ of unequal length, looking agreeably loose and rregular.

July 2. Our Intellectual Ray

CALLA PALUSTRIS (WITH ITS convolute point like the cultivated) at the outh end of Gowing's Swamp. Having found this in one place, I now find it in another. Many an object is not seen, though it falls within the range of our visual ay, because it does not come within the range of our intellectual ray, *i. e.,* we are not looking for it. So, in the largest sense, we find only the world we look for.

July 29. An Indistinct Prospect

I AM INTERESTED IN an indistinct prospect, a distant view, a mere uggestion often, revealing an almost wholly new world to me. I rejoice to get, and am apt to present, a new view. But I find it impossible to present my view to most people. In effect, it would seem that they do not wish to take a new view in any ase.

Sept. 16. A Soft White Pine Grove

WALKED THROUGH THAT BEAUTIFUL soft white pine grove on the west of the road in John Flint's pasture. These trees are large, but there is ample space between them, so that the ground is left grassy. Great pines two or more feet in diameter branch sometimes within two feet of the ground on each side, sending out large horizontal branches on which you can sit. Like great harps on which the wind makes music. There is no finer tree. The different stages of its soft glaucous foliage completely concealing the trunk and branches are separated by dark horizontal lines of shadow, the flakes of pine foliage, like a pile of light fleeces.

Sept. 24. Red Maple Blush

THE RED MAPLE HAS fairly begun to blush in some places by the river. I see one, by the canal behind Barrett's mill, all aglow against the sun. These first trees that change are most interesting, since they are seen against others still freshly green,—such brilliant red on green. I go half a mile out of my way to examine such a red banner. A single tree becomes the crowning beauty of some meadowy vale and attracts the attention of the traveller from afar. At the eleventh hour of the year, some tree which has stood mute and inglorious in some distant vale thus proclaims its character as effectually as [if] it stood by the highway-side, and it leads our thoughts away from the dusty road into those brave solitudes which it inhabits. The whole tree, thus ripening in advance of its fellows, attains a singular preëminence. I am thrilled at the sight of it, bearing aloft its scarlet standard for its regiment of green-clad foresters around. The forest is the more spirited.

Sept. 27.   Red Maple's Scarlet Flags

P. M.—TO LEE'S CLIFF by land.

Small red maples in low ground have fairly begun to burn for a week. It varies from scarlet to crimson. It looks like training-day in the meadows and swamps. They have run up their colors. A small red maple has grown, perchance, far away on some moist hillside, a mile from any road, unobserved. It has faithfully discharged the duties of a maple there, all winter and summer, neglected none of its economies, added to its stature in the virtue which belongs to a maple, by a steady growth all summer, and is nearer heaven than in the spring, never having gone gadding abroad; and now, in this month of September, when men are turned travellers, hastening to the seaside, or the mountains, or the lakes,—in this month of travelling,—this modest maple, having ripened its seeds, still without budging an inch, travels on its reputation, runs up its scarlet flag on that hillside, to show that it has finished its summer work before all other trees, and withdraws from the contest. Thus that modest worth which no scrutiny could have detected when it was most industrious, is, by the very tint of its maturity, by its very blushes, revealed at last to the most careless and distant observer. It rejoices in its existence; its reflections are unalloyed. It is the day of thanksgiving with it. At last, its labors for the year being consummated and every leaf ripened to its full, it flashes out conspicuous to the eye of the most casual observer, with all the virtue and beauty of a maple,—*Acer rubrum.* In its hue is no regret nor pining. Its leaves have been asking their parent from time to time in a whisper, "When shall we redden?" It has faithfully husbanded its sap, and builded without babbling nearer and nearer to heaven. Long since it committed its seeds to the winds and has the satisfaction of knowing perhaps that a thousand little well-behaved and promising maples of its stock are already established in business somewhere. It deserves well of Mapledom. It has afforded a shelter to the wandering bird. Its autumnal tint shows how it has spent its summer; it is the hue of its virtue.

These burning bushes stand thus along the edge of the meadows, and I distinguish them afar upon all the hillsides, here and there. Her *virtues* are as scarlet.

Oct. 2. Woods Edge for First Tints

P. M.—To Hubbard's Close and Swamp.

Veronica scutellaria still. Sitting on a rock east of Trillium Woods, I perceive that, generally speaking, it is only the edge or *pediment* of the woods that shows the bright autumnal tints yet (while the superstructure is green), the birches, very young oaks and hickories, huckleberry bushes, blackberries, etc., etc., that stand around the edges, though here and there some taller maple flames upward amid the masses of green, or some other riper and mellower tree.

Oct. 2. Brighter Tints of Leaves

This changing of the leaves—their brighter tints—must have to do with cold, for it begins in the low meadows and in frosty hollows in the woods. There is where you must look as yet for the bright tints. I see the sprouts at the base of an old red oak for four or five feet upward, investing its trunk, all clear bright red, while all above is green. The shrub oak leaves around are more yellow or scarlet than the red. At the bottom of this hollow, the young walnut leaves have just been killed by the frosts while still green, and generally the hazel leaves also, but not the oaks, cherries, etc., etc. Many little maples in those coldest places have already dropped all their leaves. Generally in low ground many maple and birch and locust leaves have fallen. Grape leaves were killed and crisped by the last frost.

Reflections of trees and vegetation on the Concord River,
Concord, Massachusetts.

Oct. 4. The River's Border

A. M.—By boat to Conantum.

River fallen again. Barberrying and graping. Many of the grapes shrivelled and killed by frost now, and the leaves mostly fallen. The yellow leaves of the white

willow thickly strew the bottom of my boat. Willows, elms, etc., shed their oldes
leaves first, even like pines. The recent and green ones are seen mottling a yellow
ish ground, especially in the willow; and, in the case of the willow, at least, thes
green ones wither and fall for the most part without turning yellow at all.

The button-bushes are generally greenish-yellow now; only the highest and mos
exposed points brown and crisp in some places. The black willow, rising abov
them, is crisped yellowish-brown, so that the general aspect of the river's brim no
is a modest or sober ripe yellowish-brown,—generally no bright colors. When
scare up a bittern from amid the weeds, I say it is the color of that bird
breast,—or body generally, for the darker part of its wings correspond to the se
pickerel-weed. Now that the pontederia is brown, the humble, weedy *green* of th
shore is *burweed,* polygonum, wool-grass, and, in some places, rushes. Such is th
river's border ordinarily,—either these weeds mingled with the sere and darl
brown pontederia or a convex raised rim of button-bushes, two to four feet hig
by a rod wide, through [which] the black willows rise one to a dozen feet highe
Here and there, to be sure, are the purple-leaved *Cornus sericea,* yellowish swee
gale, reddish rose bushes, etc., etc.

O c t .　 4 .　 L a p p i n g　 o f　 C o l o r e d　 T r e e s

N OW　 A G A I N ,　 W H E N　 O T H E R 　 trees prove so fickle, the steadfas
evergreenness of the pines is appreciated. Bright-tinted flaming scarlet or yello
maples amid pines show various segments of bright cones embosomed in gree

At Potter's Swamp, where they are all maples, it adds to the beauty of the mapl
swamp at this season that it is not seen as a simple mass of color, but, differer
trees being of different tints,—green, yellow, scarlet, crimson, and different shad
of each,—the outline of each tree is distinct to where one laps on to another. Y
a painter would hardly venture to make them thus distinct a quarter of a mile of

O c t .　 7 .　 C o n c o r d　 A f f o r d s　 N o　 B e t t e r V i e w

W H E N　 I　 T U R N　 R O U N D 　 half-way up Fair Haven Hill, by the orchard wal
and look northwest, I am surprised for the thousandth time at the beauty of th
landscape, and I sit down to behold it at my leisure. I think that Concord afford
no better view. It is always incredibly fair, but ordinarily we are mere objects i
it, and not witnesses of it. I see, through the bright October air, a valley extendin
southwest and northeast and some two miles across,—so far I can see distinctly,–
with a broad, yellow meadow tinged with brown at the bottom, and a blue rive
winding slowly through it northward, with a regular edging of low bushes on th
brink, of the same color with the meadow. Skirting the meadow are stragglin
lines, and occasionally large masses a quarter of a mile wide, of brilliant scarl
and yellow and crimson trees, backed by and mingled with green forests and gree
and hoary russet fields and hills; and on the hills around shoot up a million scarl

and orange and yellow and crimson fires amid the green; and here and there amid the trees, often beneath the largest and most graceful of those which have brown-yellow dome-like tops, are bright white or gray houses; and beyond stretches a forest, wreath upon wreath, and between each two wreaths I know lies a similar vale; and far beyond all, on the verge of the horizon, are half a dozen dark-blue mountain-summits. Large birds of a brilliant blue and white plumage are darting and screaming amid the glowing foliage a quarter of a mile below, while smaller blue birds warble faintly but sweetly around me.

Oct. 7. Walden's Rainbow-Like Belt

As I sat on the high bank at the east end of Walden this afternoon, at five o'clock, I saw, by a peculiar intention or dividing of the eye, a very striking subaqueous rainbow-like phenomenon. A passer-by might, perhaps would, have noticed that the bright-tinted shrubs about the high shore on the sunny side were reflected from the water; but, unless on the alert for such effects, he would have failed to perceive the full beauty of the phenomenon. Unless you look for reflections, you commonly will not find them. Those brilliant shrubs, which were from three to a dozen feet in height, were all reflected, dimly so far as the details of leaves, etc., were concerned, but brightly as to color, and, of course, in the order in which they stood,—scarlet, yellow, green, etc.; but, there being a slight ripple on the surface, these reflections were not true to their height though true to their breadth, but were extended downward with mathematical perpendicularity, three or four times too far, forming sharp pyramids of the several colors, gradually reduced to mere dusky points. The effect of this prolongation of the reflection was a very pleasing softening and blending of the colors, especially when a small bush of one bright tint stood directly before another of a contrary and equally bright tint. It was just as if you were to brush firmly aside with your hand or brush a fresh line of paint of various colors, or so many lumps of friable colored powders. There was, accordingly, a sort of belt, as wide as the whole height of the hill, extending downward along the whole north or sunny side of the pond, composed of exceedingly short and narrow inverted pyramids of the most brilliant colors intermixed. I have seen, indeed, similar inverted pyramids in the old drawings of tattooing about the waists of the aborigines of this country. Walden, too, like an Indian maiden, wears this broad rainbow-like belt of brilliant-colored points or cones round her waist in October. The color seems to be reflected and re-reflected from ripple to ripple, losing brightness each time by the softest possible gradation, and tapering toward the beholder, since he occupies a mere point of view. This is one of the prettiest effects of the autumnal change.

Oct. 10. Distant Colors

Generally speaking, the autumnal tints affect the color of the landscape for only two or three miles, but I distinguish maples by their color half

a mile north of Brooks Clark's, or some three miles distant, from this hill,—one
further east very bright. Also I see them in the northeast, or on or near, apparently, a road between Bedford and Billerica, at least four or five miles distant!
This is the furthest I can see them.

Oct. 12.   Elms in the Horizon

I SEE A VERY distant mountain house in a direction a little to the west of
Carlisle, and two elms in the horizon on the right of it. Measuring carefully on
the map of the county, I think it must be the Baptist Church in North Tewksbury,
within a small fraction of fourteen miles from me. I think that this is the greatest
distance at which I have seen an elm without a glass. There is another elm in the
horizon nearly north, but not so far. It looks very much larger than it is. Perhaps
it looms a little. The elm, I think, can be distinguished further than any other tree,
and, however faintly seen in the distant horizon, its little dark dome, which the
thickness of my nail will conceal, just rising above the line of the horizon, apparently not so big as a prominence on an orange, it suggests ever the same quiet rural
and domestic life passing beneath it. It is the vignette to an unseen idyllic poem.
Though that little prominence appears so dark there, I know that it is now a rich
brownish-yellow canopy of rustling leaves, whose harvest-time is already come,
sending down its showers from time to time. Homestead telegraphs to homestead
through these distant elms seen from the hilltops. I fancy I hear the house-dog's
bark and lowing of the cows asking admittance to their yard beneath it. The
tea-table is spread; the master and mistress and the hired men now have just
sat down in their shirt-sleeves. Some are so lifted up in the horizon that they
seem like portions of the earth detached and floating off by themselves into space.
Their dark masses against the sky can be seen as far, at least, as a white spire,
though it may be taller. Some of these trees, seen through a glass, are not so
large. . . .

This was what those scamps did in California. The trees were so grand and
venerable that they could not afford to let them grow a hair's breadth bigger, or
live a moment longer to reproach themselves. They were so big that they resolved
they should never be bigger. They were so venerable that they cut them right
down. It was not for the sake of the wood; it was only because they were very
grand and venerable.

Oct. 14.   Maple Leaves on the Ground

ON THE CAUSEWAY I pass by maples here and there which are bare and
smoke-like, having lost their brilliant clothing; but there it lies, nearly as bright
as ever, on one side on the ground, making nearly as regular a figure as lately on
the tree. I should rather say that I first observed the trees thus flat on the ground
like a permanent colored and substantial shadow, and they alone suggested to look

for the trees that had borne them. They preserve these bright colors on the ground but a short time, a day or so, especially if it rains.

Oct. 14.   Parti-Colored Pine Woods

SAT IN THE OLD pasture beyond the Corner Spring Woods to look at that pine wood now at the height of its change, pitch and white. Their change produces a very singular and pleasing effect. They are regularly parti-colored. The last year's leaves, about a foot beneath the extremities of the twigs on all sides, now changed and ready to fall, have their period of brightness as well as broader leaves. They are a clear yellow, contrasting with the fresh and liquid green of the terminal plumes, or this year's leaves. These two quite distinct colors are thus regularly and equally distributed over the whole tree. You have the warmth of the yellow and the coolness of the green. So it should be with our own maturity, not yellow to the very extremity of our shoots, but youthful and untried green ever putting forth afresh at the extremities, foretelling a maturity as yet unknown. The ripe leaves fall to the ground and become nutriment for the green ones, which still aspire to heaven. In the fall of the leaf, there is no fruit, there is no true maturity, neither in our science and wisdom.

Some aspens are a very fair yellow now, and trembling as in summer. I think it is they I see a mile off on Bear Garden Hill, amid the oaks and pines.

Oct. 14.   Reflections Never a True Copy

LOOKING NOW TOWARD THE north side of the pond, I perceive that the reflection of the hillside seen from an opposite hill is not so broad as the hillside itself appears, owing to the different angle at which it is seen. The reflection exhibits such an aspect of the hill, *apparently,* as you would get if your eye were placed at that part of the surface of the pond where the reflection seems to be. In this instance, too, then, Nature avoids repeating herself. Not even reflections in still water are like their substances as seen by us. This, too, accounts for my seeing portions of the sky through the trees in reflections often when none appear in the substance. Is the reflection of a hillside, however, such an aspect of it as can be obtained by the eye directed to the hill itself from any single point of view? It plainly is not such a view as the eye would get looking upward from the immediate base of the hill or water's edge, for there the first rank of bushes on the lower part of the hill would conceal the upper. The reflection of the top appears to be such a view of it as I should get with my eye at the water's edge above the edge of the reflection; but would the lower part of the hill also appear from this point as it does in the reflection? Should I see as much of the under sides of the leaves there? If not, then the reflection is never a true copy or repetition of its substance, but a new composition, and this may be the source of its novelty

and attractiveness, and of this nature, too, may be the charm of an echo. I doub[?]
if you can ever get Nature to repeat herself exactly.

Village maples.

Oct. 15. Sugar Maples in Our Streets

RAIN AT LAST, AND end of the remarkable days. The springs and river[?]
have been very low. Millers have not water enough to grind their grists.

There has been a great fall of leaves in the night on account of this moist an[?]
rainy weather; but hardly yet that touch that brings down the rock maple. Th[?]
streets are thickly strewn with elm and buttonwood and other leaves, *feuille-mort*
color. Some elms and butternuts are quite bare. Yet the sugar maples in our street[?]
are now in their prime and show unexpectedly bright and delicate tints, while som[?]
white maples by the river are nearly bare. I see, too, that all locusts did not becom[?]
crisp and fall before this without acquiring a bright color. In the churchyard the[?]
are unwithered, just turning a pale yellow. How many plants are either yellow o[?]
scarlet! Not only maples, but rose bushes, hazel bushes, etc., etc. Rue is a conspic[?]
uous pale yellow for a weed.

Oct. 16. Carpet of Pine Needles

AM SURPRISED TO FIND an abundance of witch-hazel, now at the heigh[?]
of its change, where S. Wheeler cut off, at the bend of the Assabet. The talles[?]
bushes are bare, though in bloom, but the lowest are full of leaves, many of then[?]
green, but chiefly clear and handsome yellow of various shades, from a pale lemo[?]
in the shade or within the bush to a darker and warmer yellow without. Some ar[?]
even a hue of crimson; some green, with bright yellow along the veins. Thi[?]
reminds me that, generally, plants exposed turn early, or not at all, while the sam[?]

species in the shade of the woods at a much later date assume very pure and delicate tints, as more withdrawn from the light.

You notice now many faded, almost white dicksonia ferns, and some brakes about as white.

A great part of the pine-needles have just fallen. See the carpet of pale-brown needles under this pine. How light it lies up on the grass, and that great rock, and the wall, resting thick on its top and its shelves, and on the bushes and underwood, hanging lightly! They are not yet flat and reddish, but a more delicate pale brown, and lie up light as joggle-sticks just dropped. The ground is nearly concealed by them. How beautifully they die, making cheerfully their annual contribution to the soil! They fall to rise again; as if they knew that it was not one annual deposit alone that made this rich mould in which pine trees grow. They live in the soil whose fertility and bulk they increase, and in the forests that spring from it.

The leaves that were floating before the rain have now sunk to the bottom, being wetted above as well as below.

Oct. 22.   The Crescent of Mountains

LOOK FROM THE HIGH hill, just before sundown, over the pond. The mountains are a mere cold slate-color. But what a perfect crescent of mountains we have in our northwest horizon! Do we ever give thanks for it? Even as pines and larches and hemlocks grow in communities in the wilderness, so, it seems, do mountains love society and form a community in the horizon. Though there may be two or more ranges, one behind the other, and ten or twelve miles between them, yet if the farthest are the highest, they are all seen as one group at this distance. I look up northwest toward my mountains, as a farmer to his hill lot or rocky pasture from his door. I drive no cattle to Ipswich hills. I own no pasture for them there. My eyes it is alone that wander to those blue pastures, which no drought affects. They are my flocks and herds. See how they look. They are shaped like tents, inclining to sharp peaks. What is it lifts them upward so? Why not rest level along the horizon? They seem not perfect, they seem not satisfied, until their central parts have curved upward to a sharp summit. They are a succession of pickets with scallops between. That side my pasture is well fenced. This being their upper side, I fancy they must have a corresponding under side and roots also. Might they not be dug up like a turnip? Perhaps they spring from seeds which some wind sowed. Can't the Patent Office import some of the seed of Himmaleh with its next rutabagas? Spore of mountains has fallen there; it came from the gills of an agaric. Ah, I am content to dwell there and see the sun go down behind my mountain fence.

Oct. 28.   Noble Fruit, an Apple

EVEN THE SOUREST AND crabbedest apple, growing in the most unfavorable position, suggests such thoughts as these, it [is] so noble a fruit.

Planted by a bird on a wild and rocky hillside, it bears a fruit, perchance, which foreign potentates shall hear of and send for, though the virtues of the owner of the soil may never be heard of beyond the limits of his village. It may be the choicest fruit of its kind. Every wild apple shrub excites our expectation thus. It is a prince in disguise, perhaps.

Oct. 28. A Browsed Apple Tree

SUPPOSE I SEE A single green apple, brought to perfection on some thorny shrub, far in a wild pasture where no cow has plucked it. It is an agreeable surprise. What chemistry has been at work there? It affects me somewhat like a work of art. I see some shrubs which cattle have browsed for twenty years, keeping them down and compelling them to spread, until at last they are so broad they become their own fence and some interior shoot darts upward and bears its fruit! What a lesson to man! So are human beings, referred to the highest standard, the celestial fruit which they suggest and aspire to bear, browsed on by fate, and only the most persistent and strongest genius prevails, defends itself, sends a tender scion upward at last, and drops its perfect fruit on the ungrateful earth; and that fruit, though somewhat smaller, perchance, is essentially the same in flavor and quality as if it had grown in a garden. That fruit seems all the sweeter and more palatable even for the very difficulties it has contended with.

Here, on this rugged and woody hillside, has grown an apple tree, not planted by man, no relic of a former orchard, but a natural growth like the pines and oaks. Most fruits we prize and use depend entirely on our care. Corn and grain, potatoes, peaches *(here),* and melons, etc., depend altogether on our planting, but the apple emulates man's independence and enterprise. Like him to some extent, it has migrated to this new world and is ever here and there making its way amid the aboriginal trees. It accompanies man like the ox and dog and horse, which also sometimes run wild and maintain themselves.

Oct. 31. Some Green Ferns

IN THE LEE FARM swamp, by the old Sam Barrett mill site, I see two kinds of ferns still green and much in fruit, apparently the *Aspidium spinulosum* (?) and *cristatum* (?).[2] They are also common in other swamps now. They are quite fresh in those cold and wet places and almost flattened down now. The atmosphere of the house is less congenial to them. In the summer you might not have noticed them. Now they are conspicuous amid the withered leaves. You are inclined to approach and raise each frond in succession, moist, trembling, fragile greenness. They linger thus in all moist clammy swamps under the bare maples and grape-vines and witch-hazels, and about each trickling spring which is half choked with fallen leaves. What means this persistent vitality, invulnerable to frost and wet? Why were these spared when the brakes and osmundas were stricken down? They stay as if to keep up the spirits of the cold-blooded frogs which have not yet gone into the mud; that the summer may die with decent and graceful moderation, gradually. Is not the water of the spring improved by their presence? They fall back and droop here and there, like the plumes of departing summer,—of the departing year. Even in them I feel an argument for immortality. Death is so far from being universal. The same destroyer does not destroy all. How valuable they are (with the lycopodiums) for cheerfulness. Greenness at the end of the year, after the fall of the leaf, as in a hale old age. To my eyes they are tall and noble as palm groves, and always some forest nobleness seems to have its haunt under their umbrage. Each such green tuft of ferns is a grove where some nobility dwells and walks. All that was immortal in the swamp's herbage seems here crowded into smaller compass,—the concentrated greenness of the swamp. How dear they must be to the chickadee and the rabbit! The cool, slowly retreating rear-guard of the swamp army. What virtue is theirs that enables them to resist the frost?

Nov. 2.   Reflected Surface Abstractions

Returning, I see the red oak on R. W. E.'s shore reflected in the bright sky water. In the reflection the tree is black against the clear whitish sky, though as I see it against the opposite woods it is a warm greenish yellow. But the river sees it against the bright sky, and hence the reflection is like ink. The water tells me how it looks to it seen from below. I think that most men, as farmers, hunters, fishers, etc., walk along a river's bank, or paddle along its stream, without seeing the reflections. Their minds are not abstracted from the surface, from surfaces generally. It is only a reflecting mind that sees reflections. I am aware often that I have been occupied with shallow and commonplace thoughts, looking for something superficial, when I did not see the most glorious reflections, though exactly in the line of my vision. If the fisherman was looking at the reflection, he would not know when he had a nibble! I know from my own experience that he may cast his line right over the most elysian landscape and sky, and not *catch* the slightest notion of them. You must be in an abstract mood to see reflections however distinct. I was even startled by the sight of that reflected red oak as if it were a black water-spirit. When we are enough abstracted, the opaque earth itself reflects images to us; *i. e.*, we are imaginative, see visions, etc. Such a reflection, this inky, leafy tree, against the white sky, can only be seen at this season.

Nov. 3.   Rocks as a Picture Frame

Follow up the Boulder Field northward, and it terminates in that moraine. As I return down the Boulder Field, I see the now winter-colored—*i.e.* reddish (of oak leaves)—horizon of hills, with its few white houses, four or five miles distant southward, between two of the boulders, which are a dozen rods from me, a dozen feet high, and nearly as much apart,—as a landscape between the frame of a picture. But what a picture-frame! These two great slumbering masses

Oak tree and boulders.

of rock, reposing like a pair of mastodons on the surface of the pasture, completely shutting out a mile of the horizon on each side, while between their adjacent sides, which are nearly perpendicular, I see to the now purified, dry, reddish, leafy horizon, with a faint tinge of blue from the distance. To see a remote landscape between two near rocks! I want no other gilding to my picture-frame. There they lie, as perchance they tumbled and split from off an iceberg. What better frame could you have? The globe itself, here named pasture, for ground and foreground, two great boulders for the sides of the frame, and the sky itself for the top! And for artists and subject, God and Nature! Such pictures cost nothing but eyes, and it will not bankrupt one to own them. They were not stolen by any conqueror as spoils of war, and none can doubt but they are really the works of an old master. What more, pray, will you see between any two slips of gilded wood in that pasture you call Europe and browse in sometimes? It is singular that several of those rocks should be thus split into twins. Even very low ones, just appearing above the surface, are divided and parallel, having a path between them.

It would be something to own that pasture with the great rocks in it! And yet I suppose they are considered an incumbrance only by the owner.

Nov. 3. Sun Penetrated Woods

COMING BY EBBY HUBBARD'S thick maple and pine wood, I see the rays of the sun, now not much above the horizon, penetrating quite through it to my side in very narrow and slender glades of light, peculiarly bright. It seems, then, that no wood is so dense but that the rays of the setting sun may penetrate twenty rods into it. The other day (November 1st), I stood on the sunny side of such a wood at the same season, or a little earlier. Then I saw the lit sides of the tree stems all aglow with their lichens, and observed their black shadows behind. Now I see chiefly the dark stems massed together, and it is the warm sunlight that is reduced to a pencil of light: *i.e.,* then light was the rule and shadow the exception, now shadow the rule and light the exception.

Nov. 4. A Stump with New Life

P. M.—To Pine Hill *via* Spanish Brook.
   I leave the railroad at Walden Crossing and follow the path to Spanish Brook. How swift Nature is to repair the damage that man does! When he has cut down a tree and left only a white-topped and bleeding stump, she comes at once to the rescue with her chemistry, and covers it decently with a fresh coat of gray, and in course of time she adds a thick coat of green cup and bright cockscomb lichens, and it becomes an object of new interest to the lover of nature! Suppose it were always to remain a raw stump instead! It becomes a shell on which this humble vegetation spreads and displays itself, and we forget the death of the larger in the life of the less.

Nov. 4. Mountains from Pine Hill

I climb Pine Hill just as the sun is setting, this cool evening. Sitting with my back to a thick oak sprout whose leaves still glow with life, Walden lies an oblong square endwise to, beneath me. Its surface is slightly rippled, and dusky prolonged reflections of trees extend wholly across its length, or half a mile,—I sit high. The sun is once or twice its diameter above the horizon, and the mountains north of it stand out grand and distinct, a decided purple. But when I look critically, I distinguish a whitish mist—such is the color of the denser air—about their lower parts, while their tops are dark-blue. (So the mountains too have a bloom on them; and is not the bloom on fruits equivalent to that blue veil of air which distance gives to many objects?) I see one glistening reflection on the dusky and leafy northwestern earth, seven or eight miles off, betraying a window there, though no house can be seen. It twinkles incessantly, as from a waving surface. This, probably, is the undulation of the air. Now that the sun is actually setting, the mountains are dark-blue from top to bottom. As usual, a small cloud attends the sun to the portals of the day and reflects this brightness to us, now that he is gone. But those grand and glorious mountains, how impossible to remember daily that they are there, and to live accordingly! They are meant to be a perpetual reminder to us, pointing out the way.

Nov. 5. A Transient Glimpse

SOMETIMES I WOULD RATHER get a transient glimpse or side view of a thing than stand fronting to it,—as those polypodies. The object I caught a glimpse of as I went by haunts my thoughts a long time, is infinitely suggestive, and I do not care to front it and scrutinize it, for I know that the thing that really concerns me is not there, but in my relation to that. That is a mere reflecting surface. It is not the polypody in my pitcher or herbarium, or which I may possibly persuade to grow on a bank in my yard, or which is described in botanies, that interests me, but the one that I pass by in my walks a little distance off, when in the right mood. Its influence is sporadic, wafted through the air to me. Do you imagine its fruit to stick to the back of the leaf all winter? At this season polypody is in the air. It is worth the while to walk in swamps now, to bathe your eyes with greenness. The terminal shield fern is the handsomest and glossiest green.

Start up a snipe feeding in a wet part of the Dam Meadows.

I think that the man of science makes this mistake, and the mass of mankind along with him: that you should coolly give your chief attention to the phenomenon which excites you as something independent on you, and not as it is related to you. The important fact is its effect on me. He thinks that I have no business to see anything else but just what he defines the rainbow to be, but I care not whether my vision of truth is a waking thought or dream remembered, whether it is seen in the light or in the dark. It is the subject of the vision, the truth alone, that concerns me. The philosopher for whom rainbows, etc., can be explained away never saw them. With regard to such objects, I find that it is not they themselves (with which the men of science deal) that concern me; the point of interest is somewhere *between* me and them (*i. e.* the objects). . . .

Nov. 8. A Walk in Thick Air

WHEN THE AIR IS thick and the sky overcast, we need not walk so far. We give our attention to nearer objects, being less distracted from them. I take occasion to explore some near wood which my walks commonly overshoot.

What a difference it makes between two ravines in other respects exactly similar that in the one there is a stream which drains it, while the other is dry!

Nov. 18. Perception of Nature

THERE ARE MANY WAYS of feeling one's pulse. In a healthy state the constant experience is a pleasurable sensation or sentiment. For instance, in such a state I find myself in perfect connection with nature, and the perception, or remembrance even, of any natural phenomena is attended with a gentle pleasurable excitement. Prevailing sights and sounds make the impression of beauty and music on me. But in sickness all is deranged. I had yesterday a kink in my back and a general cold, and as usual it amounted to a cessation of life. I lost for the time my *rapport* or relation to nature. Sympathy with nature is an evidence of perfect health. You cannot perceive beauty but with a serene mind.

Nov. 20. He Who Has Lived the Deepest

IN BOOKS, THAT WHICH is most generally interesting is what comes home to the most cherished private experience of the greatest number. It is not the book of him who has travelled the farthest over the surface of the globe, but of him who has lived the deepest and been the most at home. If an equal emotion is excited by a familiar homely phenomenon as by the Pyramids, there is no advantage in seeing the Pyramids. It is on the whole better, as it is simpler, to use the common language. We require that the reporter be very permanently planted before the facts which he observes, not a mere passer-by; hence the facts cannot be too homely. A man is worth most to himself and to others, whether as an observer, or poet, or neighbor, or friend, where he is most himself, most contented and at home. There his life is the most intense and he loses the fewest moments. Familiar and surrounding objects are the best symbols and illustrations of his life. If a man who has had deep experiences should endeavor to describe them in a book of travels, it would be to use the language of a wandering tribe instead of a universal language. The poet has made the best roots in his native soil of any man, and is the hardest to transplant. The man who is often thinking that it is better to be somewhere else than where he is excommunicates himself. If a man is rich and strong anywhere, it must be on his native soil. Here I have been these forty years learning the language of these fields that I may the better express myself. If I should travel to the prairies, I should much less understand them, and my past life would serve me but ill to describe them. Many a weed here stands for more of life to me than the big trees of California would if I should go there. We only need travel enough to give our intellects an airing. In spite of Malthus and the rest, there will be plenty of room in this world, if every man will mind his own business. I have not heard of any planet running against another yet.

Nov. 26. Minott's Weather-Stained House

MINOTT'S IS A SMALL, square, one-storied and unpainted house, with a hipped roof and at least one dormer-window, a third the way up the south side of a long hill which is some fifty feet high and extends east and west. A traveller of taste may go straight through the village without being detained a moment by any dwelling, either the form or surroundings being objectionable, but very few go by this house without being agreeably impressed, and many are therefore led to inquire who lives in it. Not that its form is so incomparable, nor even its weather-stained color, but chiefly, I think, because of its snug and picturesque position on the hillside, fairly lodged there, where all children like to be, and its perfect harmony with its surroundings and position. For if, preserving this form and color, it should be transplanted to the meadow below, nobody would notice it more than a schoolhouse which was lately of the same form. It is there because somebody was independent or bold enough to carry out the happy thought of placing it high on the hillside. It is the locality, not the architecture, that takes us captive. There is exactly such a site, only of course less room on either side, between this house and the next westward, but few if any, even of the admiring travellers, have thought of this as a house-lot, or would be bold enough to place a cottage there.

Without side fences or gravelled walks or flowerplats, that simple sloping bank before it is pleasanter than any front yard, though many a visitor—and many times the master—has slipped and fallen on the steep path. From its position and exposure, it has shelter and warmth and dryness and prospect. He overlooks the road, the meadow and brook, and houses beyond, to the distant woods. The spring comes earlier to that dooryard than to any, and summer lingers longest there.

CHAPTER X

YEAR
1858
AGE
40–41

Jan. 4. Down River from Fair Haven

P.M.—THE WEATHER STILL remarkably warm; the ice too soft for
skating. I go through by the Andromeda Ponds and down river from Fair Haven.
I am encouraged by the sight of men fishing in Fair Haven Pond, for it reminds
me that they have animal spirits for such adventures. I am glad to be reminded
that any go a-fishing. When I get down near to Cardinal Shore, the sun near
setting, its light is wonderfully reflected from a narrow edging of yellowish stubble
at the edge of the meadow ice and foot of the hill, an edging only two or three
feet wide, and the stubble but a few inches high. (I am looking east.) It is
remarkable because the ice is but a dull lead-color (it is so soft and sodden),

reflecting no light, and the hill beyond is a dark russet, here and there patched with snow, but this narrow intermediate line of stubble is all aglow. I get its true color and brightness best when I do not look directly at it, but a little above it toward the hill, seeing it with the lower part of my eye more truly and abstractly. It is as if all the rays slid over the ice and lodged against and were reflected by the stubble. It is surprising how much sunny light a little straw that survives the winter will reflect.

Nearing the ridge.

Feb. 7. A Hill Approach

IF POSSIBLE, COME UPON the top of a hill unexpectedly, perhaps through woods, and then see off from it to the distant earth which lies behind a bluer veil, before you can see directly down it, *i. e.* bringing its own near top against the distant landscape.

March 5. Indian Definitions

WE READ THE ENGLISH poets; we study botany and zoölogy and geology, lean and dry as they are; and it is rare that we get a new suggestion. It is ebb-tide with the scientific reports, Professor–in the chair. We would fain know something more about these animals and stones and trees around us. We are ready to skin the animals alive to come at them. Our scientific names convey a very partial information only; they suggest certain thoughts only. It does not occur to me that there are other names for most of these objects, given by a people who stood between me and them, who had better senses than our race. How little I know of that *arbor-vitæ* when I have learned only what science can tell me! It is but a word. It is not a *tree* of *life*. But there are twenty words for the tree and its different parts which the Indian gave, which are not in our botanies, which imply a more practical and vital science. He used it every day. He was well acquainted with its wood, and its bark, and its leaves. No science does more than arrange what knowledge we have of any class of objects. But, generally speaking, how much more conversant was the Indian with any wild animal or plant than we are, and in his language is implied all that intimacy, as much as ours is expressed in our language. How many words in his language about a moose, or birch bark, and the like! The Indian stood nearer to wild nature than we. The wildest and noblest quadrupeds, even the largest fresh-water fishes, some of the wildest and noblest birds and the fairest flowers have actually receded as *we* advanced, and we have but the most distant knowledge of them. A rumor has come down to us that the skin of a lion was seen and his roar heard here by an early settler. But there was a race here that slept on his skin. It was a new light when my guide gave me Indian names for things for which I had only scientific ones before. In proportion as I understood the language, I saw them from a new point of view.

March 18. A Spring Landscape

WHEN I GET TWO thirds up the hill, I look round and am for the hundredth time surprised by the landscape of the river valley and the horizon with its distant blue scalloped rim. It is a spring landscape, and as impossible a fortnight ago as the song of birds. It is a deeper and warmer blue than in winter, methinks. The snow is off the mountains, which seem even to have come again like the birds. The undulating river is a bright-blue channel between sharp-edged shores of ice retained by the willows. The wind blows strong but warm from west by north, so that I have to hold my paper tight when I write this, making the copses creak and roar; but the sharp tinkle of a song sparrow is heard through it all. But ah! the needles of the pine, how they shine, as I look down over the Holden wood and westward! Every third tree is lit with the most subdued but clear ethereal light, as if it were the most delicate frostwork in a winter morning, reflecting no heat, but only light. And as they rock and wave in the strong wind, even a mile off, the light courses up and down there as over a field of grain; *i. e.,* they are alternately light and dark, like looms above the forest, when the shuttle is thrown between the light woof and the dark web, weaving a light article,—spring goods for Nature to wear. At sight of this my spirit is like a lit tree. It runs or flashes over their parallel boughs as when you play with the teeth of a comb. The pinetops wave like squirrels' tails flashing in the air. Not only osiers but pine-needles, methinks, shine in the spring, and arrowheads and railroad rails, etc., etc. Anacreon noticed the same. Is it not the higher sun, and cleansed air, and greater animation of nature? There is a warmer red to the leaves of the shrub oak, and to the tail of the hawk circling over them.

I sit on the Cliff, and look toward Sudbury. I see its meeting-houses and its common, and its fields lie but little beyond my ordinary walk, but I never played on its common nor read the epitaphs in its graveyard, and many strangers to me dwell there. How distant in all important senses may be the town which yet is within sight! We see beyond our ordinary walks and thoughts. With a glass I might perchance read the time on its clock. How circumscribed are our walks, after all! With the utmost industry we cannot expect to know well an area more than six miles square, and yet we pretend to be travellers, to be acquainted with Siberia and Africa!

March 20. Interesting House and Grounds

IN ORDER THAT A house and grounds may be picturesque and interesting in the highest degree, they must suggest the idea of necessity, proving the devotion of the builder, not of luxury. We need to see the honest and naked life here and there protruding. What is a fort without any foe before it, that is not now sustaining and never has sustained a siege? The gentleman whose purse is always full, who can meet all demands, though he employs the most famous artists, can never make a very interesting seat. He does not carve from near enough to the bone. No man is rich enough to keep a poet in his pay.

March 28. This Hilltop I Overlook

FROM THIS HILLTOP I overlook, again bare of snow, putting on a warm, hazy spring face, this seemingly concave circle of earth, in the midst of which I was born and dwell, which in the northwest and southeast has a more distant blue rim to it, as it were of more costly manufacture. On ascending the hill next his home, every man finds that he dwells in a shallow concavity whose sheltering walls are the convex surface of the earth, beyond which he cannot see. I see those familiar features, that large type, with which all my life is associated, unchanged.

May 6. Build with Thoughts

THE THINKER, HE WHO is serene and self-possessed, is the brave, not the desperate soldier. He who can deal with his thoughts as a material, building them into poems in which future generations will delight, he is the man of the greatest and rarest vigor, not sturdy diggers and lusty polygamists. He is the man of energy, in whom subtle and poetic thoughts are bred. Common men can enjoy partially; they can go a-fishing rainy days; they can *read* poems perchance, but they have not the vigor to beget poems. They can enjoy feebly, but they cannot create. Men talk of freedom! How many are free to think? free from fear, from perturbation, from prejudice? Nine hundred and ninety-nine in a thousand are perfect slaves. How many can exercise the highest human faculties? He is the man truly— courageous, wise, ingenious—who can use his thoughts and ecstasies as the material of fair and durable creations. One man shall derive from the fisherman's story more than the fisher has got who tells it. The mass of men do not know how to cultivate the fields they traverse. The mass glean only a scanty pittance where the thinker reaps an abundant harvest. What is all your building, if you do not build with thoughts? No exercise implies more real manhood and vigor than joining thought to thought. How few men can tell what they have thought! I hardly know half a dozen who are not too lazy for this. They cannot get over some difficulty, and therefore they are on the long way round. You conquer fate by thought. If you think the fatal thought of men and institutions, you need never pull the trigger. The consequences of thinking inevitably follow. There is no more Herculean task than to think a thought about this life and then get it expressed.

May 17. Grand Mountain View

I THOUGHT YESTERDAY THAT the view of the mountains from the bare hill on the Lincoln side of Flint's Pond was very grand. Surely they do not look so grand anywhere within twenty miles of them. And I reflected what kind of life it must be that is lived always in sight of them. I looked round at some windows in the middle of Lincoln and considered that such was the privilege of the inhabitants of these chambers; but their blinds were closed, and I have but little doubt that they are *blind* to the beauty and sublimity of this prospect. I doubt if in the landscape there can be anything finer than a distant mountain-range. They are a constant elevating influence.

June 2. Start for Monadnock Climb

8:30 A.M.—START FOR MONADNOCK.

Between Shirley Village and Lunenburg, I notice, in a meadow on the right hand, close to the railroad, the *Kalmia glauca* in bloom, as we are whirled past. The conductor says that he has it growing in his garden. Blake joins me at Fitchburg. Between Fitchburg and Troy saw an abundance of wild red cherry, now apparently in prime, in full bloom, especially in burnt lands and on hillsides, a small but cheerful lively white bloom.

Arrived at Troy Station at 11.5 and shouldered our knapsacks, steering northeast to the mountain, some four miles off,—its top. It is a pleasant hilly road, leading past a few farmhouses, where you already begin to snuff the mountain, or at least up-country, air. By the roadside I plucked, now apparently in prime, the *Ribes Cynosbati,* rather downy leaved, and, near by, the same with smooth berries. I noticed, too, the *Salix lucida,* by the roadside there on high land; the *S. rostrata,* etc., were common.

Almost without interruption we had the mountain in sight before us,—its sublime gray mass—that antique, brownish-gray, Ararat color. Probably these crests of the earth are for the most part of one color in all lands, that gray color of antiquity, which nature loves; color of unpainted wood, weather-stain, time-stain; not glaring nor gaudy; the color of all roofs, the color of things that endure, and the color that wears well; color of Egyptian ruins, of mummies and all antiquity; baked in the sun, done brown. Methought I saw the same color with which Ararat and Caucasus and all earth's brows are stained, which was mixed in antiquity and receives a new coat every century; not scarlet, like the crest of the bragging cock, but that hard, enduring gray; a terrene sky-color; solidified air with a tinge of earth.

June 3. Lichens on Rocks, Monadnock

AS I WALKED OVER this plateau, I first observed, looking toward the summit, that the steep angular projections of the summit and elsewhere and the brows of the rocks were the parts chiefly covered with dark-brown lichens,— umbilicaria, etc.,—as if they were to grow on the ridge and slopes of a man's nose only. It was the steepest and most exposed parts of the high rocks alone on which they grew, where you would think it most difficult for them to cling. They also covered the more rounded brows on the sides of the mountain, especially the east side, where they were very dense, fine, crisp, and firm, like a sort of shagreen, giving a firm footing or hold to the feet where it was needed. It was these that gave that Ararat-brown color of antiquity to these portions of the mountain, which a few miles distant could not be accounted for compared with the more prevalent gray. From the sky-blue you pass through the misty gray of the rocks, to this darker and more terrene color. The temples of the mountain are covered with lichens, which color the mountain for miles.

June 3. Top of Monadnock

WE HAD THUS MADE a pretty complete survey of the top of the mountain. It is a very unique walk, and would be almost equally interesting to take though it were not elevated above the surrounding valleys. It often reminded me of my walks on the beach, and suggested how much both depend for their sublimity on solitude and dreariness. In both cases we feel the presence of some vast, titanic power. The rocks and valleys and bogs and rain-pools of the mountain are so wild and unfamiliar still that you do not recognize the one you left fifteen minutes before. This rocky region, forming what you may call the top of the mountain, must be more than two miles long by one wide in the middle, and you would need to ramble about it many times before it would begin to be familiar. There may be twenty little swamps so much alike in the main that [you] would not know whether you had seen a particular one before, and the rocks are trackless and do not present the same point. So that it has the effect of the most intricate labyrinth and artificially extended walk.

June 4. Leaving Monadnock

IT IS REMARKABLE HOW, as you are leaving a mountain and looking back at it from time to time, it gradually gathers up its slopes and spurs to itself into a regular whole, and makes a new and total impression. The lofty beaked promontory which, when you were on the summit, appeared so far off and almost equal to it, seen now against the latter, scarcely deepens the tinge of bluish, misty gray on its side. The mountain has several spurs or ridges, bare and rocky, running from it, with a considerable depression between the central peak and them; *i.e.,* they attain their greatest height half a mile or more from the central apex. There is such a spur, for instance, running off southward about a mile. When we looked back from four or five miles distant on the south, this, which had appeared like an independent summit, was almost totally lost to our view against the general misty gray of the side of the principal summit. We should not have suspected its existence if we had not just come from it, and though the mountain ranges northeasterly and southwesterly, or not far from north and south, and is much the longest in that direction, it now presented a pretty regular pyramidal outline with a broad base, as if it were broadest east and west. That is, when you are on the mountain, the different peaks and ridges appear more independent; indeed, there is a bewildering variety of ridge and valley and peak, but when you have withdrawn a few miles, you are surprised at the more or less pyramidal outline of the mountain and that the lower spurs and peaks are all subordinated to the central and principal one. The summit appears to rise and the surrounding peaks to subside, though some new prominences appear. Even at this short distance the mountain has lost most of its rough and jagged outline, considerable ravines are smoothed over, and large boulders which you must go a long way round make no impression on the eye, being swallowed up in the air.

July 2. Banks of the Merrimack

WHAT A RELIEF AND expansion of my thoughts when I come out from that inland position by the graveyard to this broad river's shore! This vista was incredible there. Suddenly I see a broad reach of blue beneath, with its curves and headlands, liberating me from the more terrene earth. What a difference it makes whether I spend my four hours' nooning between the hills by yonder roadside, or on the brink of this fair river, within a quarter of a mile of that! Here the earth is fluid to my thought, the sky is reflected from beneath, and around yonder cape is the highway to other continents. This current allies me to all the world. Be careful to sit in an elevating and inspiring place. There my thoughts were confined and trivial, and I hid myself from the gaze of travellers. Here they are expanded and elevated, and I am charmed by the beautiful river-reach. It is equal to a different season and country and creates a different mood. As you travel northward from Concord, probably the reaches of the Merrimack River, looking up or down them from the bank, will be the first inspiring sight. There is something in the scenery of a broad river equivalent to culture and civilization. Its channel conducts our thoughts as well as bodies to classic and famous ports, and allies us to all that is fair and great. I like to remember that at the end of half a day's walk I can stand on the bank of the Merrimack. It is just wide enough to interrupt the land and lead my eye and thoughts down its channel to the sea. A river is superior to a lake in its liberating influence. It has motion and indefinite length. A river touching the back of a town is like a wing, it may be unusued as yet, but ready to waft it over the world. With its rapid current it is a slightly fluttering wing. River towns are winged towns.

July 18. Convenience of the Traveller

JULY 18. SUNDAY. KEEP on through New Boston, the east side of Mount Vernon, Amherst to Hollis, and noon by a mill-pond in the woods, on Pennichook Brook, in Hollis, or three miles north of village. At evening go on to Pepperell. A marked difference when we enter Massachusetts, in roads, farms, houses, trees, fences, etc.,—a great improvement, showing an older-settled country. In New Hampshire there is a greater want of shade trees, but long bleak or sunny roads from which there is no escape. What barbarians we are! The convenience of the traveller is very little consulted. He merely has the privilege of crossing somebody's farm by a particular narrow and maybe unpleasant path. The individual retains all other rights,—as to trees and fruit, and wash of the road, etc. On the other hand, these should belong to mankind inalienably. The road should be of ample width and adorned with trees expressly for the use of the traveller. There should be broad recesses in it, especially at springs and watering-places, where he can turn out and rest, or camp if he will. I feel commonly as if I were condemned to drive through somebody's cow-yard or huckleberry pasture by a narrow lane, and if I make a fire by the roadside to boil my hasty pudding, the farmer comes running over to see if I am not burning up his stuff. You are barked along through the country, from door to door.

Aug. 6. Value of Country Life

I HEAR OF PICKERS ordered out of the huckleberry-fields, and I see stakes set up with written notices forbidding any to pick there. Some let their fields, or allow so much for the picking. *Sic transit gloria ruris.* We are not grateful enough that we have lived part of our lives before these evil days came. What becomes of the true value of country life? What if you must go to market for it? Shall things come to such a pass that the butcher commonly brings round huckleberries in his cart? It is as if the hangman were to perform the marriage ceremony, or were to preside at the communion table. Such is the inevitable tendency of *our* civilization,—to reduce huckleberries to a level with beef-steak. The butcher's item on the door is now "calf's head and huckleberries." I suspect that the inhabitants of England and of the Continent of Europe have thus lost their natural rights with the increase of population and of monopolies. The wild fruits of the earth disappear before civilization, or are only to be found in large markets. The whole country becomes, as it were, a town or beaten common, and the fruits left are a few hips and haws.

Aug. 12. High-Colored Purple Grass

THAT VERY HANDSOME HIGH-COLORED fine purple grass grows particularly on dry and rather unproductive soil just above the edge of the meadows, on the base of the hills, where the hayer does not deign to swing his scythe. He carefully gets the meadow-hay and the richer grass that borders it, but leaves this fine purple mist for the walker's harvest. Higher up the hill, perchance, grow blackberries and johnswort and neglected and withered and wiry June-grass. Twenty or thirty rods off it appears as a high-colored purple border above the meadow, like a berry's stain laid on close and thick, but if you pluck one plant you will be surprised to find how thin it is and how little color it has. What puny causes combine to produce such decided effects! There is ripeness in its color as in the poke stem. It grows in waste places, perhaps on the edge of blackberry-fields, a thin, fine, spreading grass, left by the mower. It oftenest grows in scattered rounded tufts a foot in diameter, especially on gentle slopes.

Aug. 23. Discover Something Old

THE WRITER NEEDS THE suggestion and correction that a correspondent or companion is. I sometimes remember something which I have told another as worth telling to myself, *i. e.* writing in my Journal.

Channing, thinking of walks and life in the country, says, "You don't want to discover anything new, but to discover something old," *i. e.* be reminded that such things still are.

Aug. 26. Tall Purple Grasses

TWO INTERESTING TALL PURPLISH grasses appear to be the prevailing ones now in dry and sterile neglected fields and hillsides,—*Andropogon furcatus,* forked beard grass, and apparently *Andropogon scoparius,* purple wood grass, though the last appears to have three awns like an *Aristida.* The first is a very tall and slender-culmed grass, with four or five purple finger-like spikes, raying upward from the top. It is very abundant on the hillside behind Peter's. The other is also quite slender, two to three or four feet high, growing in tufts and somewhat curving, also commonly purple and with pretty purple stigmas like the last, and it has purple anthers. When out of bloom, its appressed spikes are recurving and have a whitish hairy or fuzzy look.

These are the prevailing conspicuous flowers where I walk this afternoon in dry ground. I have sympathy with them because they are despised by the farmer and occupy sterile and neglected soil. They also by their rich purple reflections or tinges seem to express the ripeness of the year. It is high-colored like ripe grapes, and expresses a maturity which the spring did not suggest.

Only the August sun could have thus burnished these culms and leaves. The farmer has long since done his upland haying, and he will not deign to bring his scythe to where these slender wild grasses have at length flowered thinly. You often see the bare sand between them. I walk encouraged between the tufts of purple wood grass, over the sandy fields by the shrub oaks, glad to recognize these simple contemporaries. These two are almost the first grasses that I have learned to distinguish. I did not know by how many friends I was surrounded. The purple of their culms excites me like that of the pokeweed stems.

Think what refuge there is for me before August is over, from college commencements and society that isolates me! I can skulk amid the tufts of purple wood grass on the borders of the Great Fields! Wherever I walk this afternoon the purple-fingered grass stands like a guide-board and points my thoughts to more poetic paths than they have lately travelled.

A man shall, perchance, rush by and trample down plants as high as his head, and cannot be said to know that they exist, though he may have cut and cured many tons of them for his cattle. Yet, perchance, if he ever favorably attend to them, he may be overcome by their beauty.

Each humblest plant, or weed, as we call it, stands there to express some thought or mood of ours, and yet how long it stands in vain! I have walked these Great Fields so many Augusts and never yet distinctly recognized these purple companions that I have there. I have brushed against them and trampled them down, forsooth, and now at last they have, as it were, risen up and blessed me. Beauty and true wealth are always thus cheap and despised. Heaven, or paradise, might be defined as the place which men avoid. Who can doubt that these grasses which the farmer says are of no account to him find some compensation in my appreciation of them? I may say that I never saw them before, or can only recall a dim vision of them, and now wherever I go I hardly see anything else. It is the reign and presidency only of the andropogons.

Sept. 8.　Stirring About Your Affairs

It is good policy to be stirring about your affairs, for the reward of activity and energy is that if you do not accomplish the object you had professed to yourself, you do accomplish something else. So, in my botanizing or natural history walks, it commonly turns out that, going for one thing, I get another thing. "Though man proposeth, God disposeth all."

Sept. 9.　Intention of the Eye

It requires a different intention of the eye in the same locality to see different plants, as, for example, *Juncaceæ* and *Gramineæ* even; *i. e.,* I find that when I am looking for the former, I do not see the latter in their midst. How much more, then, it requires different intentions of the eye and of the mind to attend to different departments of knowledge! How differently the poet and the naturalist look at objects! A man sees only what concerns him. A botanist absorbed in the pursuit of grasses does not distinguish the grandest pasture oaks. He as it were tramples down oaks unwittingly in his walk.

Sept. 18. The Clamshell Hills

NEVERTHELESS, WHEN, TURNING MY head, I looked at the willowy edge of Cyanean Meadow and onward to the sober-colored but fine-grained Clamshell Hills, about which there was no glitter, I was inclined to think that the truest beauty was that which surrounded us but which we failed to discern, that the forms and colors which adorn our daily life, not seen afar in the horizon, are our fairest jewelry. The beauty of Clamshell Hill, near at hand, with its sandy ravines, in which the cricket chirps. This is an Occidental city, not less glorious than that we dream of in the sunset sky.

Oct. 9. To the Cliffs

COLD AND NORTHWEST WIND still. The maple swamps begin to look smoky, they are already so bare. Their fires, so faded, are pale-scarlet or pinkish. Some *Cornus sericea* looks quite greenish yet. Huckleberry leaves falling fast.

I go to the Cliffs. The air is clear, with a cold northwest wind, and the trees beginning to be bare. The mountains are darker and distincter, and Walden, seen from this hill, darker blue. It is quite Novemberish. People are making haste to gather the remaining apples this cool evening. Bay-wings flit along road.

Southwest side of Walden Pond
with railroad embankment to the shore, Concord, Massachusetts.

Oct. 10. Fungus as Inspired Matter

THE SIMPLEST AND MOST lumpish fungus has a peculiar interest to us, compared with a mere mass of earth, because it is so obviously organic and related to ourselves, however mute. It is the expression of an idea; growth according to a law; matter not dormant, not raw, but inspired, appropriated by spirit. If I take up a handful of earth, however separately interesting the particles may be, their relation to one another appears to be that of mere juxtaposition generally. I might have thrown them together thus. But the humblest fungus betrays a life akin to my own. It is a successful poem in its kind. There is suggested something superior to any particle of matter, in the idea or mind which uses and arranges the particles.

Oct. 12. Nature Is Confident

THERE ARE MANY MAPLE, birch, etc., leaves on the Assabet, in stiller places along the shore, but not yet a leaf harvest. Many swamp white oaks look crisp and brown.

I land at Pinxter Swamp. The leaves of the azaleas are falling, mostly fallen, and revealing the large blossom-buds, so prepared are they for another year. With man all is uncertainty. He does not confidently look forward to another spring. But examine the root of the savory-leaved aster, and you will find the new shoots, fair purple shoots, which are to curve upward and bear the next year's flowers, already grown half an inch or more in earth. Nature is confident.

The river is lower than before this year, or at least since spring, yet not remarkably low, and meadows and pools generally are drier.

The oak leaves generally are duller than usual this year. I think it must be that they are killed by frost before they are ripe. Some small sugar maples are still as fair as ever. You will often see one, large or small, a brilliant and almost uniform scarlet, while another close to it will be perfectly green.

Oct. 16. Oak Sprout-Land

THE OAK SPROUT-LAND ON the hillside north of Puffer's is now quite brilliant red. There is a pretty dense row of white birches along the base of the hill near the meadow, and their light-yellow spires are seen against the red and set it off remarkably, the red being also seen a little below them, between their bare stems. The green white pines seen here and there amid the red are equally important.

Oct. 18. Sugar Maples in Concord

THE LARGE SUGAR MAPLES on the Common are now at the height of their beauty. One, the earliest to change, is partly bare. This turned so early and

Specimen Sugar Maple.

so deep a scarlet that some thought that it was surely going to die. Also that one at the head of the Turnpike reveals its character now as far as you can see it. Yet about ten days ago all but one of these was quite green, and I thought they would not acquire any bright tints. A delicate but warmer than golden yellow is the prevailing color, with scarlet cheeks. They are great regular oval masses of yellow and scarlet. All the sunny warmth of the season seems to be absorbed in their leaves. There is an auction on the Common, but its red flag is hard to be discerned amid this blaze of color. The lowest and inmost leaves next the bole are of the most delicate yellow and green, as usual, like the complexion of young men brought up in the house.

Little did the fathers of the town anticipate this brilliant success when they caused to be imported from further in the country some straight poles with the tops cut off, which they called sugar maple trees,—and a neighboring merchant's clerk, as I remember, by way of jest planted beans about them. Yet these which were then jestingly called bean-poles are these days far the most beautiful objects noticeable in our streets. They are worth all and more than they have cost,— though one of the selectmen did take the cold which occasioned his death in setting them out,—if only because they have filled the open eyes of children with their rich color so unstintedly so many autumns. We will not ask them to yield us sugar in the spring, while they yield us so fair a prospect in the autumn. Wealth may be the inheritance of few in the houses, but it is equally distributed on the Common. All children alike can revel in this golden harvest. These trees, through- out the street, are at least equal to an annual festival and holiday, or a week of such,—not requiring any special police to keep the peace,—and poor indeed must be that New England village's October which has not the maple in its streets. This October festival costs no powder nor ringing of bells, but every tree is a liberty- pole on which a thousand bright flags are run up. Hundreds of children's eyes are steadily drinking in this color, and by these teachers even the truants are caught and educated the moment they step abroad. It is as if some cheap and innocent gala-day were celebrated in our town every autumn,—a week or two of such days.

What meant the fathers by establishing this *living* institution before the church,—this institution which needs no repairing nor repainting, which is continually "enlarged and repaired" by its growth? Surely trees should be set in our streets with a view to their October splendor. Do you not think it will make some odds to these children that they were brought up under the maples? Indeed, neither the truant nor the studious are at present taught colors in the schools. These are instead of the bright colors in apothecary shops and city windows. It is a pity we have not more red maples and some hickories in the streets as well. Our paint-box is very imperfectly filled. Instead of, or besides, supplying paint-boxes, I would supply these natural colors to the young.

I know of one man at least, called an excellent and peculiarly successful farmer, who has thoroughly repaired his house and built a new barn with a barn cellar, such as every farmer seems fated to have, who has not a single tree or shrub of any kind about his house or within a considerable distance of it.

No annual training or muster of soldiery, no celebration with its scarfs and banners, could import into the town a hundredth part of the annual splendor of our October. We have only to set the trees, or let them stand, and Nature will find the colored drapery,—flags of all her nations, some of whose private signals hardly the botanist can read. Let us have a good many maples and hickories and scarlet oaks, then, I say. Blaze away! Shall that dirty roll of bunting in the gun-house be all the colors a village can display? A village is not complete unless it has these trees to mark the season in it. They are as important as a town clock. Such a village will not be found to work well. It has a screw loose; an essential part is wanting. Let us have willows for spring, elms for summer, maples and walnuts and tupelos for autumn, evergreens for winter, and oaks for all seasons. What is a gallery in a house to a gallery in the streets! I think that there is not a picture-gallery in the country which would be worth so much to us as is the western view under the elms of our main street. They are the frame to a picture, and we are not in the dilemma of the Irishman who, having bought a costly gilt picture-frame at an auction, found himself obliged to buy a picture at private sale to put into it, for our picture is already painted with each sunset behind it. An avenue of elms as large as our largest, and three miles long, would seem to lead to some admirable place, though only Concord were at the end of it. Such a street as I have described would be to the traveller, especially in October, an ever-changing panorama.

A village needs these innocent stimulants of bright and cheery prospects to keep off melancholy and superstition. Show me two villages, one embowered in trees and blazing with all the glories of October, the other a merely trivial and treeless waste, and I shall be sure that in the latter will be found the most desperate and hardest drinkers. What if we were to take half as much pains in protecting them as we do in setting them out,—not stupidly tie our horses to our dahlia stems?

They are cheap preachers, permanently settled, which preach their half-century, and century, aye, and century and a half sermons, with continually increasing influence and unction, ministering to many generations of men, and the least we can do is to supply them with suitable colleagues as they grow infirm.

Oct. 19. The Lit River

THE LIT RIVER, PURLING and eddying onward, was spotted with recently fallen leaves, some of which were being carried round by eddies. Leaves are now falling all the country over: some in the swamps, concealing the water; some in woods and on hillsides, where perhaps Vulcan may find them in the spring; some by the wayside, gathered into heaps, where children are playing with them; and some are being conveyed silently seaward on rivers; concealing the water in swamps, where at length they flat out and sink to the bottom, and we never hear of them again, unless we shall see their impressions on the coal of a future geological period. Some add them to their manure-heaps; others consume them with fire. The trees repay the earth with interest for what they have taken from it. The trees are discounting.

Oct. 22. Colors Advancing Deeper

IT IS VERY AGREEABLE to observe now from an eminence the different tints of red and brown in an oak sprout-land or young woodland, the brownish predominating. The chocolate is one. Some will tell you that they prefer these more sober colors which the landscape wears at present to the bright ones it exhibited a few days ago, as some prefer the sweet brown crust to the yellow inside. It is interesting to observe how gradually but steadily the woods advance through deeper and deeper shades of brown to their fall. You can tell the young white oak in the midst of the sprout-land by its light-brown color, almost like that of the russet fields seen beyond, also the scarlet by its brighter red, but the pines are now the brightest of them all.

Apple orchards throughout the village, or on lower and rich ground, are quite green, but on this drier Fair Haven Hill all the apple trees are yellow, with a sprinkling of green and occasionally a tinge of scarlet, *i. e.* are russet.

I can see the red of young oaks as far as the horizon on some sides.

I think that the yellows, as birches, etc., are the most distinct this very thick and cloudy day in which there is no sun, but when the sun shines the reds are lit up more and glow.

The oaks stand browned and crisped (amid the pines), their bright colors for the most part burnt out, like a loaf that is baked, and suggest an equal wholesomeness. The whole tree is now not only ripe but, as it were, a fruit perfectly cooked by the sun. That same sun which called forth its leaves in the spring has now, aided by the frost, sealed up their fountains for the year and withered them. The order has gone forth for them to rest. As each tree casts its leaves it stands careless and free, like a horse freed from his harness, or like one who has done his year's work and now stands unnoticed, but with concentrated strength and contentment, ready to brave the blasts of winter without a murmur.

Oct. 22. Bright Leaves the Rule

T HESE BRIGHT LEAVES ARE not the exception but the rule, for I believe that *all* leaves, even grasses, etc., etc.,—*Panicum clandestinum,*—and mosses, as sphagnum, under favorable circumstances acquire brighter colors just before their fall. When you come to observe faithfully the changes of each humblest plant, you find, it may be unexpectedly, that each has sooner or later its peculiar autumnal tint or tints, though it may be rare and unobserved, as many a plant is at all seasons. And if you undertake to make a complete list of the bright tints, your list will be as long as a catalogue of the plants in your vicinity.

Think how much the eyes of painters, both artisans and artists, and of the manufacturers of cloth and paper, and the paper-stainers, etc., are to be educated by these autumnal colors. The stationer's envelopes may be of very various tints, yet not so various as those of the leaves of a single tree sometimes. If you want a different shade or tint of a particular color, you have only to look further within or without the tree, or the wood. The eye might thus be taught to distinguish color and appreciate a difference of tint or shade.

Oct. 24. Late October Colors

T HE BRILLIANT AUTUMNAL COLORS are red and yellow and the various tints, hues, and shades of these. Blue is reserved to be the color of the sky, but yellow and red are the colors of the earth flower. Every fruit, on ripening, and just before its fall, acquires a bright tint. So do the leaves; so the sky before the end of the day, and the year near its setting. October is the red sunset sky, November the later twilight. Color stands for all ripeness and success. We have dreamed that the hero should carry his color aloft, as a symbol of the ripeness of his virtue. The noblest feature, the eye, is the fairest-colored, the jewel of the body. The warrior's flag is the flower which precedes his fruit. He unfurls his flag to the breeze with such confidence and brag as the flower its petals. Now we shall see what kind of fruit will succeed.

The very forest and herbage, the pellicle of the earth as it were, must acquire a bright color, an evidence of its ripeness, as if the globe itself were a fruit on its stem, with ever one cheek toward the sun.

Our appetites have commonly confined our views of ripeness and its phenomena—color and mellowness and perfectness—to the fruits which we eat, and we are wont to forget that an immense harvest which we do not eat, hardly use at all, is annually ripened by nature. At our annual cattle-shows and horticultural exhibitions we make, as we think, a great show of fair fruits, destined, however, to a rather ignoble fate, fruits not worshipped for this chiefly; but round about and within our towns there is annually another show of fruits, on an infinitely grander scale, fruits which address our taste for beauty alone.

The scarlet oak, which was quite green the 12th, is now completely scarlet and apparently has been so a few days. This alone of our indigenous deciduous trees (the pitch pine is with it) is now in its glory. (I have not seen the beech, but suppose it past. The *Populus grandidentata* and sugar maple come nearest to it, but they have lost the greater part of their leaves.) Look at one, completely changed from green to bright dark-scarlet, every leaf, as if it had been dipped into a scarlet dye, between you and the sun. Was not this worth waiting for? Little did you think ten days ago that that cold green tree could assume such color as this. Its leaves still firmly attached while those of other trees are falling around it. I am the last to blush, but I blush deeper than any of ye. I bring up the rear in my red coat. The scarlet oaks, alone of oaks, have not given up the fight. Perchance their leaves, so finely cut, are longer preserved partly because they present less surface to the elements, and for a long time, if I remember rightly, some scarlet oak leaves will "hold out to burn."

Now in huckleberry pastures you see only here and there a few bright scarlet or crimson (for they vary) leaves amid or above the bare reddish stems, burning as if with condensed brightness,—as if the few that remained burned with the condensed brightness of all that have fallen. In sheltered woods you [see] some dicksonia still straw-color or pale-yellow. Some thoroughwort the same color. In the shade generally you find paler and more delicate tints, fading to straw-color and white. The deep reds and scarlets and purples show exposure to the sun. I see an intensely scarlet high blueberry—but where one leaf has overlapped another it is yellow—with a regular outline.

Oct. 25.   Leaves Are Fallen

Now that the leaves are fallen (for a few days), the long yellow buds (often red-pointed) which sleep along the twigs of the *S. discolor* are very conspicuous and quite interesting, already even carrying our thoughts forward to spring. I noticed them first on the 22d. They may be put with the azalea buds already noticed. Even bleak and barren November wears these *gems* on her breast in sign of the coming year. How many thoughts lie undeveloped, and as it were dormant, like these buds, in the minds of men!

Oct. 25.   Silvery Leaves and Pine Needles

Now, especially, we notice not only the silvery leaves of the *Salix alba* but the silvery sheen of pine-needles; *i. e.,* when its old leaves have fallen and trees generally are mostly bare, in the cool Novemberish air and light we observe and enjoy the trembling shimmer and gleam of the pine-needles. I do not know why we perceive this more at this season, unless because the air is so clear and all surfaces reflect more light; and, besides, all the needles now left are fresh ones, or the growth of this year. Also I notice, when the sun is low, the light reflected from the parallel twigs of birches recently bare, etc., like the gleam from gossamer lines. This is another Novemberish phenomenon. Call these November Lights. Hers is a cool, silvery light.

In November consider the sharp, dry rustle of withered leaves; the cool, silvery, and shimmering gleams of light, as above; the fresh bright buds formed and exposed along the twigs; walnuts.

The leaves of the *Populus grandidentata,* though half fallen and turned a pure and handsome yellow, are still wagging as fast as ever. These do not lose their color and wither on the tree like oaks and beeches and some of their allies, and hickories, too, and buttonwood, neither do maples, nor birches quite, nor willows (except the *Salix tristis* and perhaps some of the next allied),—but they are fresh and unwilted, full of sap and fair as ever when they are first strewn on the ground. I do not think of any tree whose leaves are so fresh and fair when they fall.

Oct. 27. Withering Sedges and Grasses

NOT ONLY THE LEAVES of trees and shrubs and flowers have been changing and withering, but almost countless sedges and grasses. They become pale-brown and bleached after the frost has killed them, and give that peculiar light, almost silvery, sheen to the fields in November. The colors of the fields make haste to harmonize with the snowy mantle which is soon to invest them and with the cool, white twilights of that season which is itself the twilight of the year. They become more and more the color of the frost which rests on them. Think of the interminable forest of grasses which dies down to the ground every autumn! What a more than Xerxean army of wool-grasses and sedges without fame lie down to an ignominious death, as the mowers esteem it, in our river meadows each year, and become "old fog" to trouble the mowers, lodging as they fall, that might have been the straw beds of horses and cattle, tucked under them every night!

The fine-culmed purple grass, which lately we admired so much, is now bleached as light as any of them. Culms and leaves robbed of their color and withered by cold. This is what makes November—and the light reflected from the bleached culms of grasses and the bare twigs of trees! When many hard frosts have formed and melted on the fields and stiffened grass, they leave them almost as silvery as themselves. There is hardly a surface to absorb the light.

It is remarkable that the autumnal change of our woods has left no deeper impression on our literature yet. There is no record of it in English poetry, apparently because, according to all accounts, the trees acquire but few bright colors there. Neither do I know any adequate notice of it in our own youthful literature, nor in the traditions of the Indians. One would say it was the very phenomenon to have caught a savage eye, so devoted to bright colors. In our poetry and science there are many references to this phenomenon, but it has received no such particular attention as it deserves. High-colored as are most political speeches, I do not detect any reflection, even, from the autumnal tints in them. They are as colorless and lifeless as the herbage in November.

The year, with these dazzling colors on its margin, lies spread open like an illustrated volume. The preacher does not utter the essence of its teaching.

Oct. 27. Tints of a Subtle Difference

IT IS IMPOSSIBLE TO describe the infinite variety of hues, tints, and shades, for the language affords no names for them, and we must apply the same term monotonously to twenty different things. If I could exhibit so many different trees, or only leaves, the effect would be different. When the tints are the same they differ so much in purity and delicacy that language, to describe them truly, would have not only to be greatly enriched, but as it were dyed to the same colors herself, and speak to the eye as well as to the ear. And it is these subtle differences which especially attract and charm our eyes. Where else will you study color under such advantages? What other school of design can vie with this? To describe these colored leaves you must use colored words. How tame and ineffectual must be the words with which we attempt to describe that subtle difference of tint, which so charms the eye? Who will undertake to describe in words the difference in tint between two neighboring leaves on the same tree? or of two thousand?—for by so many the eye is addressed in a glance. In describing the richly spotted leaves, for instance, how often we find ourselves using ineffectually words which merely indicate faintly our good intentions, giving them in our despair a terminal twist toward our mark,—such as reddish, yellowish, purplish, etc. We cannot make a hue of words, for they are not to be compounded like colors, and hence we are obliged to use such ineffectual expressions as reddish brown, etc. They need to be ground together.

Oct. 28. Handsome Red Oak Acorns

HOW HANDSOME THE GREAT red oak acorns now! I stand under the tree on Emerson's lot. They are still falling. I heard one fall into the water as I approached, and thought that a musquash had plunged. They strew the ground and the bottom of the river thickly, and while I stand here I hear one strike the boughs with force as it comes down, and drop into the water. The part that was covered by the cup is whitish-woolly. How munificent is Nature to create this profusion of wild fruit, as it were merely to gratify our eyes! Though inedible they are more wholesome to my immortal part, and stand by me longer, than the fruits which I eat. If they had been plums or chestnuts I should have eaten them on the spot and probably forgotten them. They would have afforded only a momentary gratification, but being acorns, I remember, and as it were *feed* on, them still.

They are untasted fruits forever in store for me. I know not of their flavor as yet
That is postponed to some still unimagined winter evening. These which we admire
but do not eat are nuts of the gods. When time is no more we shall crack them
I cannot help liking them better than horse-chestnuts, which are of a similar color
not only because they are of a much handsomer form, but because they are
indigenous. What hale, plump fellows they are! They can afford not to be useful
to me, nor to know me or be known by me. They go their way, I go mine, and
it turns out that sometimes I go *after* them.

Oct. 29. Bare Trees and Old Leaves

I LOOK NORTH FROM the causeway at Heywood's meadow. How rich some
scarlet oaks imbosomed in pines, their branches (still bright) intimately intermin
gled with the pine! They have their full effect there. The pine boughs are the green
calyx to its [*sic*] petals. Without these pines for contrast the autumnal tints would
lose a considerable part of their effect.

The white birches being now generally bare, they stand along the east side of
Heywood's meadow slender, parallel white stems, revealed in a pretty reddish
maze produced by their fine branches. It is a lesser and denser smoke (?) than the
maple one. The branches must be thick, like those of maples and birches, to give
the effect of smoke, and most trees have fewer and coarser branches, or do not
grow in such dense masses.

Nature now, like an athlete, begins to strip herself in earnest for her contest
with her great antagonist Winter. In the bare trees and twigs what a display of
muscle!

Looking toward Spanish Brook, I see the white pines, a clear green, rising amid
and above the pitch pines, which are parti-colored, glowing internally with the
warm yellow of the old leaves. Of our Concord evergreens, only the white and
pitch pines are interesting in their change, for only their leaves are bright and
conspicuous enough.

I notice a barberry bush in the woods still thickly clothed, but merely yellowish
green, not showy. Is not this commonly the case with the introduced European
plants? Have they not European habits? And are they not also late to fall, killed
before they are ripe?—*e. g.* the quince, apple, pear(?), barberry, silvery abele
privet, plum(?), white willow, weeping willow, lilac, hawthorn (the horse-chestnut
and European mountain-ash are distincter yellow, and the Scotch larch is at least
as bright as ours at same time; the Lombardy poplar is a handsome yellow (some
branches early), and the cultivated cherry is quite handsome orange (often yellow
ish), which, with exceptions in parenthesis, are inglorious in their decay.

Three Beech trees and a maple,
Concord, Massachusetts.

Oct. 31. Scarlet Oaks, Close and Far

As I sit on the Cliff there, the sun is now getting low, and the woods in Lincoln south and east of me are lit up by its more level rays, and there is brought out a more brilliant redness in the scarlet oaks, scattered so equally over the forest, than you would have believed was in them. Every tree of this species which is visible in these directions, even to the horizon, now stands out distinctly red. Some great ones lift their red backs high above the woods near the Codman place, like huge roses with a myriad fine petals, and some more slender ones, in a small grove of white pines on Pine Hill in the east, in the very horizon, alternating with the pines on the edge of the grove and shouldering them with their red coats,—an intense, burning red which would lose some of its strength, methinks, with every step you might take toward them,—look like soldiers in red amid hunters in green. This time it is *Lincoln* green, too. Until the sun thus lit them up you would not have believed that there were so many redcoats in the forest army. Looking westward, their colors are lost in a blaze of light, but in other directions the whole forest is a flower-garden, in which these late roses burn, alternating with green, while the so-called "gardeners," working here and there, perchance, beneath, with spade and water-pot, see only a few little asters amid withered leaves, for the shade that lurks amid their foliage does not report itself at this distance. They are unanimously red. The focus of their reflected [color] is in the atmosphere far on this side. Every such tree, especially in the horizon, becomes a nucleus of red, as it were, where, with the declining sun, the redness grows and glows like a cloud. It only has some comparatively dull-red leaves for a nucleus and to start it, and it becomes an intense scarlet or red mist, or fire which finds fuel for itself in the very atmosphere. I have no doubt that you would be disappointed in the brilliancy of those trees if you were to walk to them. You see a redder tree than exists. It is a strong red, which gathers strength from the air on its way to your eye. It is partly borrowed fire, borrowed of the sun. The scarlet oak asks the clear sky and the brightness of the Indian summer. These bring out its color. If the sun goes into a cloud they become indistinct.

These are my China asters, my late garden flowers. It costs me nothing for a gardener. The falling leaves, all over the forest, are protecting the roots of my plants. Only look at what is to be seen, and you will have garden enough, without deepening the soil of your yard. We have only to elevate our view a little to see the whole forest as a garden.

To my surprise, the only yellow that I see amid the universal red and green and chocolate is one large tree-top in the forest, a mile off in the east, across the pond, which by its form and color I know to be my late acquaintance the tall aspen (*tremuliformis*) of the 29th. It, too, is far more yellow at this distance than it was close at hand, and so are the Lombardy poplars in our streets. The *Salix alba*, too, looks yellower at a distance now. Their dull-brown and green colors do not report themselves so far, while the yellow *crescit eundo*, and we see the sun reflected in it. After walking for a couple of hours the other day through the woods, I came to the base of a tall aspen, which I do not remember to have seen before, standing in the midst of the woods in the next town, still thickly leaved and turned to greenish yellow. It is perhaps the largest of its species that I know. It was by merest accident that I stumbled on it, and if I had been sent to find it, I should have thought it to be, as we say, like looking for a needle in a haymow. All summer, and it chances for so many years, it has been concealed to me; but now, walking in a different direction, to the same hilltop from which I saw the scarlet oaks, and looking off just before sunset, when all other trees visible for miles around are reddish or green, I distinguish my new acquaintance by its yellow color. Such is its fame, at last, and reward for living in that solitude and obscurity. It is the most distinct tree in all the landscape, and would be the cynosure of all eyes here. Thus it plays its part in the choir. I made a minute of its locality, glad to know where so large an aspen grew. Then it seemed peculiar in its solitude and obscurity. It seemed the obscurest of trees. Now it was seen to be equally peculiar for its distinctness and prominence. Each tree (in October) runs up its flag and we know [what] colors it sails under. The sailor sails, and the soldier marches, under a color which will report his virtue farthest, and the ship's "private signals" must be such as can be distinguished at the greatest distance. The eye, which distinguishes and appreciates color, is itself the seat of color in the human body.

It is as if it recognized me too, and gladly, coming half-way to meet me, and now the acquaintance thus propitiously formed will, I trust, be permanent.

Of the three (?) mocker-nuts on Conantum top only the southernmost is bare, the rest are thickly leaved yet. The *Viburnum Lentago* is about bare.

That hour-glass apple shrub near the old Conantum house is full of small yellow fruit. Thus it is with them. By the end of some October, when their leaves have fallen, you see them glowing with an abundance of wild fruit, which the cows cannot get at over the bushy and thorny hedge which surrounds them. Such is their pursuit of knowledge through difficulties. Though they may have taken the hour-glass form, think not that their sands are run out. So is it with the rude, neglected genius from amid the country hills; he suffers many a check at first, browsed on by fate, springing in but a rocky pasture, the nursery of other creatures there, and he grows broad and strong, and scraggy and thorny, hopelessly stunted, you would say, and not like a sleek orchard tree all whose forces are husbanded and the precious early years not lost, and when at first, within this rind and hedge, the man shoots up, you see the thorny scrub of his youth about him, and he walks like an hour-glass, aspiring above, it is true, but held down and impeded by the rubbish of old difficulties overcome, and you seem to see his sands running out. But at length, thanks to his rude culture, he attains to his full stature, and every vestige of the thorny hedge which clung to his youth disappears, and he bears golden crops of Porters or Baldwins, whose fame will spread through all orchards for generations to come, while that thrifty orchard tree which was his competitor will, perchance, have long since ceased to bear its engrafted fruit and decayed.

Nov. 1.   Larches in Yellow Pyramids

P.M.—To Poplar Hill.

Many black oaks are bare in Sleepy Hollow. Now you easily detect where larches grow, *viz.* in the swamp north of Sleepy Hollow. They are far more distinct than at any other season. They are very regular soft yellow pyramids, as I see them from the Poplar Hill. Unlike the pines there is no greenness left to alternate with their yellow, but they are a uniform yellow, and they differ from other yellow trees in the generally regular pyramidal outline, *i. e.* these middling-sized trees. These trees now cannot easily be mistaken for any other, because they are the only conspicuously yellow trees now left in the woods, except a very few aspens of both kinds, not one in a square mile, and these are of a very different hue as well as form, the birches, etc., having fallen. The larch, apparently, will soon be the only yellow tree left in the woods. It is almost quite alone now. But in the summer it is not easy to distinguish them either by their color or form at a distance.

If you wish to count the scarlet oaks, do it now. Stand on a hilltop in the woods, when the sun is an hour high and the sky is clear, and every one within range of your vision will be revealed. You might live to the age of Methusaleh and never find a tithe of them otherwise.

We are not wont to see our dooryard as a part of the earth's surface. The gardener does not perceive that some ridge or mound in his garden or lawn is related to yonder hill or the still more distant mountain in the horizon, is, per-chance, a humble spur of the last. We are wont to look on the earth still as a sort of chaos, formless and lumpish. I notice from this height that the curving moraine forming the west side of Sleepy Hollow is one of several arms or fingers which stretch away from the hill range that runs down the north side of the Boston road, turning northward at the Court-House; that this finger-like moraine is continued northward by itself almost to the river, and points plainly enough to Ponkawtasset Hill on the other side, even if the Poplar Hill range itself did not indicate this connection; and so the sloping cemetery lots on the west of Sleepy Hollow are related to the distant Ponkawtasset.

N o v .   1 .   N o v e m b e r   T h o u g h t s

AS THE AFTERNOONS GROW shorter, and the early evening drives us home to complete our chores, we are reminded of the shortness of life, and become more pensive, at least in this twilight of the year. We are prompted to make haste and finish our work before the night comes. I leaned over a rail in the twilight on the Walden road, waiting for the evening mail to be distributed, when such thoughts visited me. I seemed to recognize the November evening as a familiar thing come round again, and yet I could hardly tell whether I had ever known it or only divined it. The November twilights just begun! It appeared like a part of a panorama at which I sat spectator, a part with which I was perfectly familiar just coming into view, and I foresaw how it would look and roll along, and prepared to be pleased. Just such a piece of art merely, though infinitely sweet and grand, did it appear to me, and just as little were any active duties required of me. We are independent on all that we see. The hangman whom I have *seen* cannot hang me. The earth which I have *seen* cannot bury me. Such doubleness and distance does sight prove. Only the rich and such as are troubled with ennui are implicated in the maze of phenomena. You cannot see anything until you are clear of it. The long railroad causeway through the meadows west of me, the still twilight in which hardly a cricket was heard, the dark bank of clouds in the horizon long after sunset, the villagers crowding to the post-office, and the hastening home to supper by candle-light, had I not seen all this before! What new sweet was I to extract from it? Truly they mean that we shall learn our lesson well. Nature gets thumbed like an old spelling-book. The almshouse and Frederick were still as last November. I was no nearer, methinks, nor further off from my friends. Yet I sat the bench with perfect contentment, unwilling to exchange the familiar vision that was to be unrolled for any treasure or heaven that could be imagined. Sure to keep just so far apart in our orbits still, in obedience to the laws of attraction and repulsion, affording each other only steady but indispensable starlight. It was as if I was promised the greatest novelty the world has ever seen or shall see, though the utmost possible novelty would be the difference between me and myself a year ago. This alone encouraged me, and was my fuel for the approaching winter. That we may behold the panorama with this slight improvement or change, this is what we sustain life for with so much effort from year to year.

And yet there is no more tempting novelty than this new November. No going to Europe or another world is to be named with it. Give me the old familiar walk, post-office and all, with this ever new self, with this infinite expectation and faith, which does not know when it is beaten. We'll go nutting once more. We'll pluck the nut of the world, and crack it in the winter evenings. Theatres and all other sightseeing are puppet-shows in comparison. I will take another walk to the Cliff, another row on the river, another skate on the meadow, be out in the first snow, and associate with the winter birds. Here I am at home. In the bare and bleached crust of the earth I recognize my friend.

One actual Frederick that you know is worth a million only read of. Pray, am I altogether a bachelor, or am I a widower, that I should go away and leave my bride? This Morrow that is ever knocking with irresistible force at our door, there is no such guest as that. I will stay at home and receive company.

I want nothing new, if I can have but a tithe of the old secured to me. I will spurn all wealth beside. Think of the consummate folly of attempting to go away from *here!* When the constant endeavor should be to get nearer and nearer *here.* Here are all the friends I ever had or shall have, and as friendly as ever. Why, I never had any quarrel with a friend but it was just as sweet as unanimity could be. I do not think we budge an inch forward or backward in relation to our friends. How many things can you go away from? They see the comet from the northwest coast just as plainly as we do, and the same stars through its tail. Take the shortest way round and stay at home. A man dwells in his native valley like a corolla in its calyx, like an acorn in its cup. *Here,* of course, is all that you love, all that you expect, all that you are. Here is your bride elect, as close to you as she can be got. Here is all the best and all the worst you can imagine. What more do you want? Bear hereaway then! Foolish people imagine that what they imagine is somewhere else. That stuff is not made in any factory but their own.

Nov. 4. Looking and Seeing

IF, ABOUT THE LAST of October, you ascend any hill in the outskirts of the town and look over the forest, you will see, amid the brown of other oaks, which are now withered, and the green of the pines, the bright-red tops or crescents of the scarlet oaks, very equally and thickly distributed on all sides, even to the horizon. Complete trees standing exposed on the edges of the forest, where you have never suspected them, or their tops only in the recesses of the forest surface, or perhaps towering above the surrounding trees, or reflecting a warm rose red from the very edge of the horizon in favorable lights. All this you will see, and much more, if you are prepared to see it,—if you *look* for it. Otherwise, regular and universal as this phenomenon is, you will think for threescore years and ten that all the wood is at this season sere and brown. Objects are concealed from our view not so much because they are out of the course of our visual ray (continued) as because there is no intention of the mind and eye toward them. We do not realize how far and widely, or how near and narrowly, we are to look. The greater part of the phenomena of nature are for this reason concealed to us all our lives. Here, too, as in political economy, the supply answers to the demand. Nature does not cast pearls before swine. There is just as much beauty visible to us in the

landscape as we are prepared to appreciate,—not a grain more. The actual objects
which one person will see from a particular hilltop are just as different from those
which another will see as the persons are different. The scarlet oak must, in a sense,
be in your eye when you go forth. We cannot see anything until we are possessed
with the idea of it, and then we can hardly see anything else. In my botanical
rambles I find that first the idea, or image, of a plant occupies my thoughts, though
it may at first seem very foreign to this locality, and for some weeks or months
I go thinking of it and expecting it unconsciously, and at length I surely see it,
and it is henceforth an actual neighbor of mine. This is the history of my finding
a score or more of rare plants which I could name.

Take one of our selectmen and put him on the highest hill in the township, and
tell him to look! What, probably, would he see? What would he *select* to look at?
Sharpening his sight to the utmost, and putting on the glasses that suited him best,
aye, using a spy-glass if he liked, straining his optic nerve to its utmost, and making
a full report. Of course, he would see a Brocken spectre of himself. Now take Julius
Cæsar, or Emanuel Swedenborg, or a Fiji-Islander, and set him up there! Let them
compare notes afterward. Would it appear that they had enjoyed the same prospect? For aught we know, as strange a man as any of these is always at our elbows.
It does not appear that anybody saw Shakespeare when he was about in England
looking off, but only some of his raiment.

Why, it takes a sharpshooter to bring down even such trivial game as snipes
and woodcocks; he must take very particular aim, and know what he is aiming
at. He would stand a very small chance if he fired at random into the sky, being
told that snipes were flying there. And so it is with him that shoots at beauty.
Not till the sky falls will he catch larks, unless he is a trained sportsman. He will
not bag any if he does not already know its seasons and haunts and the color of
its wing,—if he has not dreamed of it, so that he can *anticipate* it; then, indeed,
he flushes it at every step, shoots double and on the wing, with both barrels,
even in corn-fields. The sportsman trains himself, dresses, and watches un-
weariedly, and loads and primes for his particular game. He prays for it, and so
he gets it. After due and long preparation, schooling his eye and hand, dreaming
awake and asleep, with gun and paddle and boat, he goes out after meadow-
hens,—which most of his townsmen never saw nor dreamed of,—paddles for
miles against a head wind, and therefore he gets them. He had them half-way
into his bag when he started, and has only to shove them down. The fisherman,
too, dreams of fish, till he can almost catch them in his sink-spout. The hen
scratches, and finds her food right under where she stands; but such is not the
way with the hawk.

Nov. 7.   Houses Reflected in River

ROUNDING THE ISLAND JUST after sunset, I see not only the houses
nearest the river but our own reflected in the river by the Island. From what

various points of view and in what unsuspected lights and relations we sooner or later see the most familiar objects! I see houses reflected in the river which stand a mile from it, and whose inhabitants do not consider themselves near the shore.

Nov. 8.   Twigs in Misty Masses

THOSE TREES AND BUSHES which grow in dense masses and have many fine twigs, being bare, make an agreeable misty impression where there are a myriad retreating points to receive the eye, not a hard, abrupt wall; just as, in the sky, the visual ray is cushioned on clouds, unless it is launched into the illimitable ether. The eye is less worn and wearied, not to say wounded, by looking at these mazes where the seer is not often conscious of seeing anything. It is well that the eye is so rarely caught and detained by any object in one whole hemisphere of its range, *i. e.* the sky. It enjoys everlasting holiday on this side. Only the formless clouds and the objectless ether are presented to it. For they are nervous who see many faces in the clouds. Corresponding to the clouds in the sky are those mazes now on the earth. Nature disposes of her naked stems so softly as not to put our eyes out. She makes them a smoke, or stationary cloud, on this side or that, of whose objective existence we rarely take cognizance. She does not expect us to notice them. She calls our attention to the maple swamp more especially in October.

A most wild place.

Nov. 8. Nature's Many Scenes

NATURE HAS MANY SCENES to exhibit, and constantly draws a curtain
over this part or that. She is constantly repainting the landscape and all surfaces,
dressing up some scene for our entertainment. Lately we had a leafy wilderness,
now bare twigs begin to prevail, and soon she will surprise us with a mantle of
snow. Some green she thinks so good for our eyes, like blue, that she never banishes
it entirely, but has created evergreens.

It is remarkable how little any but a lichenist will observe on the bark of trees.
The mass of men have but the vaguest and most indefinite notion of mosses, as
a sort of shreds and fringes, and the world in which the lichenist dwells is much
further from theirs than one side of this earth from the other. They see bark as
if they saw it not. These objects which, though constantly visible, are rarely looked
at are a sort of eye-brush.

Each phase of nature, while not invisible, is yet not too distinct and obtru-
sive. It is there to be found when we look for it, but not demanding our attention. It is like a silent but sympathizing companion in whose company we retain
most of the advantages of solitude, with whom we can walk and talk, or be
silent, naturally, without the necessity of talking in a strain foreign to the place.

Nov. 8. Fruit of the Sumach

I THINK I ADMIRE again about this time the still bright-red or crimson fruit
of the sumach, now when not only its own but most other leaves have fallen and
there are few bright tints, it is now so distinct on its twigs. Your attention is not
distracted by its brilliant leaves now.

Nov. 8. Keep Some Old Woods

I STAND IN EBBY Hubbard's yellow birch swamp, admiring some gnarled
and shaggy picturesque old birches there, which send out large knee-like limbs
near the ground, while the brook, raised by the late rain, winds fuller than usual
through the rocky swamp. I thought with regret how soon these trees, like the
black birches that grew on the hill near by, would be all cut off, and there would
be almost nothing of the old Concord left, and we should be reduced to read old
deeds in order to be reminded of such things,—deeds, at least, in which some old
and revered bound trees are mentioned. These will be the only proof at last that
they ever existed. Pray, farmers, keep some old woods to match the old deeds.
Keep them for history's sake, as specimens of what the township was. Let us not
be reduced to a mere paper evidence, to deeds kept in a chest or secretary, when
not so much as the bark of the paper birch will be left for evidence, about its
decayed stump.

Nov. 11. The Scarlet Oak Leaf

THE SCARLET OAK LEAF! What a graceful and pleasing outline! a combination of graceful curves and angles.

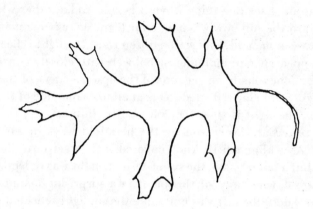

These deep bays in the leaf are agreeable to us as the thought of deep and smooth and secure havens to the mariner. But both your love of repose and your spirit of adventure are addressed, for both bays and headlands are represented,—sharp-pointed rocky capes and rounded bays with smooth strands. To the sailor's eye it is a much indented shore, and in his casual glance he thinks that if he doubles its sharp capes he will find a haven in its deep rounded bays. If I were a drawing-master, I would set my pupils to copying these leaves, that they might learn to draw firmly and gracefully. It is a shore to the aerial ocean, on which the windy surf beats. How different from the white oak leaf with its rounded headlands, on which no lighthouse need be placed!

Nov. 12. The Word "Ripe"

I THINK THAT THE change to some higher color in a leaf is an evidence that it has arrived at a late and more perfect and final maturity, answering to the maturity of fruits, and not to that of green leaves, etc., etc., which merely serve a purpose. The word "ripe" is thought by some to be derived from the verb "to reap," according to which that is ripe which is ready to be reaped. The fall of the leaf is preceded by a ripe old age.

Nov. 17. The November Lights

LEAVING MY BOAT, I walk through the low wood west of Dove Rock, toward the scarlet oak. The very sunlight on the pale-brown bleached fields is an interesting object these cold days. I naturally look toward [it] as to a wood-fire. Not only different objects are presented to our attention at different seasons of the year, but we are in a frame of body and of mind to appreciate different objects at different seasons. I see one thing when it is cold and another when it is warm.

Looking toward the sun now when an hour high, there being many small alders and birches between me and it for half a dozen rods, the light reflected from their twigs has the appearance of an immense cobweb with closely concentric lines, of which I see about one fourth, on account of the upward curve of the twigs on each side, and the light not being reflected to me at all from one side of the trees directly in front of me. The light is thus very pleasantly diffused.

We are interested at this season by the manifold ways in which the light is reflected to us. Ascending a little knoll covered with sweet-fern, shortly after, the sun appearing but a point above the sweet-fern, its light was reflected from a dense mass of the bare downy twigs of this plant in a surprising manner which would not be believed if described. It was quite like the sunlight reflected from grass and weeds covered with hoar frost. Yet in an ordinary light these are but dark or dusky looking twigs with scarcely a noticeable downiness. Yet as I saw it, there was a perfect halo of light resting on the knoll as I moved to right or left. A myriad of surfaces are now prepared to reflect the light. This is one of the hundred silvery lights of November. The setting sun, too, is reflected from windows more brightly than at any other season. "November Lights" would be a theme for me.

Nov. 20. Across the Tony Wheeler Pasture

I GO ACROSS THE great Tony Wheeler pasture. It is a cool but pleasant November afternoon. The glory of November is in its silvery, sparkling lights. I think it is peculiar among the months for the amount [of] sparkling white light reflected from a myriad of surfaces. The air is so clear, and there are so many bare, polished, bleached or hoary surfaces to reflect the light. Few things are more exhilarating, if it is only moderately cold, than to walk over bare pastures and see the abundant sheeny light like a universal halo, reflected from the russet and bleached earth. The earth shines perhaps more than in spring, for the reflecting surfaces are less dimmed now. It is not a red but a white light. In the woods and about swamps, as Ministerial, also, there are several kinds of twigs, this year's shoots of shrubs, which have a slight down or hairiness, hardly perceptible in ordinary lights though held in the hand, but which, seen toward the sun, reflect a cheering silvery light. Such are not only the sweet-fern, but the hazel in a less degree, alder twigs, and even the short huckleberry twigs, also lespedeza stems

It is as if they were covered with a myriad fine spiculæ which reflect a dazzling white light, exceedingly warming to the spirits and imagination. This gives a character of snug warmth and cheerfulness to the swamp, as if it were a place where the sun consorted with rabbits and partridges.

Dec. 11. The Tawny Copse

P.M.—To Walden.

An overcast afternoon and rather warm. The snow on the ground in pastures brings out the warm red in leafy oak woodlands by contrast. These are what Thomson calls "the tawny copse." So that they suggest both shelter and warmth. All browns, indeed, are warmer now than a week ago. These oak woodlands half a mile off, commonly with pines intermingled, look like warm coverts for birds and other wild animals. How much warmer our woodlands look and *are* for these withered leaves that still hang on! Without them the woods would be dreary, bleak, and wintry indeed. Here is a manifest provision for the necessities of man and the brutes. These leaves remain to keep us warm, and to keep the earth warm about their roots. While the oak leaves look redder and warmer, the pines look much darker since the snow has fallen (the hemlocks darker still). A mile or two distant they are dark-brown, or almost black, as, still further, is all woodland, and in the most distant horizon have a blue tinge like mountains, from the atmosphere. The boughs of old and bare oak woods are gray and in harmony with the white ground, looking as if snowed on.

Dec. 13. Leather-Colored Oak Leaves

A damp day brings out the color of oak leaves, somewhat as of lichens. They are of a brighter and deeper leather-color, richer and more wholesome, hanging more straightly down than ever. They look peculiarly clean and wholesome, their tints brought out and their lobes more flattened out, and they show to great advantage, these trees hanging still with leather-colored leaves in this mizzling rain, seen against the misty sky. They are again as it were full-veined with some kind of brown sap.

CHAPTER XI

YEAR
1859
AGE
41–42

Jan. 9. Outline of Hills

AT SUNDOWN TO WALDEN.

Standing on the middle of Walden I see with perfect distinctness the form and outlines of the low hills which surround it, though they are wooded, because they are quite white, being covered with snow, while the woods are for the most part bare or very thin-leaved. I see thus the outline of the hills eight or ten rods back through the trees. This I can never do in the summer, when the leaves are thick and the ground is nearly the same color with them. These white hills are now seen as through a veil of stems. Immediately after the wood was cut off, this outline, of course, was visible at all seasons, but the wood, springing up again, concealed it, and now the snow has come to reveal the lost outline.

The sun has been set some minutes, and as I stand on the pond looking west-ward toward the twilight sky, a soft, satiny light is reflected from the ice in flakes here and there, like the light from the under side of a bird's wing. It is worth the while to stand here at this hour and look into the soft western sky, over the pines whose outlines are so rich and distinct against the clear sky. I am inclined to measure the angle at which [a] pine bough meets the stem. That soft, still, cream-colored sky seems the scene, the stage or field, for some rare drama to be acted on.

Jan. 10. Pink Light on the Snow

ABOUT HALF AN HOUR before sunset this intensely clear cold evening (thermometer at five-6°), I observe all the sheets of ice (and they abound every-where now in the fields), when I look from one side about at right angles with the sun's rays, reflect a green light. This is the case even when they are in the shade. I walk back and forth in the road waiting to see the pink. The windows on the skirts of the village reflect the setting sun with intense brilliancy, a dazzling glitter, it is so cold. Standing thus on one side of the hill, I begin to see a pink light reflected from the snow there about fifteen minutes before the sun sets. This gradually deepens to purple and violet in some places, and the pink is very distinct, especially when, after looking at the simply white snow on other sides, you turn your eyes to the hill. Even after all direct sunlight is withdrawn from the hilltop, as well as from the valley in which you stand, you see, if you are prepared to discern it, a faint and delicate tinge of purple or violet there. This was in a very clear and cold evening when the thermometer was −6°. This is one of the phenom-ena of the winter sunset, this distinct pink light reflected from the brows of snow-clad hills on one side of you as you are facing the sun.

Jan. 19. Oak Leaves with Pines

I LOOK DOWN THE whole length of the meadows to Ball's Hill, etc. In a still, warm winter day like this, what warmth in the withered oak leaves, thus far away, mingled with pines! They are the redder for the warmth and the sun. At this season we do not want any more color.

Feb. 3. Creating a Theme

THE WRITER MUST TO some extent inspire himself. Most of his sentences may at first lie dead in his essay, but when all are arranged, some life and color will be reflected on them from the mature and successful lines; they will appear to pulsate with fresh life, and he will be enabled to eke out their slumbering sense, and make them worthy of their neighborhood. In his first essay on a given theme, he produces scarcely more than a frame and groundwork for his sentiment and poetry. Each clear thought that he attains to draws in its train many divided thoughts or perceptions. The writer has much to do even to create a theme for himself. Most that is first written on any subject is a mere groping after it, mere rubble-stone and foundation. It is only when many observations of different periods have been brought together that he begins to grasp his subject and can make one pertinent and just observation.

Feb. 16. Hen-Hawk and the Pine

MY EYES NIBBLE THE piny sierra which makes the horizon's edge, as a hungry man nibbles a cracker.

The hen-hawk and the pine are friends. The same thing which keeps the hen-hawk in the woods, away from the cities, keeps me here. That bird settles with confidence on a white pine top and not upon your weathercock. That bird will not be poultry of yours, lays no eggs for you, forever hides its nest. Though willed, or *wild,* it is not willful in its wildness. The unsympathizing man regards the wildness of some animals, their strangeness to him, as a sin; as if all their virtue consisted in their tamableness. He has always a charge in his gun ready for their extermination. What we call wildness is a civilization other than our own. The hen-hawk shuns the farmer, but it seeks the friendly shelter and support of the pine. It will not consent to walk in the barn-yard, but it loves to soar above the clouds. It has its own way and is beautiful, when we would fain subject it to our will. So any surpassing work of art is strange and wild to the mass of men, as is genius itself.

March 7. Ripeness

THERE IS NO RIPENESS which is not, so to speak, something ultimate in itself, and not merely a perfected means to a higher end. In order to be ripe it must serve a transcendent use. The ripeness of a leaf, being perfected, leaves the tree at that point and never returns to it. It has nothing to do with any other fruit which the tree may bear, and only the genius of the poet can pluck it.

The fruit of a tree is neither in the seed nor the timber,—the full-grown tree,—but it is simply the highest use to which it can be put.

March 11. Our Unconscious Leavings

FIND OUT AS SOON as possible what are the best things in your composition, and then shape the rest to fit them. The former will be the midrib and veins of the leaf.

There is always some accident in the best things, whether thoughts or expressions or deeds. The memorable thought, the happy expression, the admirable deed are only partly ours. The thought came to us because we were in a fit mood; also we were unconscious and did not know that we had said or done a good thing. We must walk consciously only part way toward our goal, and then leap in the dark to our success. What we do best or most perfectly is what we have most thoroughly learned by the longest practice, and at length it falls from us without our notice, as a leaf from a tree. It is the *last* time we shall do it,—our unconscious leavings.

March 12.   Rich Tints of Brown

IT IS A REGULAR spring rain, such as I remember walking in,—windy but warm. It alternately rains hard and then holds up a little. A similar alternation we see in the waves of water and all undulating surfaces,—in snow and sand and the clouds (the mackerel sky). Now you walk in a comparative lull, anticipating fair weather, with but a slight drizzling, and anon the wind blows and the rain drives down harder than ever. In one of these lulls, as I passed the Joe Hosmer (rough-cast) house, I thought I never saw any bank so handsome as the russet hillside behind it. It is a very barren, exhausted soil, where the cladonia lichens abound, and the lower side is a flowing sand, but this russet grass with its weeds, being saturated with moisture, was in this light the richest brown, methought, that I ever saw. There was the pale brown of the grass, red browns of some weeds (sarothra and pinweed probably), dark browns of huckleberry and sweet-fern stems, and the very visible green of the cladonias thirty rods off, and the rich brown fringes where the broken sod hung over the edge of the sand-bank. I did not see the browns of withered vegetation so rich last fall, and methinks these terrestrial lichens were never more fair and prominent. On some knolls these vivid and rampant lichens as it were dwarf the oaks. A peculiar and unaccountable light seemed to fall on that bank or hillside, though it was thick storm all around. A sort of Newfoundland sun seemed to be shining on it. It was such a light that you looked around for the sun that might be shining on it. Both the common largest and the very smallest hypericums *(Sarothra)* and the pinweeds were very rich browns at a little distance, coloring whole fields, and also withered and fallen ferns, reeking wet. It was a prospect to excite a reindeer. These tints of brown were as softly and richly fair and sufficing as the most brilliant autumnal tints. In fair and dry weather these spots may be commonplace, but now they are worthy to tempt the painter's brush. The picture should be the side of a barren lichen-clad hill with a flowing sand-bank beneath, a few blackish huckleberry bushes here and there, and bright white patches of snow here and there in the ravines, the hill running east and west and seen through the storm from a point twenty or thirty rods south. This kind of light, the air being full of rain and all vegetation dripping with it, brings out the browns wonderfully.

March 13. Intensity of Wet Browns

I CANNOT EASILY FORGET the beauty of those terrestrial browns in the rain yesterday. The withered grass was not of that very pale hoary brown that it is to-day, now that it is dry and lifeless, but, being perfectly saturated and dripping with the rain, the whole hillside seemed to reflect a certain yellowish light, so that you looked around for the sun in the midst of the storm. All the yellow and red and leather-color in the fawn-colored weeds was more intense than at any other season. The withered ferns which fell last fall—pinweeds, sarothra, etc.—were actually a *glowing* brown for the same reason, being all dripping wet. The cladonias crowning the knolls had visibly expanded and erected themselves, though seen twenty rods off, and the knolls appeared swelling and bursting as with yeast. All these hues of brown were most beautifully blended, so that the earth appeared covered with the softest and most harmoniously spotted and tinted tawny fur coat of any animal. The very bare sand slopes, with only here and there a thin crusting of mosses, was [*sic*] a richer color than ever it is.

In short, in these early spring rains, the withered herbage, thus saturated, and reflecting its brightest withered tint, seems in a certain degree to have revived, and sympathizes with the fresh greenish or yellowish or brownish lichens in its midst, which also seem to have withered. It seemed to me—and I think it may be the truth—that the abundant moisture, bringing out the highest color in the brown surface of the earth, generated a certain degree of light, which, when the rain held up a little, reminded you of the sun shining through a thick mist.

Oak leaves which have sunk deep into the ice now are seen to be handsomely spotted with black (of fungi or lichens?), which spots are rarely perceived in dry weather.

All that vegetable life which loves a superfluity of moisture is now rampant, cold though it is, compared with summer. Radical leaves are as bright as ever they are.

The barrenest surfaces, perhaps, are the most interesting in such weather as yesterday, when the most terrene colors are seen. The wet earth and sand, and especially subsoil, are very invigorating sights.

March 19. Wind Through the White Pines

THE MEADOWS ARE ALL in commotion. The ducks are now concealed by the waves, if there are any floating there. While the sun is behind a cloud, the surface of the flood is almost uniformly yellowish or blue, but when the sun comes out from behind the cloud, a myriad dazzling white crests to the waves are seen. The wind makes such a din about your ears that conversation is difficult; your words are blown away and do not strike the ear they were aimed at. If you walk by the water, the tumult of the waves confuses you. If you go by a tree or enter the woods, the din is yet greater. Nevertheless this universal commotion is very interesting and exciting. The white pines in the horizon, either single trees or whole woods, a mile off in the southwest or west, are particularly interesting. You not only see the regular bilateral form of the tree, all the branches distinct like the frond of a fern or a feather (for the pine, even at this distance, has not merely beauty of outline and color,—it is not merely an amorphous and homogeneous or continuous mass of green,—but shows a regular succession of flattish leafy boughs or stages, in flakes one above another, like the veins of a leaf or the leaflets of a frond; it is this richness and symmetry of detail which, more than its outline, charms us), but that fine silvery light reflected from its needles (perhaps their under sides) incessantly in motion. As a tree bends and waves like a feather in the gale, I see it alternately dark and light, as the sides of the needles, which reflect the cool sheen, are alternately withdrawn from and restored to the proper angle, and the light appears to flash upward from the base of the tree incessantly. In the intervals of the flash it is often as if the tree were withdrawn altogether from sight. I see one large pine wood over whose whole top these cold electric flashes are incessantly passing off harmlessly into the air above. I thought at first of some fine spray dashed upward, but it is rather like broad flashes of pale, cold light. Surely you can never see a pine wood so expressive, so speaking. This reflection of light from the waving crests of the earth is like the play and flashing of electricity. No deciduous tree exhibits these fine effects of light. Literally incessant sheets, not of heat- but cold-lightning, you would say were flashing there. Seeing some just over the roof of a house which was far on this side, I thought at first that it was something like smoke even—though a rare kind of smoke—that went up from the house. In short, you see a play of light over the whole pine, similar in its cause, but far grander in its effects, than that seen in a waving field of grain. Is not this wind an awaking to life and light [of] the pines after their winter slumber? The wind is making passes over them, magnetizing and electrifying them. Seen at midday, even, it is still the light of dewy morning alone that is reflected from the needles of the pine. This is the brightening and awakening of the pines, a phenomenon perchance connected with the flow of sap in them. I feel somewhat like the young Astyanax at sight of his father's flashing crest. As if in this wind-storm of March a certain electricity was passing from heaven to earth through the pines and calling them to life.

That first general exposure of the russet earth, March 16th, after the soaking rain of the day before, which washed off most of the snow and ice, is a remarkable era in an ordinary spring. The earth casting off her white mantle and appearing in her homely russet garb. This russet—including the leather-color of oak leaves—is peculiar and not like the russet of the fall and winter, for it reflects the spring light or sun, as if there were a sort of sap in it. When the strong northwest winds first blow, drying up the superabundant moisture, the withered grass and leaves do not present a merely weather-beaten appearance, but a washed and combed springlike face. The knolls forming islands in our meadowy flood are never more interesting than then. This is when the earth is, as it were, re-created, raised up to the sun, which was buried under snow and ice.

March 23. A Diversified Landscape

WE CROSS TO LEE'S shore and sit upon the bare rocky ridge overlooking the flood southwest and northeast. It is quite sunny and sufficiently warm. I see one or two of the small fuzzy gnats in the air. The prospect thence is a fine one, especially at this season, when the water is high. The landscape is very agreeably diversified with hill and vale and meadow and cliff. As we look southwest, how attractive the shores of russet capes and peninsulas laved by the flood! Indeed, that large tract east of the bridge is now an island. How fair that low, undulating russet land! At this season and under these circumstances, the sun just come out and the flood high around it, russet, so reflecting the light of the sun, appears to me the most agreeable of colors, and I begin to dream of a russet fairyland and elysium. How dark and terrene must be green! but this smooth russet surface reflects almost all the light. That broad and low but firm island, with but few trees to conceal the contour of the ground and its outline, with its fine russet sward, firm and soft as velvet, reflecting so much light,—all the undulations of the earth, its nerves and muscles, revealed by the light and shade, and even the sharper ridgy edge of steep banks where the plow has heaped up the earth from year to year,— this is a sort of fairyland and elysium to my eye. The tawny couchant island! Dry land for the Indian's wigwam in the spring, and still strewn with his arrow-points. The sight of such land reminds me of the pleasant spring days in which I have walked over such tracts, looking for these relics. How well, too, this smooth, firm, light-reflecting, tawny earth contrasts with the darker water which surrounds it,—or perchance lighter sometimes! At this season, when the russet colors prevail, the contrast of water and land is more agreeable to behold. What an inexpressibly soft curving line is the shore! Or if the water is perfectly smooth and yet rising, you seem to see it raised an eighth of an inch with swelling lip above the immediate shore it kisses, as in a cup or the of [sic] a saucer. Indian isles and promontories. Thus we sit on that rock, hear the first wood frog's croak, and dream of a russet elysium. Enough for the season is the beauty thereof. Spring has a beauty of its own which we would not exchange for that of summer, and at this moment, if I imagine the fairest earth I can, it is still russet, such is the color of its blessed isles, and they are surrounded with the phenomena of spring.

March 23. Under the Spring Sun

I THINK I HAVE already noticed within a week how very agreeably and strongly the green of small pines contrasts with the russet of a hillside pasture now. Perhaps there is no color with which green contrasts more strongly.

    I see the shadow of a cloud—and it chances to be a hollow ring with sunlight in its midst—passing over the hilly sprout-land toward the Baker house, a sprout-land of oaks and birches; and, owing to the color of the birch twigs, perhaps, this shadow turns all from russet to a decided dark-purplish color as it moves along. And then, as I look further along eastward in the horizon, I am surprised to see strong purple and violet tinges in the sun, from a hillside a mile off densely covered with full-grown birches. It is the steep old corn-field hillside of Jacob Baker's. I would not have believed that under the spring sun so many colors were brought out. It is not the willows only that shine, but, under favorable circumstances, many other twigs, even a mile or two off. The dense birches, so far that their white stems are not distinct, reflect deep, strong purple and violet colors from the distant hillsides opposite to the sun. Can this have to do with the sap flowing in them?

Fair Haven Bay and open wooded slope
on the east side near Concord, Massachusetts.

March 28. Water and Land

HOW CHARMING THE CONTRAST of land and water, especially a temporary island in the flood, with its new and tender shores of waving outline, so withdrawn yet habitable, above all if it rises into a hill high above the water and contrasting with it the more, and if that hill is wooded, suggesting wildness! Our vernal lakes have a beauty to my mind which they would not possess if they were more permanent. Everything is in rapid flux here, suggesting that Nature is alive to her extremities and superficies. To-day we sail swiftly on dark rolling waves or paddle over a sea as smooth as a mirror, unable to touch the bottom, where mowers work and hide their jugs in August; coasting the edge of maple swamps, where alder tassels and white maple flowers are kissing the tide that has risen to meet them. But this particular phase of beauty is fleeting. Nature has so many shows for us she cannot afford to give much time to this. In a few days, perchance, these lakes will have all run away to the sea. Such are the pictures

which she paints. When we look at our masterpieces we see only dead paint and
its vehicle, which suggests no liquid life rapidly flowing off from beneath. In the
former case—in Nature—it is constant surprise and novelty. In many arrangements there is a wearisome monotony. We know too well what [we] shall have for
our Saturday's dinner, but each day's feast in Nature's year is a surprise to us and
adapted to our appetite and spirits. She has arranged such an order of feasts as
never tires. Her motive is not economy but satisfaction.

As we sweep past the north end of Poplar Hill, with a sand-hole in it, its now
dryish, pale-brown mottled sward clothing its rounded slope, which was lately
saturated with moisture, presents very agreeable hues. In this light, in fair
weather, the patches of now dull-greenish mosses contrast just regularly enough
with the pale-brown grass. It is like some rich but modest-colored Kidderminster
carpet, or rather the skin of a monster python tacked to the hillside and stuffed
with earth. These earth colors, methinks, are never so fair as in the spring. Now
the green mosses and lichens contrast with the brown grass, but ere long the
surface will be uniformly green. I suspect that we are more amused by the effects
of color in the skin of the earth now than in summer. Like the skin of a python,
greenish and brown, a fit coat for it to creep over the earth and be concealed in.
Or like the skin of a pard, the great leopard mother that Nature is, where she lies
at length, exposing her flanks to the sun. I feel as if I could land to stroke and
kiss the very sward, it is so fair. It is homely and domestic to my eyes like the
rug that lies before my hearth-side. Such ottomans and divans are spread for us
to recline on. Nor are these colors mere thin superficial figures, vehicles for paint,
but wonderful living growths,—these lichens, to the study of which learned men
have devoted their lives,—and libraries have been written about them. The earth
lies out now like a leopard, drying her lichen and moss spotted skin in the sun,
her sleek and variegated hide. I know that the few raw spots will heal over. Brown
is the color for me, the color of our coats and our daily lives, the color of the poor
man's loaf. The bright tints are pies and cakes, good only for October feasts, which
would make us sick if eaten every day.

April 15. The Farmer's Life

CONSIDER HOW MUCH IS annually spent on the farmer's life: the beauty
of his abode, which has inspired poets since the world was made; the hundreds of
delicate and beautiful flowers scattered profusely under his feet and all around
him, as he walks or drives his team afield,—he cannot put his spade into uncul-
tivated, nor into much cultivated, ground without disturbing some of them; a
hundred or two of equally beautiful birds to sing to him morning and evening, and
some at noonday, a good part of the year; a perfect sky arched over him, a perfect
carpet spread under him, etc., etc.! And can the farmer speak or think carelessly
of these gifts? Will he find it in his heart to curse the flowers and shoot the birds?

April 23. Live in the Present

THERE IS A SEASON for everything, and we do not notice a given phenomenon except at that season, if, indeed, it can be called the same phenomenon at any other season. There is a time to watch the ripples on Ripple Lake, to look for arrowheads, to study the rocks and lichens, a time to walk on sandy deserts; and the observer of nature must improve these seasons as much as the farmer his. So boys fly kites and play ball or hawkie at particular times all over the State. A wise man will know what game to play to-day, and play it. We must not be governed by rigid rules, as by the almanac, but let the season rule us. The moods and thoughts of man are revolving just as steadily and incessantly as nature's. Nothing must be postponed. Take time by the forelock. Now or never! You must live in the present, launch yourself on every wave, find your eternity in each moment. Fools stand on their island opportunities and look toward another land. There is no other land; there is no other life but this, or the like of this. Where the good husbandman is, there is the good soil. Take any other course, and life will be a succession of regrets. Let us see vessels sailing prosperously before the wind, and not simply stranded barks. There is no world for the penitent and regretful.

May 27. Houses of the Poor

WENT BY TEMPLE'S. FOR rural interest, give me the houses of the poor, with simply a cool spring, a good deal of weather-stained wood, and a natural door-stone; a house standing somewhere in nature, and not merely in an atmosphere of art, on a measured lot; on a hillside, perchance, obviously not made by any gardener, amid rocks not placed there by a landscape gardener for effect; with nothing "pretty" about it, but life reduced to its lowest terms and yet found to be beautiful. This is a good foundation or board to spring from. All that the natives erect themselves above that will be a genuine growth.

June 15. A Country House

SAW NEAR MILL, ON the wooded hillside, a regular old-fashioned country house, long and low, one story unpainted, with a broad green field, half orchard, for all yard between it and the road,—a part of the hillside,—and much June-grass before it. This is where the men who save the country are born and bred. Here is the pure fountain of human life.

Sept. 24. This Old Carlisle Road

GOING ALONG THIS OLD Carlisle road,—road for walkers, for berry-pickers, and no more worldly travellers; road for Melvin and Clark, not for the sheriff nor butcher nor the baker's jingling cart; road where all wild things and fruits abound, where there are countless rocks to jar those who venture there in wagons; which no jockey, no wheelwright in his right mind, drives over, no little spidery gigs and Flying Childers; road which leads to and through a great but not famous garden, zoölogical and botanical garden, at whose *gate* you never arrive,— as I was going along there, I perceived the grateful scent of the dicksonia fern now partly decayed, and it reminds me of all up-country with its springy moun- tainsides and unexhausted vigor. Is there any essence of dicksonia fern, I wonder? Surely that giant who, my neighbor expects, is to bound up the Alleghanies will have his handkerchief scented with that. In the lowest part of the road the dicksonia by the wall-sides is more than half frost-bitten and withered,—a sober Quaker-color, brown crape!—though not so tender or early [?] as the cinnamon fern; but soon I rise to where they are more yellow and green, and so my route is varied. On the higher places there are very handsome tufts of it, all yellowish outside and green within. The sweet fragrance of decay! When I wade through by narrow cow-paths, it is as if I had strayed into an ancient and decayed herb-garden. Proper for old ladies to scent their handkerchiefs with. Nature perfumes her garments with this essence now especially. She gives it to those who go a-barberrying and on dank autumnal walks. The essence of this as well as of new-mown hay, surely! The very scent of it, if you have a decayed frond in your chamber, will take you far up country in a twinkling. You would think you had gone after the cows there, or were lost on the mountains. It will make you as cool and well as a frog,—a wood frog, *Rana sylvatica.* It is the scent the earth yielded in the saurian period, before man was created and fell, before milk and water were invented, and the mints. Far wilder than they. *Rana sylvatica* passed judgment on it, or rather that peculiar-scented *Rana palustris.* It was in his reign it was introduced. That is the scent of the Silurian Period precisely, and a modern beau may scent his handkerchief with it. Before man had come and the plants that chiefly serve him. There were no *Rosaceœ* nor mints then. So the earth smelled in the Silurian (?) Period, before man was created and any soil had been debauched with manure. The saurians had their handkerchiefs scented with it. For all the ages are represented still and you can smell them out.

A man must attend to Nature closely for many years to know when, as well as where, to look for his objects, since he must always anticipate her a little. Young men have not learned the phases of Nature; they do not know what constitutes a year, or that one year is like another. I would know when in the year to expect certain thoughts and moods, as the sportsman knows when to look for plover.

Sept. 24. Road-That Old Carlisle One

ROAD—THAT OLD CARLISLE ONE —that leaves towns behind; where you put off worldly thoughts; where you do not carry a watch, nor remember the proprietor; where the proprietor is the only trespasser,—looking after *his* ap- ples!—the only one who mistakes his calling there, whose title is not good; where fifty may be a-barberrying and you do not see one. It is an endless succession of glades where the barberries grow thickest, successive yards amid the barberry bushes where you do not see out. There I see Melvin and the robins, and many a-nut-brown maid *sashé*-ing [*sic*] to the barberry bushes in hoops and crinoline, and none of them see me. The world-surrounding hoop! faery rings! Oh, the jolly cooper's trade it is the best of any! Carried to the furthest isles where civilized man penetrates. This the girdle they've put round the world! Saturn or Satan set the example. Large and small hogsheads, barrels, kegs, worn by the misses that go to that lone schoolhouse in the Pinkham notch. The lonely horse in its pasture is glad to see company, comes forward to be noticed and takes an apple from your hand. Others are called *great* roads, but this is greater than they all. The road is only laid out, offered to walkers, not *accepted* by the town and the travelling world. To be represented by a dotted line on charts, or drawn in lime-juice, undiscoverable to the uninitiated, to be held to a warm imagination. No guide-boards indicate it. No odometer would indicate the miles a wagon had run there. Rocks which the druids *might* have raised—if they could. There I go searching for malic acid of the right quality, with my tests. The process is simple. Place the fruit between your jaws and then endeavor to make your teeth meet. The very earth contains it. The Easterbrooks Country contains malic acid.

To my senses the dicksonia fern has the most wild and primitive fragrance, quite unalloyed and untamable, such as no human institutions give out,—the early morning fragrance of the world, antediluvian, strength and hope imparting. They who scent it can never faint. It is ever a new and untried field where it grows, and only when we think original thoughts can we perceive it. If we keep that on [*sic*] our boudoir we shall be healthy and evergreen as hemlocks. Older than, but related to, strawberries. Before strawberries were, it was, and it will outlast them. Good for the trilobite and saurian in us; death to dandies. It yields its scent most morning and evening. Growing without manure; older than man; refreshing him; preserving his original strength and innocence. When the New Hampshire farmer, far from travelled roads, has cleared a space for his mountain home and conducted the springs of the mountain to his yard, already it grows about the sources of that spring, before any mint is planted in his garden. There his sheep and oxen and he too scent it, and he realizes that the world is new to him. There the pastures are rich, the cattle do not die of disease, and the men are strong and free. The wild original of strawberries and the rest.

Sept. 29. A Handsome Juniper

Juniperus repens berries are quite green yet. I see some of last year's *dark*-purple ones at the base of the branchlets. There is a very large specimen on the side of Fair Haven Hill, above Cardinal Shore. This is very handsome this bright afternoon, especially if you stand on the lower and sunny side, on account of the various ways in which its surging flakes and leafets, green or silvery, reflect the light. It is as if we were giants, and looked down on an evergreen forest from whose flaky surface the light is variously reflected. Though so low, it is so dense and rigid that neither men nor cows think of wading through it. We get a bird's-eye view of this evergreen forest, as a hawk sailing over, looking into its unapproachable clefts and recesses, reflecting a green or else a cheerful silvery light.

Oct. 3.   Ground Strewn Aspen Leaves

I SEE THE GROUND strewn with *Populus grandidentata* leaves in one place on the old Carlisle road, where one third are fallen. These yellow leaves are all thickly brown-spotted and are very handsome, somewhat leopard-like. It would seem that they begin to decay in spots at intervals all over the leaf, producing a very pretty effect. Think of the myriad variously tinted and spotted and worm-eaten leaves which now combine to produce the general impression of autumn! The ground is here strewn with thousands, any one of which, if you carry it home, it will refresh and delight you to behold. If we have not the leopard and jaguar and tiger in our woods, we have all their spots and rosettes and stripes in our autumn-tinted leaves.

Oct. 3.   A Gray Roof and Plume of Smoke

LOOKING FROM THE HOG-PASTURE over the valley of Spencer Brook westward, we see the smoke rising from a huge chimney above a gray roof amid the woods, at a distance, where some family is preparing its evening meal. There are few more agreeable sights than this to the pedestrian traveller. No cloud is fairer to him than that little bluish one which issues from the chimney. It suggests all of domestic felicity beneath. There beneath, we suppose, that life is lived of which we have only dreamed. In our minds we clothe each unseen inhabitant with all the success, with all the serenity, which we can conceive of. If old, we imagine him serene; if young, hopeful. Nothing can exceed the perfect peace which reigns there. We have only to see a gray roof with its plume of smoke curling up amid the trees to have this faith. There we suspect no coarse haste or bustle, but serene labors which proceed at the same pace with the declining day. *There* is no hireling in the barn nor in the kitchen. Why does any distant prospect ever charm us? Because we instantly and inevitably imagine a life to be lived there such as is not lived elsewhere, or where we are. We presume that success is the rule. We forever carry a perfect sampler in our minds. Why are distant valleys, why lakes, why mountains in the horizon, ever fair to us? Because we realize for a moment that they may be the home of man, and that man's life may be in harmony with them. Shall I say that we thus forever delude ourselves? We do not suspect that *that* farmer goes to the depot with his milk. *There* the milk is not watered. We are constrained to imagine a life in harmony with the scenery and the hour. The sky and clouds, and the earth itself, with their beauty forever preach to us, saying,

Such an abode we offer you, to such and such a life we encourage you. *There* is not haggard poverty and harassing debt. There is not intemperance, moroseness, meanness, or vulgarity. Men go about sketching, painting landscapes, or writing verses which celebrate man's opportunities. To go into an actual farmer's family at evening, see the tired laborers come in from their day's work thinking of their wages, the sluttish help in the kitchen and sink-room, the indifferent stolidity and patient misery which only the spirits of the youngest children rise above,—that suggests one train of thoughts. To look down on that roof from a distance in an October evening, when its smoke is ascending peacefully to join the kindred clouds above,—that suggests a different train of thoughts. We think that we see these fair abodes and are elated beyond all speech, when we see only our own roofs, perchance. We are ever busy hiring house and lands and peopling them in our imaginations. There is no beauty in the sky, but in the eye that sees it. Health, high spirits, serenity, these are the great landscape-painters. Turners, Claudes, Rembrandts are nothing to them. We never see any beauty but as the garment of some virtue. Men love to walk in those picture-galleries still, because they have not quite forgotten their early dreams. When I see only the roof of a house above the woods and do not know whose it is, I presume that one of the worthies of the world dwells beneath it, and for a season I am exhilarated at the thought. I would fain sketch it that others may share my pleasure. But commonly, if I see or know the occupant, I am affected as by the sight of the almshouse or hospital.

Wild apples are perhaps at their height, or perhaps only the earlier ones.

Those *P. grandidentata* leaves are wildly rich. So handsomely formed and floridly scalloped, to begin with,—a fine chrome yellow now richly spotted with dark brown like a leopard's skin,—they cover the still green sward by the roadside and the gray road thick as a pavement, each one worthy to be admired as a gem or work of Oriental art.

Oct. 4. Knowledge and Perception

IT IS ONLY WHEN we forget all our learning that we begin to know. I do not get nearer by a hair's breadth to any natural object so long as I presume that I have an introduction to it from some learned man. To conceive of it with a total apprehension I must for the thousandth time approach it as something totally strange. If you would make acquaintance with the ferns you must forget your botany. You must get rid of what is commonly called *knowledge* of them. Not a single scientific term or distinction is the least to the purpose, for you would fain perceive something, and you must approach the object totally unprejudiced. You must be aware that *no thing* is what you have taken it to be. In what book is this world and its beauty described? Who has plotted the steps toward the discovery of beauty? You have got to be in a different state from common. Your greatest success will be simply to perceive that such things are, and you will have no communication to make to the Royal Society. If it were required to know the position of the fruit-dots or the character of the indusium, nothing could be easier

than to ascertain it; but if it is required that you be affected by ferns, that they amount to anything, signify anything, to you, that they be another sacred scripture and revelation to you, helping to redeem your life, this end is not so surely accomplished. In the one case, you take a sentence and analyze it, you decide if it is printed in large [*sic*] primer or small pica; if it is long or short, simple or compound, and how many clauses it is composed of; if the i's are all dotted, or some for variety without dots; what the color and composition of the ink and the paper; and it is considered a fair or mediocre sentence accordingly, and you assign its place among the sentences you have seen and kept specimens of. But as for the meaning of the sentence, that is as completely overlooked as if it had none. This is the Chinese, the Aristotelean, method. But if you should ever perceive the meaning you would disregard all the rest. So far science goes, and it punctually leaves off there,—tells you finally where it is to be found and its synonyms, and rests from its labors.

Oct. 15. A Town Park or Forest

EACH TOWN SHOULD HAVE a park, or rather a primitive forest, of five hundred or a thousand acres, where a stick should never be cut for fuel, a common possession forever, for instruction and recreation. We hear of cow-commons and ministerial lots, but we want *men*-commons and lay lots, inalienable forever. Let us keep the New World *new,* preserve all the advantages of living in the country. There is meadow and pasture and wood-lot for the town's poor. Why not a forest and huckleberry-field for the town's rich? All Walden Wood might have been preserved for our park forever, with Walden in its midst, and the Easterbrooks Country, an unoccupied area of some four square miles, might have been our huckleberry-field. If any owners of these tracts are about to leave the world without natural heirs who need or deserve to be specially remembered, they will do wisely to abandon their possession to all, and not will them to some individual who perhaps has enough already. As some give to Harvard College or another institution, why might not another give a forest or huckleberry-field to Concord? A town is an institution which deserves to be remembered. We boast of our system of education, but why stop at schoolmasters and schoolhouses? We are all school-masters, and our schoolhouse is the universe. To attend chiefly to the desk or schoolhouse while we neglect the scenery in which it is placed is absurd. If we do not look out we shall find our fine schoolhouse standing in a cow-yard at last.

Nov. 26. Cutting New Paths

P.M.—WALK OVER THE Colburn Farm wood-lot south [of] the road.

I find, sometimes, after I have been lotting off a large wood-lot for auction, that I have been cutting new paths to walk in. I cut lines an inch [*sic*] or two long in arbitrary directions, in and around some dense wood-lot which perhaps is not crossed once a month by any mortal, nor has been for thirty or fifty years, and thus I open to myself new works [*sic*],—enough in a lot of forty acres to occupy me for an afternoon. A forty-acre wood-lot which otherwise would not detain a walker more than half an hour, being thus opened and carved out, will entertain him for half a day.

In this case there was a cultivated field here some thirty years ago, but, the wood being suffered to spring up, from being open and revealed this part of the earth became a covert and concealed place. Excepting an occasional hunter who crossed it maybe once in several months, nobody has walked there, nobody has penetrated its recesses. The walker habitually goes round it, or follows the single cart-path that winds through it. Woods, both the primitive and those which are suffered to spring up in cultivated fields, thus preserve the mystery of nature. How private and sacred a place a grove thus becomes!—merely because its denseness excludes man. It is worth the while to have these thickets on various sides of the town, where the rabbit lurks and the jay builds its nest.

When I ran out the boundary lines of this lot, I could commonly distinguish the line, not merely by the different growth of wood, but often by a kind of ditch which I think may have been produced by the plow, which heaped up the soil along the side of the field when it was cultivated. I could also detect trees variously bent and twisted, which probably had made part of a hedge fence when young, and others which were scarred by the fencing-stuff that had been fastened to them.

Dec. 12. View Over Pile of Wood

AS I TALKED WITH the woodchopper who had just cleared the top of
Emerson's I got a new view of the mountains over his pile of wood in the
foreground. They were very grand in their snowy mantle, which had a slight tinge
of purple. But when afterward I looked at them from a higher hill, where there
was no wood-pile in the foreground, they affected me less. It is now that these
mountains, in color as well as form, most resemble the clouds.

Chapter XII
Year
1860 and 1861
Age
42–44

860

Jan. 4. Observations Make A Chain

A MAN RECEIVES ONLY what he is ready to receive, whether physically or intellectually or morally, as animals conceive at certain seasons their kind only. We hear and apprehend only what we already half know. If there is something which does not concern me, which is out of my line, which by experience or by genius my attention is not drawn to, however novel and remarkable it may be, if it is spoken, we hear it not, if it is written, we read it not, or if we read it, it does not detain us. Every man thus *tracks himself* through life, in all his hearing and reading and observation and travelling. His observations make a chain. The phenomenon or fact that cannot in any wise be linked with the rest which he has observed, he does not observe. By and by we may be ready to receive what we cannot receive now. I find, for example, in Aristotle something about the spawning, etc., of the pout and perch, because I know something about it already and have my attention aroused; but I do not discover till very late that he has made other equally important observations on the spawning of other fishes, because I am not interested in those fishes.

Jan. 30. Natural Parks

I GO THROUGH THE piny field northwest of M. Miles's. There are no more beautiful natural parks than these pastures in which the white pines have sprung up spontaneously, standing at handsome intervals, where the wind chanced to let the seed lie at last, and the grass and blackberry vines have not yet been killed by them.

Feb. 13. Unto Him That Hath

THE SCRIPTURE RULE, "UNTO him that hath shall be given," is true of composition. The more you have thought and written on a given theme, the more you can still write. Thought breeds thought. It grows under your hands.

March 14. Walden Ice Melted

AS I STAND THERE, I see some dark ripples already drop and sweep over the surface of the pond, as they will ere long over Ripple Lake and other pools in the wood. No sooner has the ice of Walden melted than the wind begins to play in dark ripples over the surface of the virgin water. It is affecting to see Nature so tender, however old, and wearing none of the wrinkles of age. Ice dissolved is the next moment as perfect water as if it had been melted a million years. To see that which was lately so hard and immovable now so soft and impressible! What if our moods could dissolve thus completely? It is like a flush of life in a cheek that was dead. It seems as if it must rejoice in its own newly acquired fluidity, as it affects the beholder with joy. Often the March winds have no chance to ripple its face at all.

March 19. Cheerful Pitch Pine

GOING ALONG THE TURNPIKE, I look over to the pitch pines on Moore's hillside,—ground bare as it has been since February 23, except a slight whitening or two,—and it strikes me that this pine, take the year round, is the most cheerful tree and most living to look at and have about your house, it is so sunny and full of light, in harmony with the yellow sand there and the spring sun. The deciduous trees are apparently dead, and the white pine is much darker, but the pitch pine has an ingrained sunniness and is especially valuable for imparting warmth to the landscape at this season. Yet men will take pains to cut down these trees and set imported larches in their places! The pitch pine shines in the spring somewhat as the osiers do.

March 26. Yellow Sand and Pines

ONE OF THE MOST interesting sights this afternoon is the color of the yellow sand in the sun at the bottom of Nut Meadow and Second Division Brooks. The yellow sands of a lonely brook seen through the rippling water, with the shadows of the ripples like films passing over it.

By degrees you pass from heaven to earth up the trunk of the white pine. See the flash of its boughs reflecting the sun, each light or sunny above and shaded beneath, even like the clouds with their dark bases, a sort of mackerel sky of pine boughs.

June 4. Fully Expanded Leaves

ONE ASKS ME TO-DAY when it is that the leaves are fully expanded, so that the trees and woods look dark and heavy with leaves. I answered that there were leaves on many if not on most trees already fully expanded, but that there were not many on a tree, the shoots having grown only some three inches, but by and by they will have grown a foot or two and there will be ten times as many leaves. Each tree (or most trees) now holds out many little twigs, some three inches long, with two or three fully expanded leaves on it, between us and the sun, making already a grateful but thin shade, like a coarse sieve, so open that we see the fluttering of each leaf in its shadow; but in a week or more the twigs will have so extended themselves, and the number of fully expanded leaves be so increased, that the trees will look heavy and dark with foliage and the shadow be dark and opaque,—a gelid shade.

Hazy, and mountains concealed.

I notice to-day, for example, that most maple, birch, willow, alder, and elm leaves are fully expanded, but most oaks and hickories, ash trees, etc., are not quite.

June 8. Mountains as Pyramids

AS I LOOK AT the mountains in the horizon, I am struck by the fact that they are all pyramidal—pyramids, more or less low—and have a peak. Why have the mountains usually a peak? This is not the common form of hills. They do not so impress us at least.

July 15. The Cultivated Grasses

ON HILL.—NO CROPS clothe the earth with richer hues and make a greater impression of luxuriousness than the cultivated grasses. Field after field, densely packed like the squares of a checker-board, all through and about the villages, paint the earth with various shades of green and other colors. There is the rich glaucous green of young grain now, of various shades, depending on its age and kind; the flashing blades of corn which does not yet hide the bare ground; the yellowing tops of ripening grain; the dense uniform red of red-top, the most striking and high-colored of all (that is, cultivated); the very similar purple of the fowl-meadow (the most deep-piled and cumulous-looking, like down) along the low river-banks; the very dark and dusky, as it were shadowy, green of herd's-grass at a distance, as if clouds were always passing over it,—close at hand it is of a dark purplish or slaty purple, from the color of its anthers; the fresh light green where June-grass has been cut, and the fresh dark green where clover has been cut; and the hard, dark green of pastures (red-top) generally,—not to speak of the very light-colored wiry fescue there.

Farm fields.

July 22. Beauty of Farmer's Crops

YESTERDAY HAVING BEEN A rainy day, the air is now remarkably clear and cool and you rarely see the horizon so distinct. The surface of the earth, especially looking westward,—grass grounds, pastures, and meadows,—is remarkably beautiful. I stand in Heywood's pasture west of the leek and, leaning over the wall, look westward. All things—grass, etc.—are peculiarly fresh this season on account of the copious rains.

The next field on the west slopes gently from both east and west to a meadow in the middle. So, as I look over the wall, it is first dark-green, where white clover has been cut (still showing a myriad low white heads which resound with the hum of bees); next, along the edge of the bottom or meadow, is a strip or belt three or four rods wide of red-top, uncut, perfectly distinct; then the cheerful bright-yellow sedge of the meadow, yellow almost as gamboge; then a corresponding belt of red-top on its upper edge, quite straight and rectilinear like the first; then a glaucous-green field of grain still quite low; and, in the further corner of the field, a much darker square of green than any yet, all brilliant in this wonderful light. You thus have a sort of terrestrial rainbow, thus:

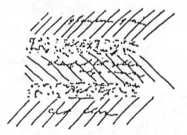

The farmer accustomed to look at his crops from a mercenary point of view is not aware how beautiful they are. This prospect was really exciting, even as a rainbow is. Then the next pasture on the northwest, where it sloped toward me gently, a smooth velvet or impalpable green slope, with here and there the lightest cobwebby touch of lighter green like a dew on it, where a little fescue grass still made an impression in spite of the cows. These soft, indefinite lighter touches on the dark-green enamelled slope! It was like a delicately watered surface, and here and there stood on it a few young hickories, their stems and their umbrage both as black as a coal; and further, just this side the wall over which the clear light came, some low bushes, probably sumach, reflected a hoary, silvery light. You can tell the crops afar off by their color. The next, more springy pasture on the north was all lit up with yellow ferns.

July 23. Under Sides of the Leaves

SO FAR AS LEAVES are concerned, one of the most noticeable phenomena of this green-leaf season is the conspicuous reflection of light in clear breezy days from the silvery under sides of some.

All trees and shrubs which have light-colored or silvery under sides to their leaves, but especially the swamp white oak and the red maple, are now very bright and conspicuous in the strong wind after the rain of the morning. Indeed, now that the leaves are so numerous they are more noticeable than ever, but you must be on the windward side. Some, as the *Salix alba,* are thus silvered only at the top

and extremities, the younger leaves alone being sufficiently appressed to show
their under sides. But the two kinds first mentioned are the most generally conspicuous, and these forming commonly the front rank,—especially at the base of
hills,—behind which grow other oaks, and birches, pines, etc., you see the whole
outline of these trees, waving and rustling in the breeze against that darker green,
suggesting frostwork, or as if etched in silver on a green ground. To be sure, most,
if not all leaves, not to mention grasses, are a paler green beneath, and hence the
oaks and other trees behind show various shades of green, which would be more
observed if it were not for these stronger contrasts. Though the wind may not be
very strong nor incessant, you appear to see *only* the under sides of those first
named, and they make a uniform impression, as if their leaves, having been turned
up, were permanently held so. Before the wind arose, the wooded shore and
hillsides were an almost uniform green, but now the whole outline of the swamp
white oaks and maples is revealed by the wind—a sort of magic, a "presto
change"—distinctly against trees whose leaves are nearly of the same color with
the upper sides of these.

Some of the swamp white oaks, whose leaves are but slightly turned up, look
as if crisped by frost. The grape leaf also, where it occurs, is sufficiently conspicuous. Thus the leaves take an airing. It is like etching on silverware. If you look
sharply, you perceive also the paler under sides of the oaks and birches in the
background contrasting with the darker upper sides of their lower leaves. In a
maple swamp every maple-top stands now distinguished thus from the birches in
their midst. Before they were confounded, but a wind comes and lifts their leaves,
showing their lighter under sides, and suddenly, as by magic, the maple stands out
from the birch. There is a great deal of life in this landscape. What an airing the
leaves get! Perchance it is necessary that their under sides be thus exposed to the
light and air in order that they may be hardened and darkened by it.

Aug. 6.   Pastures on Monadnock

EVENING AND MORNING WERE the most interesting seasons, especially
the evening. Each day, about an hour before sunset, I got sight, as it were
accidentally, of an elysium beneath me. The smoky haze of the day, suggesting
a furnace-like heat, a trivial dustiness, gave place to a clear transparent enamel,
through which houses, woods, farms, and lakes were seen as in [a] picture indescribably fair and expressly made to be looked at. At any hour of the day, to be
sure, the surrounding country looks flatter than it is. Even the great steep,
furrowed, and rocky pastures, red with hardhack and raspberries, which creep so
high up the mountain amid the woods, in which you think already that you are
halfway up, perchance, seen from the top or brow of the mountain are not for a
long time distinguished for elevation above the surrounding country, but they look
smooth and tolerably level, and the cattle in them are not noticed or distinguished
from rocks unless you search very particularly. At length you notice how the
houses and barns keep a respectful, and at first unaccountable, distance from these

near pastures and woods, though they *are* seemingly flat, that there is a broad
neutral ground between the roads and the mountain; and yet when the truth
flashes upon you, you have to imagine the long, ascending path through them.

To speak of the landscape generally, the open or cleared land looks like a
thousand little swells or tops of low rounded hills,—tent-like or like a low hay-cap
spread,—tawny or green amid the woods. As you look down on this landscape you
little think of the hills where the traveller walks his horse. The woods have not
this swelling look. The most common color of open land (from apex at 5 P.M.) is
tawny brown, the woods dark green. At midday the darker green of evergreens
amid the hardwoods is quite discernible half a dozen miles off. But, as the most
interesting view is at sunset, so it is the part of [the] landscape nearest to you and
most immediately beneath the mountain, where, as usual, there is that invisible
gelid haze to glass it.

Aug. 9.   The Peak of Monadnock

THEY WHO SIMPLY CLIMB to the peak of Monadnock have seen but little
of the mountain. I came not to look *off from* it, but to look *at* it. The view of the
pinnacle itself from the plateau below surpasses any view which you get from the
summit. It is indispensable to see the top itself and the sierra of its outline from
one side. The great charm is not to look off from a height but to walk over this
novel and wonderful rocky surface. Moreover, if you would enjoy the prospect,
it is, methinks, most interesting when you look from the edge of the plateau
immediately down into the valleys, or where the edge of the lichen-clad rocks, only
two or three rods from you, is seen as the lower frame of a picture of green fields,
lakes, and woods, suggesting a more stupendous precipice than exists. There are
much more surprising effects of this nature along the edge of the plateau than on
the summit. It is remarkable what haste the visitors make to get to the top of the
mountain and then look away from it.

Aug. 9.   Mountain Bogs and Swamps

THOUGH THERE IS LITTLE or no soil upon the rocks, owing apparently
to the coolness, if not moisture, you have rather the vegetation of a swamp than
that of sterile rocky ground below. For example, of the six prevailing trees and
shrubs—low blueberry, black spruce, lambkill, black choke-berry, wild holly, and
Viburnum nudum—all but the first are characteristic of swampy and low ground,
to say nothing of the commonness of wet mosses, the two species of cotton-grass,
and some other plants of the swamp and meadow. Little meadows and swamps
are scattered all over the mountain upon and amid the rocks. You are continually
struck with the proximity of gray and lichen-clad rock and mossy bog. You tread
alternately on wet moss, into which you sink, and dry, lichen-covered rocks. You
will be surprised to see the vegetation of a swamp on a little shelf only a foot or
two over,—a bog a foot wide with cotton-grass waving over it in the midst of

cladonia lichens so dry as to burn like tinder. The edges of the little swamps—if not their middle—are commonly white with cotton-grass. The *Arenaria Grœn-landica* often belies its name here, growing in wet places as often as in dry ones, together with eriophorum.

Aug. 9. Outline of a Mountain

THERE WAS A GOOD view of the mountain from just above the pond, some two miles from Troy. The varying outline of a mountain is due to the crest of different spurs, as seen from different sides. Even a small spur, if you are near, may conceal a much larger one and give its own outline to the mountain, and at the same time one which extends directly toward you is not noticed at all, however important, though, as you travel round the mountain, this may gradually come into view and finally its crest may be one half or more of the outline presented. It may partly account for the peaked or pyramidal form of mountains that one crest may be seen through the gaps of another and so fill up the line.

Oct. 9. Brilliancy of Red Maples

THOUGH THE RED MAPLES have not their common brilliancy on account of the very severe frost about the end of September, some are very interesting. You cannot judge a tree by seeing it from one side only. As you go round or away from it, it may overcome you with its mass of glowing scarlet or yellow light. You need to stand where the greatest number of leaves will transmit or reflect to you most favorably. The tree which looked comparatively lifeless, cold, and merely parti-colored, seen in a more favorable light as you are floating away from it, may affect you wonderfully as a warm, glowing drapery. I now see one small red maple which is all a pure yellow within and a bright red scarlet on its outer surface and prominences. It is a remarkably distinct painting of scarlet on a yellow ground. It is an indescribably beautiful contrast of scarlet and yellow. Another is yellow and green where this was scarlet and yellow, and in this case the bright and liquid green, now getting to be rare, is by contrast as charming a color as the scarlet.

Oct. 16. Communities of Trees

P.M.—TO WHITE POND and neighborhood.

As a consequence of the different manner in which trees which have winged seeds and those which have not are planted,—the [former] being blown together in one direction by the wind, the latter being dispersed irregularly by animals,—I observe that the former, as pines (which (the white) are said in the primitive wood to grow in communities), white birches, red maples, alders, etc., often grow in more or less regular rounded or oval or conical patches, as the seeds fell, while oaks, chestnuts, hickories, etc., simply form woods of greater or less extent whether by themselves or mixed; *i. e.,* they do not naturally spring up in an oval form (or elliptical) unless they derive it from the pines under which they were planted.

For example, take this young white pine wood half a dozen years old, which has sprung up in a pasture adjacent to a wood of oaks and pines mixed. It has the form of a broad crescent, or half-moon, with its diameter resting on the old wood near where a large white pine stood. It is true most such groves are early squared by our plows and fences, for we square these circles every day in our rude practice. And in the same manner often they fall in a sprout-land amid oaks, and I, looking from a hilltop, can distinguish in distant old woods still, of pine and oak mixed, these more exclusive and regular communities of pine, a dozen or more rods wide, while it is the oak commonly that fills up the irregular crevices, beside occupying extensive spaces itself. So it happens that, as the pines themselves and their fruit have a more regularly conical outline than deciduous trees, the groves they form also have.

Our wood-lots, of course, have a history, and we may often recover it for a hundred years back, though we *do* not. A small pine lot may be a side of such an oval, or a half, or a square in the inside with all the curving sides cut off by fences. Yet if we attended more to the history of our lots we should manage them more wisely.

Looking round, I observe at a distance an oak wood-lot some twenty years old, with a dense narrow edging of pitch pines about a rod and a half wide and twenty-five or thirty years old along its whole southern side, which is straight and thirty or forty rods long, and, next to it, an open field or pasture. It presents a very singular appearance, because the oak wood is broad and has no pines within it, while the narrow edging is perfectly straight and dense, and pure pine. It is the more remarkable at this season because the oak is all red and yellow and the pine all green. I understand it and read its history easily before I get to it. I find, as I expected, a fence separating the pines from the oaks, or that they belong to different owners. I also find, as I expected, that eighteen or twenty years ago a pitch pine wood had stood where the oaks are, and was then cut down, for there are their old stumps. But before they were cut, their seeds were blown into the neighbor's field, and the little pines came up all along its edge, and they grew so thickly and so fast that that neighbor refrained at last from plowing them up or cutting them off, for just this rod and a half in width, where they were thickest, and moreover, though there are no sizable oaks mixed with these pines, the whole surface even of this narrow strip is as usual completely stocked with little seedling oaks less than a foot high. But I ask, if the neighbor so often lets this narrow edging grow up, why not often, by the same rule, let them spread over the whole of his field? When at length he sees how they have grown, does he not often regret that he did not do so? Or why be dependent, even to this extent, on these windfalls from our neighbors' trees, or an accident? Why not control our own woods and destiny more? (This was north from the lane beyond Conant's handsome wood.) There are many such problems in forest geometry to be solved.

Oct. 16. This Double Forest

THUS THIS DOUBLE FOREST was advancing to conquer new (or old) land, sending forward their children on the wings of the wind, while already the oak seedlings from the oak wood behind had established themselves beneath the old pines ready to supplant them. The pines were the vanguard. They stood up to fire with their children before them, while the little oaks kneeled behind and between them. The pine is the pioneer, the oak the more permanent settler who lays out his improvements. Pines are by some considered lower in the scale of trees—in the order of development—than oaks.

Oct. 17. Noblest Trees, First Extinct

THE NOBLEST TREES AND those which it took the longest to produce, and which are the longest-lived, as chestnuts, hickories (?), oaks, are the first to become extinct under our present system and the hardest to reproduce, and their place is taken by pines and birches, of feebler growth than the primitive pines and birches, for want of a change of soil.

There is many a tract now bearing a poor and decaying crop of birches, or perhaps of oaks, dying when a quarter grown and covered with fungi and excrescences, where two hundred years ago grew oaks or chestnuts of the largest size.

Oct. 17. Natural Succession of Trees

APPARENTLY THE PINE WOODS are a natural nursery of oaks, from whence we might easily transplant them to our grounds, and thus save some of those which annually decay, while we let the pines stand. Experience has proved, at any rate, that these oaks will bear exposure to the light. It is remarkable that for the most part there are no seedling oaks in the open grassy fields and pastures. The acorns are little likely to succeed if dropped there. Those springing up in such places appear to have been dropped or buried by animals when on their way with them to another covert.

I examine under the pitch pines by Thrush Alley to see how long the oaks live under dense pines. The oldest oaks there are about eight or ten years old. I see none older under these and other dense pines, even when the pines are thirty or more years old, though I have no doubt that oaks began to grow there more than twenty years ago. Hence they must have died, and I suppose I could find their great roots in the soil if I should dig for them. I should say that they survived under a very dense pine wood only from six to ten years. This corresponds exactly with the experience of the English planters, who begin to shred the branches of the nursing pines when the oaks are six or seven years old and to remove the pines altogether when the oaks are eight to ten years old.

But in openings amid the pines, though only a rod in diameter, or where the pines are thin, and also on their edges, the oaks shoot up higher and become trees, and this shows how mixed woods of pine and oak are produced. If the pines are quite small or grow but thinly, fewer acorns will be planted amid them, it is true, but more will come to trees, and so you have a mixed wood. Or when you thin out a pine wood, the oaks spring up here and there; or when you thin an oak wood, the pines plant themselves and grow up in like manner.

It is surprising how many accidents these seedling oaks will survive. We have seen [?] that they commonly survive six to ten years under the thickest pines and acquire stout and succulent roots. Not only they bear the sudden exposure to the light when the pines are cut, but, in case of a more natural succession, when a fire runs over the lot and kills pines and birches and maples, and oaks twenty feet high, these little oaks are scarcely injured at all, and they will still be just as high the next year, if not in the fall of the same year if the fire happens early in the spring. Or if in the natural course of events a fire does not occur nor a hurricane, the soil may at last be exhausted for pines, but there are always the oaks ready to take advantage of the least feebleness and yielding of the pines.

Hereabouts a pine wood, or even a birch wood, is no sooner established than the squirrels and birds begin to plant acorns in it. First the pines, then the oaks; and coniferous trees, geologists tell us, are older, as they are lower in the order of development,—were created before oaks.

I observe to-day a great many pitch pine plumes cut off by squirrels and strewn under the trees, as I did yesterday.

I count the rings of a great white pine sawed off in Laurel Glen a few years ago,—about one hundred and thirty. This, probably, was really of the second growth, at least, but probably now even the second growth is all gone in this town. We may presume that any forest tree here a hundred and thirty years old belongs to the second growth, at least. We may say that all pines and oaks of this age or *growth* are now extinct in this town, and the present generation are not acquainted with large trees of these species.

Oct. 19. Pines and Oaks Together

It is evident to any who attend to the matter that pines are here the natural nurses of the oaks, and therefore they grow together. By the way, how nearly identical is the range of our pines with the range of our oaks? Perhaps oaks extend beyond them southward, where there is less danger of frost.

The *new* woodlands, *i. e.*, forests that spring up where there were no trees before, are pine (or birch or maple), and accordingly you may see spaces of bare pasture sod between the trees for many years. But oaks, in masses, are not seen springing up thus with old sod between them. They form a sprout-land, or stand amid the stumps of a recent pine lot.

It will be worth the while to compare seedling oaks with sprout-lands, to see which thrive best.

I see, on the side of Fair Haven Hill, pines which have spread, apparently from the north, one hundred rods, and the hillside begins to wear the appearance of woodland, though there are many cows feeding amid the pines. The custom with us is to let the pines spread thus into the pasture, and at the same time to let the cattle wander there and contend with the former for the possession of the ground, from time to time coming to the aid of the cattle with a bush-whack. But when, after some fifteen or twenty years, the pines have fairly prevailed over us both, though they have suffered terribly and the ground is strewn with their dead, we then suddenly turn about, coming to the aid of the pines with a whip, and drive the cattle out. They shall no longer be allowed to scratch their heads on them, and we fence them in. This is the actual history of a great many of our wood-lots. While the English have taken great pains to learn how to create forests, this is peculiarly our mode. It is plain that we have thus both poor pastures and poor forests.

Oct. 19. White Oak Acorn

THE WHITE OAK ACORN has very little bitterness and is quite agreeable to eat. When chestnuts are away I am inclined to think them as good as they. At any rate it braces my thought more, and does me more good to eat them, than it does to eat chestnuts. I feel the stronger even before I have swallowed one. It gives me heart and back of oak.

Oct. 20. Old Oak and Pine Wood

I NEXT EXAMINED EBBY Hubbard's old oak and pine wood. The trees may be a hundred years old. The older or decaying trees have been cut out from time to time, neglecting these more recent stumps. The very oldest evidences of a tree were a hollow three or four feet across, in which you often slumped,—a hollow place in which squirrels have their holes covered with many layers of leaves, and perhaps with young oaks springing up in it, for the acorns rolled into it. But if you dug there, from under the moss (there was commonly a little green moss around it) and leaves and soil, in the midst of the virgin mould which the tree had turned to, you pulled up flakes and shoulder-blades of wood that might still be recognized for oak, portions preserved by some quality which they concentrated, like the fat leaves or veins of the pine,—the oak of oak. But for the most part it was but the mould and mildew of the grave,—the grave of a tree which was cut or died eighty or a hundred years ago there. It is with the graves of trees as with those of men,—at first an upright stump (for a monument), in course of time a mere mound, and finally, when the corpse has decayed and shrunk, a depression in the soil. In such a hollow it is better to plant a pine than an oak. The only other ancient traces of trees were perhaps the semiconical mounds which had been heaved up by trees which fell in some hurricane.

Oct. 20.   Woodland Classifications

1st. THERE IS THE primitive wood, woodland which was woodland when the township was settled, and which has not been cut at all. Of this I know of none in Concord. Where is the nearest? There is, perhaps, a large tract in Winchendon.

2d. Second growth, the woodland which has been cut but once,—true second growth. This country has been so recently settled that a large part of the older States is covered now with this second growth, and the same name is occasionally still applied, though falsely, to those wood-lots which have been cut twice or many more times. Of this second growth I think that we have considerable left, and I remember much more. These are our forests which contain the largest and oldest trees,—shingle pines (very few indeed left) and oak timber.

3d. Primitive woodland, *i. e.,* which has always been woodland, never cultivated or converted into pasture or grain-field, nor burned over intentionally. Of two kinds, first, that which has only been thinned from time to time, and secondly, that which has been cut clean many times over. A larger *copsewood.*

4th. Woodland which has been cleared one or more times, enough to raise a crop of grain on it, burned over and perhaps harrowed or even plowed, and suffered to grow up again in a year or two. Call this "interrupted woodland" or "tamed."

5th. *New woods,* or which have sprung up *de novo* on land which has been cultivated or cleared long enough to kill all the roots in it. (The 3d, 4th, and 5th are a kind of copsewood.)

6th. Artificial woods, or those which have been set out or raised from the seed, artificially.

It happens that we have not begun to set out and plant till all the primitive wood is gone. All the *new woods* (or 5th kind) whose beginning I can (now) remember are pine or birch (maple, etc., I have not noticed enough). I suspect that the greater part (?) of our woodland is the 3d kind, or primitive woodland, never burned over intentionally nor plowed, though much of it is the 4th kind. Probably almost all the large wood cut ten or fifteen years ago (and since) here was second growth, and most that we had left was cut then.

Oct. 22.   White Pines Under Oaks

IN THE DEEP CUT big wood (Stow's), pines and oaks, there are thousands of little white pines as well as many oaks. After a mixed wood like this you may have a mixed wood, but after dense pines, commonly oak chiefly, yet not always; for, to my surprise, I find that in the pretty dense pitch pine wood of Wheeler's blackberry-field, where there are only several white pines old enough to bear, and accordingly more than a thousand pitch pine seeds to one white pine one, yet there are countless white pines springing up under the pitch pines (as well as many oaks), and very few or scarcely any little pitch pines, and they sickly, or a thousand white pine seedlings to one pitch pine,—the same proportion reversed (in inverse proportion). It is the same in the pigeon-place lot east of this. So if you should cut these pitch pines you would have next a white pine wood with some oaks in it, the pines taking the lead. Indeed, these white pines bid fair to supplant the pitch pines at last, for they grow well and steadily. This reminds me that, though I often see little white pines under pines and under oaks, I rarely if ever (unless I am mistaken) see many young pitch pines there. How is it? Do the pitch pines require more light and air?

Oct. 22. Squirrels: Planters of Forests

YET WHAT IS THE character of our gratitude to these squirrels, these planters of forests? We regard them as vermin, and annually shoot and destroy them in great numbers, because—if we have any excuse—they sometimes devour a little of our Indian corn, while, perhaps, they are planting the nobler oak-corn (acorn) in its place. In various parts of the country an army of grown-up boys assembles for a squirrel hunt. They choose sides, and the side that kills the greatest number of thousands enjoys a supper at the expense of the other side, and the whole neighborhood rejoices. Would it [not] be far more civilized and humane, not to say godlike, to recognize once in the year by some significant symbolical ceremony the part which the squirrel plays, the great service it performs, in the economy of the universe?

Oct. 27. Mixed Woods

TO SPEAK FROM RECOLLECTION of pines and oaks, I should say that our woods were chiefly pine and oak mixed, but we have also (to speak of the large growth, or trees) pure pine and pure oak woods. How are these three produced? Are not the pure pine woods commonly new woods, *i. e.* pioneers? After oaks have once got established, it must be hard to get them out without clearing the land. A pure oak wood may be obtained by cutting off at once and clean a pure and dense pine wood, and again sometimes by cutting the same oak wood. But pines are continually stealing into oaks, and oaks into pines, where respectively they are not too dense, as where they are burned or otherwise thinned, and so mixed woods may arise.

Oct. 29. New Pitch Pine Wood

HENRY SHATTUCK'S IS A *new* pitch pine wood, say thirty years old. The western, or greater, part contains not a single seed-bearing white pine. It is a remarkable proof of my theory, for it contains thousands of little white pines but scarcely one little pitch pine. It is also well stocked with minute oak seedlings. It is a dense wood, say a dozen rods wide by three or four times as long, running east

White Pine and hardwoods.

and west, with an oak wood on the north, from which the squirrels brought the acorns. A strip of nearly the same width of the pitch pine was cut apparently within a year on the south (a part of the above), and has just been harrowed and sown with rye, and still it is all dotted over with the little oak seedlings between the [stumps], which are perhaps unnoticed by Shattuck, but if he would keep his plow and fire out he would still have a pretty green patch there by next fall. A thousand little red flags (changed oak leaves) already wave over the green rye amid the stumps. The farmer stumbles over these in his walk, and sweats while he endeavors to clear the land of them, and yet wonders how oaks ever succeed to pines, as if he did not consider what *these* are. Where these pines are dense they are slender and tall. On the edge or in open land they are more stout and spreading.

Oct. 31. These Oak Forests

Yes, these dense and stretching oak forests, whose withered leaves now redden and rustle on the hills for many a New England mile, were all planted by the labor of animals. For after some weeks of close scrutiny I cannot avoid the conclusion that our modern oak woods sooner or later spring up from an acorn, not where it has fallen from its tree, for that is the exception, but where it has been dropped or placed by an animal. Consider what a vast work these forest-planters are doing!

Nov. 5.　Trees That Grow Slowly

I AM STRUCK BY the fact that the more slowly trees grow at first, the sounder they are at the core, and I think that the same is true of human beings. We do not wish to see children precocious, making great strides in their early years like sprouts, producing a soft and perishable timber, but better if they expand slowly at first, as if contending with difficulties, and so are solidified and perfected. Such trees continue to expand with nearly equal rapidity to an extreme old age.

An upstate pasture.

Nov. 5.　Pasture Oaks

IT IS EVIDENT THAT the pasture oaks are commonly the survivors or relics of old oak woods,—not having been set out of course, nor springing up often in the bare pasture, except sometimes along fences. I see that on the outskirts of Wetherbee's and Blood's lots are some larger, more spreading and straggling trees, which are not to be distinguished from those. Such trees are often found as stragglers beyond a fence in an adjacent lot. Or, as an old oak wood is very gradually thinned out, it becomes open, grassy, and park-like, and very many owners are inclined to respect a few larger trees on account of old associations, until at length they begin to value them for shade for their cattle. These are oftenest white oaks. I think that they grow the largest and are the hardiest. This final arrangement is in obedience to the demand of the cow. She says, looking at the oak woods: "Your tender twigs are good, but grass is better. Give me a few at intervals for shade and shelter in storms, and let the grass grow far and wide between them."

Nov. 8. Persevering Nature

I NOTICE ALONG THE Corner road, beyond Abiel Wheeler's, quite a
number of little white pines springing up against the south wall, whose seed must
have been blown from Hubbard's Grove some fifty rods east. They extend along
a quarter of a mile at least. Also a wet and brushy meadow some forty rods in front
of Garfield's is being rapidly filled with white pines whose seeds must have been
blown an equal distance.

We need not be surprised at these results when we consider how persevering
Nature is, and how much time she has to work in, though she works slowly. A great
pine wood may drop many millions of seeds in one year, and if only half a dozen
are conveyed a quarter of a mile and lodge against some fence, and only one comes
up and lives there, yet in the course of fifteen or twenty years there are fifteen
or twenty young trees there, and they begin to make a show and betray their
origin.

Nov. 10. Boxboro Oak Woods

HOW LITTLE THERE IS on an ordinary map! How little, I mean, that
concerns the walker and the lover of nature. Between those lines indicating roads
is a plain blank space in the form of a square or triangle or polygon or segment
of a circle, and there is naught to distinguish this from another area of similar size
and form. Yet the one may be covered, in fact, with a primitive oak wood, like
that of Boxboro, waving and creaking in the wind, such as may make the reputation of a county, while the other is a stretching plain with scarcely a tree on it.
The waving woods, the dells and glades and green banks and smiling fields, the
huge boulders, etc., etc., are not on the map, nor to be inferred from the map.

That grand old oak wood is just the most remarkable and memorable thing in
Boxboro, and yet if there is a history of this town written anywhere, the history
or even mention of this is probably altogether omitted, while that of the first (and
may be last) parish is enlarged on.

What sort of cultivation, or civilization and improvement, is ours to boast of,
if it turns out that, as in this instance, unhandselled nature is worth more even
by our modes of valuation than our improvements are,—if we leave the land
poorer than we found it? Is it good economy, to try it by the lowest standards,
to cut down all our forests, if a forest will pay into the town treasury a greater
tax than the farms which may supplant it,—if the oaks by steadily growing
according to their nature leave our improvements in the rear?

How little we insist on truly grand and beautiful natural features! How many
have ever heard of the Boxboro oak woods? How many have ever explored them?
I have lived so long in this neighborhood and but just heard of this noble forest,—
probably as fine an oak wood as there is in New England, only eight miles west
of me.

I noticed young white pines springing up in the more open places and dells. There were considerable tracts of large white pine wood and also pine and oak mixed, especially on the hills. So I see that the character of a primitive wood may gradually change, as from oak to pine, the oaks at last decaying and not being replaced by oaks.

Nov. 16. Disposition of the Trees

HERE, TOO, COMING TO water, I see the swamp white oak rising out of it, elm-like in its bark and trunk. Red maples also appear here with them. It is interesting to see thus how surely the character of the ground determines the growth. It is evident that in a wood that has been let alone for the longest period the greatest regularity and harmony in the disposition of the trees will be observed, while in our ordinary woods man has often interfered and favored the growth of other kinds than are best fitted to grow there naturally. To some, which he does not want, he allows no place at all.

Nov. 22. Glorious November Weather

THIS IS A VERY beautiful November day,—a cool but clear, crystalline air, through which even the white pines with their silvery sheen are an affecting sight. It is a day to behold and to ramble over the hard (stiffening) and withered surface of the tawny earth. Every plant's down glitters with a silvery light along the Marlborough road,—the sweet-fern, the lespedeza, and bare blueberry twigs, to say nothing of the weather-worn tufts of *Andropogon scoparius.* A thousand bare twigs gleam like cobwebs in the sun. I rejoice in the bare, bleak, hard, and barren-looking surface of the tawny pastures, the firm outline of the hills, so convenient to walk over, and the air so bracing and wholesome. Though you are finger-cold toward night, and you cast a stone on to your first ice, and see the unmelted crystals under every bank, it is glorious November weather, and only November fruits are out. On some hickories you see a thousand black nuts against the sky.

Nov. 22. Independent of Luxuries

IT IS GLORIOUS TO consider how independent man is of all enervating luxuries; and the poorer he is in respect to them, the richer he is. Summer is gone with all its infinite wealth, and still nature is genial to man. Though he no longer bathes in the stream, or reclines on the bank, or plucks berries on the hills, still he beholds the same inaccessible beauty around him. What though he has no juice of the grape stored up for him in cellars; the air itself is wine of an older vintage, and far more sanely exhilarating, than any cellar affords. It is ever some gouty senior and not a blithe child that drinks, or cares for, that so famous wine.

Though so many phenomena which we lately admired have now vanished, others are more remarkable and interesting than before. The smokes from distant chimneys, not only greater because more fire is required, but more distinct in the cooler atmosphere, are a very pleasing sight, and conduct our thoughts quickly to the roof and hearth and family beneath, revealing the homes of men.

Maynard's yard and frontage, and all his barns and fences, are singularly neat and substantial, and the highroad is in effect converted into a private way through his grounds. It suggests unspeakable peace and happiness. Yet, strange to tell, I noticed that he had a tiger instead of a cock for a vane on his barn, and he himself looked overworked. He had allowed the surviving forest trees to grow into ancestral trees about his premises, and so attach themselves to him as if he had planted them. The dusty highway was so subdued that it seemed as if it were lost there. He had all but stretched a bar across it. Each traveller must have felt some misgivings, as if he were trespassing.

Nov. 25.   Young Pasture Trees

HOW COMMONLY YOU SEE pitch pines, white pines, and birches filling up a pasture, and, when they are a dozen or fifteen years old, shrub and other oaks beginning to show themselves, inclosing apple trees and walls and fences gradually and so changing the whole aspect of the region. These trees do not cover the whole surface equally at present, but are grouped very agreeably after natural laws which they obey. You remember, perhaps, that fifteen years ago there was not a single tree in this pasture,—not a germinating seed of one,—and now it is a pretty dense forest ten feet high. I confess that I love to be convinced of this inextinguishable vitality in Nature. I would rather that my body should be buried in a soil thus wide-awake than in a mere inert and dead earth. The cow-paths, the hollows where I slid in the winter, the rocks, are fast being enveloped and becoming rabbit-walks and hollows and rocks in the woods.

Nov. 26.   Wild Fruits

THE VALUE OF THESE wild fruits is not in the mere possession or eating of them, but in the sight or enjoyment of them. The very derivation of the word "fruit" would suggest this. It is from the Latin *fructus*, meaning that which is *used* or *enjoyed.* If it were not so, then going a-berrying and going to market would be nearly synonymous expressions. Of course it is the spirit in which you do a thing which makes it interesting, whether it is sweeping a room or pulling turnips. Peaches are unquestionably a very beautiful and palatable fruit, but the gathering of them for the market is not nearly so interesting as the gathering of huckleberries for your own use.

Dec. 30.   Blueberries

IN MAY AND JUNE all our hills and fields are adorned with a profusion of the pretty little more or less bell-shaped flowers of this family, commonly turned toward the earth and more or less tinged with red or pink and resounding with the hum of insects, each one the forerunner of a berry the most natural, wholesome, palatable that the soil can produce.

The early low blueberry, which I will call "bluet," adopting the name from the Canadians, is probably the prevailing kind of whortleberry in New England, for the high blueberry and huckleberry are unknown in many sections. In many New Hampshire towns a neighboring mountain-top is the common berry-field of many villages, and in the berry season such a summit will be swarming with pickers. A hundred at once will rush thither from all the surrounding villages, with pails and buckets of all descriptions, especially on a Sunday, which is their leisure day. When camping on such ground, thinking myself quite out of the world, I have had my solitude very unexpectedly interrupted by such an advent, and found that the week-days were the only Sabbath-days there.

For a mile or more on such a rocky mountain-top this will be the prevailing shrub, occupying every little shelf from several rods down to a few inches only in width, and then the berries droop in short wreaths over the rocks, sometimes the thickest and largest along a seam in a shelving rock,—either that light mealy-blue, or a shining black, or an intermediate blue, without bloom. When, at that season, I look from Concord toward the blue mountain-tops in the horizon, I am reminded that near at hand they are equally blue with berries.

The mountain-tops of New England, often lifted above the clouds, are thus covered with this beautiful blue fruit, in greater profusion than in any garden.

What though the woods be cut down, this emergency was long ago foreseen and provided for by Nature, and the interregnum is not allowed to be a barren one. She is full of resources: she not only begins instantly to heal that scar, but she consoles (compensates?) and refreshes us with fruits such as the forest did not produce. To console us she heaps our baskets with berries.

The timid or ill-shod confine themselves to the land side, where they get comparatively few berries and many scratches, but the more adventurous, making their way through the open swamp, which the bushes overhang, wading amid the water andromeda and sphagnum, where the surface quakes for a rod around, obtain access to those great drooping clusters of berries which no hand has disturbed. There is no wilder and richer sight than is afforded from such a point of view, of the edge of a blueberry swamp where various wild berries are intermixed.

861

Jan. 3. Preservation of Natural Features

WHAT ARE THE NATURAL features which make a township handsome? A river, with its waterfalls and meadows, a lake, a hill, a cliff or individual rocks, a forest, and ancient trees standing singly. Such things are beautiful; they have a high use which dollars and cents never represent. If the inhabitants of a town were wise, they would seek to preserve these things, though at a considerable expense; for such things educate far more than any hired teachers or preachers, or any at present recognized system of school education. I do not think him fit to be the founder of a state or even of a town who does not foresee the use of these things, but legislates chiefly for oxen, as it were.

Far the handsomest thing I saw in Boxboro was its noble oak wood. I doubt if there is a finer one in Massachusetts. Let her keep it a century longer, and men will make pilgrimages to it from all parts of the country; and yet it would be very like the rest of New England if Boxboro were ashamed of that woodland.

I have since heard, however, that she is contented to have that forest stand instead of the houses and farms that might supplant [it], because the land pays a much larger tax to the town now than it would then.

I said to myself, if the history of this town is written, the chief stress is probably laid on its parish and there is not a word about this forest in it.

It would be worth the while if in each town there were a committee appointed to see that the beauty of the town received no detriment. If we have the largest boulder in the county, then it should not belong to an individual, nor be made into door-steps.

As in many countries precious metals belong to the crown, so here more precious natural objects of rare beauty should belong to the public.

Not only the channel but one or both banks of every river should be a public highway. The only use of a river is not to float on it.

Think of a mountain-top in the township—even to the minds of the Indians a sacred place—only accessible through private grounds! a temple, as it were, which you cannot enter except by trespassing and at the risk of letting out or letting in somebody's cattle! in fact the temple itself in this case private property and standing in a man's cow-yard,—for such is commonly the case!

Jan. 8. Huckleberry Cake

THEY TAUGHT US NOT only the use of corn and how to plant it, but also of whortleberries and how to dry them for winter, and made us baskets to put them in. We should have hesitated long to eat some kinds, if they had not set us the example, knowing by old experience that they were not only harmless but salutary. I have added a few to my number of edible berries by walking behind an Indian in Maine, who ate such as I never thought of tasting before. Of course they made a much greater account of wild fruits than we do.

It appears from the above evidence that the Indians used their dried berries commonly in the form of huckleberry cake, and also of huckleberry porridge or pudding.

What we call huckleberry cake, made of Indian meal and huckleberries, was evidently the principal cake of the aborigines, and was generally known and used by them all over this part of North America, as much or more than plum-cake by us. They enjoyed it all alone ages before our ancestors heard of Indian meal or huckleberries.

We have no national cake so universal and well known as this was in all parts of the country where corn and huckleberries grew.

If you had travelled here a thousand years ago, it would probably have been offered you alike on the Connecticut, the Potomac, the Niagara, the Ottawa, and the Mississippi.

Jan. 14. Nature the Tortoise

NATURE IS SLOW BUT sure; she works no faster than need be; she is the tortoise that wins the race by her perseverance; she knows that seeds have many other uses than to reproduce their kind. In raising oaks and pines, she works with a leisureliness and security answering to the age and strength of the trees. If every acorn of this year's crop is destroyed, never fear! she has more years to come. It is not necessary that a pine or an oak should bear fruit every year, as it is that a pea-vine should. So, botanically, the greatest changes in the landscape are produced more gradually than we expected. If Nature has a pine or an oak wood to produce, she manifests no haste about it.

Thus we should say that oak forests are produced by a kind of accident, *i. e.* by the failure of animals to reap the fruit of their labors. Yet who shall say that they have not a fair knowledge of the value of their labors—that the squirrel when it plants an acorn, or the jay when it lets one slip from under its foot, has not a transient thought for its posterity?

Nov. 3. Storm-Marked Causeway

AFTER A VIOLENT EASTERLY storm in the night, which clears up at noon (November 3, 1861), I notice that the surface of the railroad causeway, composed of gravel, is singularly marked, as if stratified like some slate rocks, on their edges, so that I can tell within a small fraction of a degree from what quarter the rain came. These lines, as it were of stratification, are perfectly parallel, and straight as a ruler, diagonally across the flat surface of the causeway for its whole length.

Behind each little pebble, as a protecting boulder, an eighth or a tenth of an inch in diameter, extends northwest a ridge of sand an inch or more, which it has protected from being washed away, while the heavy drops driven almost horizontally have washed out a furrow on each side, and on all sides are these ridges, half an inch apart and perfectly parallel.

All this is perfectly distinct to an observant eye, and yet could easily pass unnoticed by most. Thus each wind is self-registering.

EDITOR'S NOTE:
This Nov. 3, 1861 journal entry
was the very last made by Thoreau.
Although his health
had deteriorated considerably
at this point in time,
it is noteworthy
that his ability to observe
and to write
seems undiminished.